OECD/G20 Base Erosion and Profit Shifting Project

Prevention of Tax Treaty Abuse – Sixth Peer Review Report on Treaty Shopping

INCLUSIVE FRAMEWORK ON BEPS: ACTION 6

OECD
BETTER POLICIES FOR BETTER LIVES

This document, as well as any data and map included herein, are without prejudice to the status of or sovereignty over any territory, to the delimitation of international frontiers and boundaries and to the name of any territory, city or area.

The statistical data for Israel are supplied by and under the responsibility of the relevant Israeli authorities. The use of such data by the OECD is without prejudice to the status of the Golan Heights, East Jerusalem and Israeli settlements in the West Bank under the terms of international law.

Note by the Republic of Türkiye
The information in this document with reference to "Cyprus" relates to the southern part of the Island. There is no single authority representing both Turkish and Greek Cypriot people on the Island. Türkiye recognises the Turkish Republic of Northern Cyprus (TRNC). Until a lasting and equitable solution is found within the context of the United Nations, Türkiye shall preserve its position concerning the "Cyprus issue".

Note by all the European Union Member States of the OECD and the European Union
The Republic of Cyprus is recognised by all members of the United Nations with the exception of Türkiye. The information in this document relates to the area under the effective control of the Government of the Republic of Cyprus.

Please cite this publication as:
OECD (2024), *Prevention of Tax Treaty Abuse – Sixth Peer Review Report on Treaty Shopping: Inclusive Framework on BEPS: Action 6*, OECD/G20 Base Erosion and Profit Shifting Project, OECD Publishing, Paris, https://doi.org/10.1787/36cebf8e-en.

ISBN 978-92-64-34132-6 (print)
ISBN 978-92-64-76091-2 (PDF)
ISBN 978-92-64-76583-2 (HTML)
ISBN 978-92-64-65509-6 (epub)

OECD/G20 Base Erosion and Profit Shifting Project
ISSN 2313-2604 (print)
ISSN 2313-2612 (online)

Photo credits: Cover © ninog-Fotolia.com.

Corrigenda to OECD publications may be found on line at: www.oecd.org/about/publishing/corrigenda.htm.

Foreword

The integration of national economies and markets has increased substantially in recent years, putting a strain on the international tax rules, which were designed more than a century ago. Weaknesses in the current rules create opportunities for base erosion and profit shifting (BEPS), requiring bold moves by policy makers to restore confidence in the system and ensure that profits are taxed where economic activities take place and value is created.

Following the release of the report Addressing Base Erosion and Profit Shifting in February 2013, OECD and G20 countries adopted a 15-point Action Plan to address BEPS in September 2013. The Action Plan identified 15 actions along three key pillars: introducing coherence in the domestic rules that affect cross-border activities, reinforcing substance requirements in the existing international standards, and improving transparency as well as certainty.

After two years of work, measures in response to the 15 actions were delivered to G20 Leaders in Antalya in November 2015. All the different outputs, including those delivered in an interim form in 2014, were consolidated into a comprehensive package. The BEPS package of measures represents the first substantial renovation of the international tax rules in almost a century. Once the new measures become applicable, it is expected that profits will be reported where the economic activities that generate them are carried out and where value is created. BEPS planning strategies that rely on outdated rules or on poorly co-ordinated domestic measures will be rendered ineffective.

Implementation is now the focus of this work. The BEPS package is designed to be implemented via changes in domestic law and practices, and in tax treaties. With the negotiation of a multilateral instrument (MLI) having been finalised in 2016 to facilitate the implementation of the treaty related BEPS measures, over 90 jurisdictions are covered by the MLI. The entry into force of the MLI on 1 July 2018 paves the way for swift implementation of the treaty related measures. OECD and G20 countries also agreed to continue to work together to ensure a consistent and co-ordinated implementation of the BEPS recommendations and to make the project more inclusive. Globalisation requires that global solutions and a global dialogue be established which go beyond OECD and G20 countries.

A better understanding of how the BEPS recommendations are implemented in practice could reduce misunderstandings and disputes between governments. Greater focus on implementation and tax administration should therefore be mutually beneficial to governments and business. Proposed improvements to data and analysis will help support ongoing evaluation of the quantitative impact of BEPS, as well as evaluating the impact of the countermeasures developed under the BEPS Project.

As a result, the OECD established the OECD/G20 Inclusive Framework on BEPS (Inclusive Framework), bringing all interested and committed countries and jurisdictions on an equal footing in the Committee on Fiscal Affairs and all its subsidiary bodies. The Inclusive Framework, which already has more than 135 members, is monitoring and peer reviewing the implementation of the minimum standards as well as completing the work on standard setting to address BEPS issues. In addition to BEPS members, other international organisations and regional tax bodies are involved in the work of the Inclusive Framework, which also consults business and the civil society on its different work streams.

This report was approved by the Inclusive Framework on 25 January 2024 and prepared for publication by the OECD Secretariat.

Acknowledgments

This document was prepared by the Tax Treaties and International Cooperation Unit of the OECD Centre for Tax Policy and Administration. The data included in this document was submitted by the delegates of Working Party 1 (WP1), in its Inclusive Framework on BEPS (IF) format, of each jurisdiction that is a member of the IF. The sixth edition of this report was prepared by Jessica Di Maria and Sara Shearmur, advisors in the Tax Treaties and International Cooperation Unit of the OECD Centre for Tax Policy and Administration. The authors would like to thank the delegates of WP1 for their input.

The authors would also like to thank Lee Harley, Co-Head of the Tax Treaties and International Cooperation Unit, as well as Yves Van Brussel, Kazuya Shimizu, Stefano Neirotti and Shemsije Jashari for analysing the relevant data and for their contribution in preparing the report; Caroline Devlin-Genin for her help with matters relating to the Multilateral Convention to Implement Tax Treaty Related Measures to Prevent BEPS; and Lisa-Marie Stamm for her help with the French version of the report. The authors are especially grateful to Ria Sandilands and Milton Pérez Rivera for their assistance with coordination and communication, as well as to Karena Garnier and Carrie Tyler for their help in preparing this publication.

Table of contents

Executive Summary

1. The minimum standard on treaty shopping included in the Report on Action 6 is one of the four BEPS minimum standards. Action 6 of the BEPS Project identified treaty abuse, and in particular treaty shopping, as one of the principal sources of BEPS concerns. Owing to the seriousness of treaty shopping, jurisdictions have agreed to adopt, as a minimum standard, measures to address it, and to subject their efforts to an annual peer review (OECD, 2017[1]). (OECD, 2021[2]). The Inclusive Framework on BEPS published reports for each of the five peer review processes carried out in 2018, 2019, 2020, 2021 and 2022 (OECD, 2019[3]) (OECD, 2020[4]) (OECD, 2021[5]) (OECD, 2022[6]) [(OECD, 2023)].

2. This 2023 peer review report reflects the sixth peer review process on the implementation of the Action 6 minimum standard. It contains the aggregate results of the peer review, background information on treaty shopping in Chapter 7, and the "jurisdictional sections" which provide detailed information on the implementation of the minimum standard for each member of the Inclusive Framework in Chapter 8.

3. This sixth peer review process was governed by the revised peer review methodology, discussed in Section 2 below, which was first implemented in 2021.

4. In total, as at 31 May 2023, around 1,360 agreements concluded by members of the Inclusive Framework complied with the minimum standard. This represents an increase of around 30% as compared to 2022.

5. As in previous years, this year's peer review shows that in 2023, the *Multilateral Convention to Implement Tax Treaty Related Measures to Prevent Base Erosion and Profit* Shifting (BEPS MLI) continues to be a significant driver in expanding the implementation of the minimum standard for the jurisdictions that have ratified it.

6. The number of compliant agreements concluded between members of the Inclusive Framework and covered by the BEPS MLI has continued to increase steadily, growing by around 30% between 2021-2022, and by another 30% between 2022-2023. As at 31 May 2023, over 1,120 out of the 1,270 compliant agreements concluded between members of the Inclusive Framework have been brought into compliance through the BEPS MLI (with around 630 additional agreements between members of the Inclusive Framework that will become compliant under the BEPS MLI, once all Signatories to the BEPS MLI will have ratified it). Jurisdictions that have not signed or ratified the BEPS MLI have made significantly slower progress, in general, compared with those that have.

7. More broadly, as at 31 May 2023, over 2,400 agreements concluded between members of the Inclusive Framework are either compliant, subject to a complying instrument, subject to steps taken by at least one treaty partner to implement the minimum standard, or the object of a general statement by one treaty partner that it intends to use the detailed limitation-on-benefits rule (LOB), together with a mechanism to address conduit arrangements, to implement the minimum standard in all its bilateral agreements.

8. This year's peer review also provides updates on progress made by jurisdictions to give effect to their plans, developed in 2021 or 2022, to implement the minimum standard in non-compliant agreements concluded with other members of the Inclusive Framework, that are not already subject to a complying

instrument or general statement on the detailed LOB, and in respect of which no steps have been taken to implement the minimum standard (and where no reasons were provided why, for that member, the agreement does not give rise to material treaty-shopping concerns). In some cases, new implementation plans have also been developed. The majority of implementation plans involve the application of the BEPS MLI to the concerned agreements. Once all plans to implement the minimum standard are in effect, the minimum standard will be implemented, or on course to being implemented, in nearly all of the agreements concluded between members of the Inclusive Framework.

9. Finally, similar to last year, this year's peer review continues to show that many jurisdictions have followed the recommendations made in last year's peer review, in particular by completing the steps for the entry into effect of the provisions of the BEPS MLI, as applicable.

Context and background to the peer review

10. This sixth report on the implementation of the Action 6 minimum standard reflects the third peer review process carried out under the revised peer review methodology.

11. The peer review processes for 2018, 2019 and 2020 were carried out following an agreed approach that was set out in a document published on 29 May 2017, and that formed the basis on which the peer review process was undertaken (the 2017 Peer Review Documents) (OECD, 2017[1]). The 2017 Peer Review Documents included the Terms of Reference which set out the criteria for assessing the implementation of the Action 6 minimum standard, and the methodology setting out the procedural mechanism by which the review would be conducted.

12. In 2021, members of the Inclusive Framework on BEPS approved a revised methodology in the 2021 Peer Review Document (OECD, 2021[2])[1], which has governed the conduct of the peer reviews of the Action 6 minimum standard as of 2021. The changes to the peer review methodology were agreed as part of the review process that was set out in of the 2017 Peer Review Documents. Paragraph 14 of the 2017 Peer Review Documents provided that the methodology for the review of the implementation of the minimum standard on treaty shopping would be reviewed in 2020 in light of the experience in conducting that review.

13. The objective of the revised methodology (explained in further detail in Chapter 7) has been to establish a framework through which assistance would be given to a member jurisdiction that had non-compliant agreements with members of the Inclusive Framework that could, on its own assessment, create treaty-shopping opportunities and for which the jurisdiction had not yet taken steps to bring them into compliance with the minimum standard. Under this revised methodology, jurisdictions' progress in implementing the minimum standard has been measured in greater detail.

14. As in previous years, jurisdictions were required to complete a peer review questionnaire by 31 May 2023, reporting on the status of the implementation of the minimum standard in all of their comprehensive income tax agreements in force on that date (including agreements with jurisdictions that are not Inclusive Framework members). For each agreement listed, members indicated whether or not it complied with the minimum standard and, if not, whether it was on course to becoming compliant with the minimum standard.

15. Jurisdictions were invited to report additional information for every agreement with a jurisdiction member of the Inclusive Framework that neither complied with the minimum standard nor was subject to a complying instrument (e.g. the BEPS MLI or a signed amending instrument resulting from bilateral negotiations). Jurisdictions that have signed the BEPS MLI but not ratified it have also been invited to provide additional information on their ratification process.

16. As part of the new framework, jurisdictions have formulated plans, where relevant, for the implementation of the minimum standard in certain of their agreements. This concerns agreements

concluded with other members of the Inclusive Framework that are not compliant or subject to a complying instrument, for which no steps have yet been taken to implement the minimum standard, and where no statement has been made that a treaty partner intends to use a detailed limitation-on-benefits provision as part of the implementation of the minimum standard in all its bilateral tax agreements. Jurisdictions have also been invited to provide updates on progress made to give effect to such plans developed in the context of the 2021 or 2022 peer review processes, and to signal difficulties encountered in that respect, if any.

17. The assistance provided to jurisdictions under the revised methodology also includes the issuance of recommendations, contained in this report. These recommendations are, where relevant: to formulate a plan for the implementation of the minimum standard if one was not already in existence; and to complete the steps to have the BEPS MLI take effect where a jurisdiction is using the BEPS MLI to implement the minimum standard.

18. The implementation plans and recommendations are further discussed, respectively, in Chapters 3 and 4 below, as well as the jurisdictional sections of the concerned jurisdictions, in Chapter 8.

References

OECD (2022), *Prevention of Tax Treaty Abuse – Fourth Peer Review Report on Treaty Shopping: Inclusive Framework on BEPS: Action 6*, OECD/G20 Base Erosion and Profit Shifting Project, OECD Publishing, Paris, https://www.oecd-ilibrary.org/sites/3dc05e6a-en/index.html?itemId=/content/publication/3dc05e6a-en. [6]

OECD (2021), *BEPS Action 6 on Preventing the Granting of Treaty Benefits in Inappropriate Circumstances – Revised Peer Review Documents*, OECD/G20 Base Erosion and Profit Shifting Project, OECD, Paris, http://www.oecd.org/tax/beps/beps-action-6-preventing-the-granting-of-treaty-benefits-in-inappropriate-circumstances-revised-peer-review-documents.pdf. [2]

OECD (2021), *Prevention of Tax Treaty Abuse – Third Peer Review Report on Treaty Shopping : Inclusive Framework on BEPS: Action 6*, OECD/G20 Base Erosion and Profit Shifting Project, OECD Publishing, Paris, https://doi.org/10.1787/d6cecbb8-en. [5]

OECD (2020), *Prevention of Treaty Abuse – Second Peer Review Report on Treaty Shopping: Inclusive Framework on BEPS: Action 6*, OECD/G20 Base Erosion and Profit Shifting Project, OECD Publishing, Paris, https://doi.org/10.1787/d656738d-en. [4]

OECD (2019), *Prevention of Treaty Abuse - Peer Review Report on Treaty Shopping: Inclusive Framework on BEPS: Action 6*, OECD/G20 Base Erosion and Profit Shifting Project, OECD Publishing, Paris, https://doi.org/10.1787/9789264312388-en. [3]

OECD (2017), *BEPS Action 6 on Preventing the Granting of Treaty Benefits in Inappropriate Circumstances – Peer Review Documents*, OECD/G20 Base Erosion and Profit Shifting Project, OECD, Paris, http://www.oecd.org/tax/beps/beps-action-6-preventing-the-granting-of-treaty-benefits-in-inappropriatecircumstance-peer-review-documents.pdf. [1]

Note

[1] Approved by the Inclusive Framework in the 2021 Peer Review Document on 17 February 2021.

1 Implementation of the minimum standard: Aggregate data and key figures

19. This section sets out the aggregate data on the implementation of the minimum standard on treaty shopping included in the Report on Action 6 (OECD, 2015[1]).

To comply with the minimum standard, jurisdictions are required to do two things in their tax agreements: include an express statement on double non-taxation (generally in the preamble) and adopt one of three measures to address treaty shopping. The minimum standard does not specify how these two things should be implemented (e.g. through the BEPS MLI or bilaterally) (OECD, 2015[1]).[1]

20. Aggregate data on the jurisdictions' progress towards implementing the minimum standard is provided below. Detailed information on each jurisdiction's progress is provided in the jurisdictional sections in Chapter 8. The information that can be found in the "Conclusion" section in some of the jurisdictional sections in Chapter 8 further highlights the following:

- Members of the Inclusive Framework that have signed but not ratified the BEPS MLI are recommended to complete the steps to have the BEPS MLI take effect as soon as possible (Section 5 below);
- Similarly, some of the parties to the BEPS MLI that have made a reservation under the BEPS MLI to delay its entry into effect until the completion of internal procedures are recommended to complete the steps to have the BEPS MLI take effect as soon as possible (Chapter 4 below).[2]
- An implementation plan must be developed for agreements concluded with other members of the Inclusive Framework that are not compliant, not subject to a complying instrument or to a general statement on the detailed LOB, for which no steps have been taken to implement the minimum standard and no reasons have been given on why, for a jurisdiction, the agreement does not give rise to material treaty shopping concerns. Once a plan is in place, a jurisdiction must provide an annual update if changes occur. Where no implementation plan has been developed in respect of such agreements, jurisdictions are recommended to develop a plan for the implementation of the minimum standard (Chapters 3 and 4 below).
- The OECD Secretariat stands ready to discuss with any jurisdiction that has developed, or that needs to develop, a plan for the implementation of the minimum standard to see how support could best be provided to bring the concerned agreements into compliance with the minimum standard.

Aggregate data and key figures

21. In total, the 142 jurisdictions of the Inclusive Framework[3] reported 2,510 agreements (including 6 multilateral agreements) in force on 31 May 2023 among themselves, and about 850 additional

agreements between members of the Inclusive Framework and non-members.[4] Eight member jurisdictions had no comprehensive tax agreements in force.[5]

22. The data collected on the implementation of the Action 6 minimum standard showed that, on 31 May 2023, 124 jurisdictions of the Inclusive Framework had some agreements that already complied with the minimum standard, that were subject to a complying instrument, in respect of which steps had been taken to implement the minimum standard, or that were subject to a general statement on the detailed LOB.[6]

23. The agreements between members of the Inclusive Framework and non-members are not subject to the peer review and the aggregate results in this chapter focus on the 2,510 agreements (including 6 multilateral agreements) entered into among members of the Inclusive Framework. The jurisdictional sections in Chapter 8 nevertheless indicate the reported status of the implementation of the minimum standard in agreements outside the scope of the peer review.[7]

Compliant agreements

24. On 31 May 2023, over 1,270 bilateral agreements, and two multilateral agreements, between members of the Inclusive Framework complied with the minimum standard. Around 85 additional agreements not subject to this review (i.e. agreements between members of the Inclusive Framework and non-members) also complied with the minimum standard, bringing the total number of compliant agreements concluded by members of the Inclusive Framework to nearly 1,360 agreements. This represents an increase of around 30% compared to 2022.

25. In all compliant agreements, the preamble statement and the principal purpose test (PPT) were implemented to meet the minimum standard. In 52 of those agreements, the PPT was supplemented with a LOB provision.

26. The chart below illustrates the progress made, since the launch of the first Action 6 peer review process in 2018, in the implementation of the minimum standard in bilateral agreements between members of the Inclusive Framework. Over five years, the number of bilateral agreements between members of the Inclusive Framework that comply with the minimum standard increased from only 13 agreements in 2018 to over 1 270 agreements in 2023. As shown below, this increase is due mostly to the entry into effect of the provisions of the BEPS MLI.

Figure 1.1. Compliant bilateral agreements between members of the Inclusive Framework

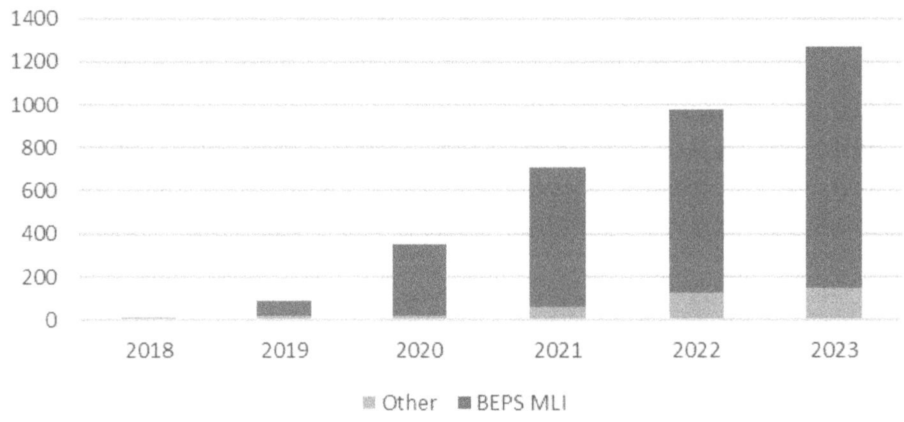

Agreements subject to compliant instrument

27. Many jurisdictions in the Inclusive Framework have agreements currently subject to a signed complying instrument that is not yet in force (in the case of a bilateral amending instrument) or the provisions of which are not yet in effect (in the case of the BEPS MLI), but that would implement the minimum standard. These agreements are on course to shortly becoming compliant with the minimum standard.

28. On 31 May 2023, around 630 bilateral agreements (of 2,504 bilateral agreements) between members of the Inclusive Framework were set to become covered tax agreements under the BEPS MLI (i.e. both Contracting Jurisdictions have listed the agreement under the BEPS MLI and, as a result, the BEPS MLI will modify the agreement once in effect) and thereby to become compliant with the minimum standard. These agreements will comply with the minimum standard once the relevant provisions of the BEPS MLI take effect, following ratification by both Contracting Jurisdictions.[8]

29. A further 22 agreements between members of the Inclusive Framework are subject to a bilateral amending instrument that is not yet in force. This number, equivalent to 3.5% of the number of agreements set to become covered tax agreements under the BEPS MLI, highlights the comparative effectiveness of the BEPS MLI in implementing the minimum standard.

30. For the agreements listed under the BEPS MLI, all 96 members of the Inclusive Framework that are parties and signatories to the BEPS ML[I9] are implementing the preamble statement and the PPT. Thirteen jurisdictions[10] have also opted to apply the simplified LOB through the BEPS MLI to supplement the PPT when possible. Seven additional jurisdictions agreed to accept a simplified LOB in agreements with partners that opted for it under the BEPS MLI.

Steps taken to implement the minimum standard (incl. general statement on the detailed LOB)

31. As provided in the revised peer review methodology, jurisdictions in the Inclusive Framework report any steps taken to implement the minimum standard in their non-compliant agreements that are not already subject to a complying instrument. These are steps that will enable the agreement to become subject to a complying instrument. For example, a jurisdiction will be considered to have taken a step to implement the minimum standard in an agreement under the BEPS MLI if it has signed the BEPS MLI and listed that agreement to be covered, but its treaty partner has not done the same. (Where both treaty partners have signed the BEPS MLI and listed an agreement to be covered, the BEPS MLI would instead be considered a complying instrument for that agreement; the agreement would later be reported as compliant with the minimum standard, by application of the BEPS MLI, once its provisions start to take effect.) Other steps also include entering into bilateral renegotiations with a treaty partner, agreeing to enter into such renegotiations, or contacting a treaty partner with a draft protocol, with these steps intended to implement the minimum standard.

32. While some jurisdictions have chosen only one method in their steps to implement the minimum standard (e.g. by listing all their agreements under the BEPS MLI), other jurisdictions have tailored their approach across their treaty network (e.g. by pursuing bilateral renegotiations of some agreements, and using the BEPS MLI for other agreements).

33. Since 2021, the number of agreements subject to steps taken by at least one treaty partner to implement the minimum standard has fluctuated (from around 620 in 2021, to around 520 in 2022, and around 650 in 2023). From one year to the next, the number of agreements subject to such steps is reduced by instances where progress is made to enable an agreement to become subject to a complying instrument (noting that once an agreement is subject to a complying instrument, it is no longer reported as being subject to steps taken to implement the minimum standard); concurrently, this number is increased by

instances where progress is made by at least one treaty partner to start to give effect to a plan to implement the minimum standard in an agreement.

34. As observed in 2021 and 2022, joining the BEPS MLI and listing an agreement to be covered remains the more widely applied step taken for the implementation of the minimum standard in non-compliant agreements, covering more than 450 such agreements concluded between members of the Inclusive Framework. Jurisdictions have also taken steps other than under the BEPS MLI to implement the minimum standard in about 200 agreements (including about 120 agreements for which a treaty partner has taken concurrent steps under the BEPS MLI). As discussed further below (Section 6) treaty partners may have taken different steps to implement the minimum standard in a given agreement, and may at this stage still be in the process of deciding which method to pursue (e.g. BEPS MLI or bilateral negotiations).

35. It is also possible for a jurisdiction to make a general statement that it intends to use the detailed LOB as part of its commitment to implement the minimum standard in all of its bilateral agreements. The detailed LOB provision is not included in the BEPS MLI and requires substantive bilateral discussions and customisation to each tax agreement, which could take several years. If a jurisdiction makes such a statement, its treaty partners will not generally provide any additional information about their tax agreement with that jurisdiction.

36. In total, this year over 2 400 agreements concluded between members of the Inclusive Framework are compliant, subject to a complying instrument or to steps taken by at least one treaty partner to implement the minimum standard, or are the object of a general statement by a treaty partner on the detailed limitation-on-benefits provision.

Provisions used to implement the minimum standard

37. As with previous years, this year's peer review shows that among the three alternative methods to implement the second component of the minimum standard[11], the PPT alone remains much the most widely used. The majority of jurisdictions has chosen to implement the minimum standard using this alternative. Indeed, it is the only provision capable on its own of satisfying the second component of the minimum standard and can be implemented using the BEPS MLI.

38. About 85 agreements are or will be brought into compliance with the minimum standard using the PPT supplemented by a detailed or simplified LOB. The BEPS MLI can be used to implement the PPT together with a simplified LOB and 13 jurisdictions[12] have chosen this option. An additional seven have agreed to implement the simplified BEPS MLI LOB in cases where their treaty partner has chosen to adopt that measure.[13]

39. Moreover, 63 agreements are covered by a general statement by one treaty partner that it intends to use the detailed LOB as part of its commitment to implement the minimum standard in all their bilateral agreements in force on 31 May 2023.

Methods of implementation

40. As in previous years, the BEPS MLI continues to be the preferred method of implementing the minimum standard. However, a jurisdiction that prefers to implement the minimum standard through a detailed limitation on benefits provision cannot use the BEPS MLI to do so. As of 31 May 2023, one hundred jurisdictions have joined the BEPS MLI (including 96 members of the Inclusive Framework)[14], 81 have ratified it[15], and the BEPS MLI would, once fully in effect, implement the minimum standard in more than 1,900 bilateral agreements, thus modifying the majority of agreements concluded between members of the Inclusive Framework.

41. As in previous years, jurisdictions that have not signed or ratified the BEPS MLI have generally made significantly slower progress compared with those that have.

42. Nevertheless, participation in the BEPS MLI is not a minimum standard and jurisdictions may have different preferences, as specified in the Terms of Reference. The way in which the minimum standard will be implemented in each bilateral agreement must be agreed between the contracting jurisdictions.

References

OECD (2015), *Preventing the Granting of Treaty Benefits in Inappropriate Circumstances, Action 6 - 2015 Final Report*, OECD/G20 Base Erosion and Profit Shifting Project, OECD Publishing, Paris, https://doi.org/10.1787/9789264241695-en. [1]

Notes

[1] The Action 6 Final Report further states that (i) a jurisdiction is required to implement the minimum standard in a treaty only if asked to do so by another member of the Inclusive Framework; (ii) the decision on which of the three methods to adopt has to be agreed (a solution cannot be imposed); and (iii) reflecting treaties' bilateral nature, there is no time limit within which a jurisdiction has to attain the minimum standard.

[2] The reservation under Article 35(7) BEPS MLI delays the entry into effect of the provisions of the BEPS MLI with respect to a Covered Tax Agreement until the reserving Party notifies (under Article 35(7)(b) BEPS MLI) that it has completed its internal procedures for such entry into effect. Several Parties to the BEPS MLI have made this reservation but have not yet made any notification under Article 35(7)(b) BEPS MLI. As a result, their agreements cannot yet be brought into compliance with the minimum standard under the BEPS MLI.

[3] The data reflected in this report also includes data on the agreements concluded by Uzbekistan. Noting that Uzbekistan joined the Inclusive Framework on 9 June 2023, which is after the reference date for this year's peer review exercise (31 May 2023), its treaty partners have not been expected to provide any additional information about their agreements with Uzbekistan.

[4] In 2022, the Inclusive Framework members reported 2,426 agreements entered into between members of the Inclusive Framework. The additional agreements reviewed in 2023 include new agreements entered into between members of the Inclusive Framework between 1 June 2022, and 31 May 2023, and the relevant existing agreements of the new members of the Inclusive Framework, which agreements were not subject to the 2022 Peer Review.

[5] Anguilla, the Bahamas, the Cayman Islands, the Cook Islands, Djibouti, Haiti, Honduras and Turks and Caicos Islands have no agreements in force.

[6] On 31 May 2023, 100 jurisdictions were signatories or parties to the BEPS MLI, but four of them (Cyprus, Fiji, Kuwait and Lesotho) were not members of the Inclusive Framework. Thus, as of 31 May 2023, 96 members of the Inclusive Framework were signatories or parties to the BEPS MLI. Eswatini and Azerbaijan, members of the Inclusive Framework, signed the MLI on 27 September 2023 and 20 November 2023, respectively. Kuwait, a signatory to the BEPS MLI, became a member of the Inclusive Framework on 15 November 2023. Therefore, as of that date, 102 jurisdictions were signatories or parties to the BEPS MLI, of which 99 are members of the Inclusive Framework. A number of additional members of the Inclusive Framework, although not signatories or parties to the BEPS MLI, have concluded amending protocols to implement the minimum standard.

[7] A "complying instrument" could be the BEPS MLI or a suitable new amending protocol yet to enter into force. It could also be a completely new agreement that has not yet entered into force.

[8] And, where relevant, the notification pursuant to Article 35(7)(b) BEPS MLI (see further explanations in footnote 3).

[9] Noting that Eswatini and Azerbaijan signed BEPS MLI on 27 September 2023 and 20 November 2023, respectively, and that Kuwait, a signatory to the BEPS MLI, became a member of the Inclusive Framework on 15 November 2023. As of that date, 99 members of the Inclusive Framework have joined the BEPS MLI.

[10] A fourteenth jurisdiction, Eswatini, signed the BEPS MLI on 27 September 2023 and has also opted to apply the simplified LOB.

[11] These are: the PPT, the PPT supplemented by a detailed or simplified LOB, or a detailed LOB together with an anti-conduit mechanism.

[12] See note 10.

[13] As allowed under Article 7(7) BEPS MLI.

[14] Eswatini and Azerbaijan signed the BEPS MLI on 27 September 2023 and 20 November 2023, respectively. Kuwait, a signatory to the BEPS MLI, became a member of the Inclusive Framework on 15 November 2023. As of that date, 102 jurisdictions have joined the BEPS MLI, including 99 members of the Inclusive Framework.

[15] Armenia, Côte d'Ivoire, Papua New Guinea and Tunisia deposited their instruments of ratification of the BEPS MLI after 31 May 2023. As of 1 December 2023, 85 jurisdictions have ratified the BEPS MLI.

2 Key role of the BEPS MLI

Ratification of the BEPS MLI

43. Since the provisions of the BEPS MLI first started to take effect, in 2019, the BEPS MLI has rapidly strengthened the bilateral tax treaty network of jurisdictions that ratified it. The number of agreements between members of the Inclusive Framework that became compliant with the BEPS MLI has increased steadily by the hundreds each year, exceeding 1,120 as of 31 May 2023. This number continues to increase, on an ongoing basis, as additional Signatories ratify the BEPS MLI. As in previous years, the peer review continues to reveal an important difference in the progress made on implementing the minimum standard by jurisdictions that have ratified the BEPS MLI compared with other jurisdictions.

44. Over the past year, eight jurisdictions that are members of the Inclusive Framework have ratified the BEPS MLI: Armenia, Bulgaria, Côte d'Ivoire, Mexico, Papua New Guinea, South Africa, Tunisia and Viet Nam. [1]

45. On average, around 55% of the treaty networks of jurisdictions for which the BEPS MLI started to take effect as of 1 January 2023,[2] are compliant with the minimum standard in 2023, as shown in the Table 2.1.

46. For the jurisdictions that ratified the BEPS MLI after October 2022,[3] the relevant provisions of the BEPS MLI had generally not yet started to take effect for their agreements on 31 May 2023. This is because provisions of the BEPS MLI can generally only start to take effect for an agreement after a period of time that follows the latest of the dates on which the BEPS MLI enters into force for each of the partners to an agreement. This period could roughly amount to a year from the latest ratification.[4]

47. As observed in prior peer reviews, while the jurisdictions that ratified the BEPS MLI made good progress in the implementation of the minimum standard, those that did not sign or ratify the BEPS MLI made comparatively little progress, in general, in implementing the minimum standard. Only around 15% of the agreements concluded by those jurisdictions are compliant.

48. The successive peer reviews therefore continue to demonstrate the importance of swift ratification of the BEPS MLI. All signatories to the BEPS MLI that have not yet ratified it are therefore encouraged to do so.

Table 2.1. Treaty networks and ratification of the BEPS MLI

Jurisdiction	Date of BEPS MLI Signing	Date of BEPS MLI Ratification	Agreements in force on 31 May 2023	Compliant agreements on 31 May 2023	% of network compliant	% of network with IF members compliant
Albania	28 May 2019	22 September 2020	43	27	63%	65%
Andorra	07 June 2017	29 September 2021	10	10	100%	100%
Armenia	07 June 2017	25 September 2023	52	3	6%	7%
Australia	07 June 2017	26 September 2018	45	29	64%	71%
Austria	07 June 2017	22 September 2017	90	40	44%	51%
Bahrain	27 November 2020	23 February 2022	45	23	51%	67%
Barbados	24 January 2018	21 December 2020	30	19	63%	67%
Belgium	07 June 2017	26 June 2019	95	55	58%	68%
Belize	11 January 2019	07 April 2022	5	2	40%	40%
Bosnia-Herzegovina	30 October 2019	16 September 2020	38	22	58%	64%
Bulgaria	07 June 2017	16 September 2022	71	41	58%	66%
Burkina Faso	07 June 2017	30 October 2020	4	2	50%	50%
Cameroon	11 July 2017	21 April 2022	6	4	67%	67%
Canada	07 June 2017	29 August 2019	94	50	53%	62%
Chile	07 June 2017	26 November 2020	36	28	78%	80%
China (People's Republic of)	07 June 2017	25 May 2022	105	60	57%	67%
Costa Rica	07 June 2017	22 September 2020	4	1	25%	25%
Côte d'Ivoire	24 January 2018	25 September 2023	11	0	0%	0%
Croatia	07 June 2017	18 February 2021	66	45	68%	75%
Curaçao	07 June 2017	29 March 2019	4	1	25%	33%
Czechia[1]	07 June 2017	13 May 2020	95	48	51%	56%
Denmark	07 June 2017	30 September 2019	71	41	57%	64%
Egypt	07 June 2017	30 September 2020	59	34	58%	69%
Estonia[2]	29 June 2018	15 January 2021	62	19	31%	32%
Finland	07 June 2017	25 February 2019	74	48	64%	72%
France	07 June 2017	26 September 2018	120	59	49%	62%
Georgia	07 June 2017	29 March 2019	57	33	58%	62%
Germany[2]	07 June 2017	18 December 2020	94	12	13%	14%
Greece	07 June 2017	30 March 2021	57	42	74%	77%
Guernsey	07 June 2017	12 February 2019	14	13	93%	92%

Jurisdiction	Date of BEPS MLI Signing	Date of BEPS MLI Ratification	Agreements in force on 31 May 2023	Compliant agreements on 31 May 2023	% of network compliant	% of network with IF members compliant
Hong Kong (China)[2]	07 June 2017	25 May 2022	43	34	79%	83%
Hungary	07 June 2017	25 March 2021	83	55	66%	73%
Iceland	07 June 2017	26 September 2019	41	31	76%	75%
India	07 June 2017	25 June 2019	96	54	56%	67%
Indonesia[2]	07 June 2017	28 April 2020	70	31	44%	55%
Ireland	07 June 2017	29 January 2019	74	55	74%	78%
Isle of Man	07 June 2017	25 October 2017	10	9	90%	90%
Israel	07 June 2017	13 September 2018	60	39	65%	71%
Japan	07 June 2017	26 September 2018	79	57	72%	80%
Jersey	07 June 2017	15 December 2017	15	10	67%	69%
Jordan	19 December 2019	29 September 2020	39	21	54%	71%
Kazakhstan	25 June 2018	24 June 2020	55	30	55%	63%
Korea	07 June 2017	13 May 2020	94	57	61%	69%
Latvia	07 June 2017	29 October 2019	64	44	69%	75%
Liechtenstein	07 June 2017	19 December 2019	21	21	100%	100%
Lithuania	07 June 2017	11 September 2018	58	41	71%	76%
Luxembourg	07 June 2017	09 April 2019	84	62	74%	77%
Malaysia	24 January 2018	18 February 2021	74	44	59%	73%
Malta	07 June 2017	18 December 2018	78	56	72%	76%
Mauritius	05 July 2017	18 October 2019	44	23	52%	64%
Mexico	07 June 2017	15 March 2023	60	3	5%	4%
Monaco	07 June 2017	10 January 2019	11	8	73%	80%
Netherlands	07 June 2017	29 March 2019	94	59	63%	70%
New Zealand	07 June 2017	27 June 2018	40	27	68%	73%
Norway	07 June 2017	17 July 2019	84	26	30%	33%
Oman	26 November 2019	07 July 2020	37	17	46%	59%
Pakistan	07 June 2017	18 December 2020	66	38	58%	72%
Panama	24 January 2018	05 November 2020	17	13	76%	76%
Papua New Guinea	23 January 2019	31 August 2023	10	0	0%	0%
Poland	07 June 2017	23 January 2018	82	52	63%	73%
Portugal	07 June 2017	28 February 2020	78	50	64%	73%
Qatar	04 December 2018	23 December 2019	80	44	55%	66%
Romania[2]	07 June 2017	28 February 2022	88	1	1%	1%

Jurisdiction	Date of BEPS MLI Signing	Date of BEPS MLI Ratification	Agreements in force on 31 May 2023	Compliant agreements on 31 May 2023	% of network compliant	% of network with IF members compliant
Russian Federation[2]	07 June 2017	18 June 2019	83	41	49%	60%
San Marino	07 June 2017	11 March 2020	25	18	72%	71%
Saudi Arabia	18 September 2018	23 January 2020	56	30	54%	63%
Senegal	07 June 2017	10 May 2022	20	12	60%	67%
Serbia	07 June 2017	05 June 2018	64	43	67%	72%
Seychelles	07 June 2017	14 February 2021	29	20	69%	73%
Singapore	07 June 2017	21 December 2018	93	62	67%	78%
Slovak Republic	07 June 2017	20 September 2018	70	41	59%	67%
Slovenia	07 June 2017	22 March 2018	60	42	70%	76%
South Africa	07 June 2017	30 September 2022	79	44	56%	66%
Spain[2]	07 June 2017	28 September 2021	93	54	58%	67%
Sweden[2]	07 June 2017	22 June 2018	83	9	11%	12%
Switzerland[2]	07 June 2017	29 August 2019	108	24	22%	23%
Thailand	09 February 2022	31 March 2022	61	34	56%	66%
Tunisia	24 January 2018	24 July 2023	56	0	0%	0%
Ukraine	23 July 2018	08 August 2019	73	41	56%	66%
United Arab Emirates	27 June 2018	29 May 2019	110	54	49%	58%
United Kingdom	07 June 2017	29 June 2018	132	73	55%	68%
Uruguay	07 June 2017	06 February 2020	23	17	74%	77%
Viet Nam	09 February 2022	23 May 2023	76	0	0%	0%

1. Czechia has 95 agreements in force. These 95 agreements relate to 96 jurisdictions, because Czechia continues to apply the agreement with former Serbia and Montenegro to both Serbia and Montenegro. Czechia has listed this agreement to be covered under the BEPS MLI only in respect of Serbia. The agreement complies with the minimum standard only in relation to Serbia.
2. Estonia, Germany, Hong Kong (China), Indonesia, Romania, the Russian Federation, Spain, Sweden and Switzerland made a reservation under Article 35(7) of the BEPS MLI to delay the entry into effect of the BEPS MLI after completing their internal procedures.

Gaps in coverage of BEPS MLI

49. Although the coverage of the BEPS MLI is vast, certain gaps remain. These gaps exist because the BEPS MLI is a flexible instrument that allows each signatory to decide which of its agreements it wishes to cover under the BEPS MLI. Thus, at the time of signature, signatories are required to deposit lists of agreements they want to modify. The BEPS MLI only modifies bilateral agreements listed by both treaty partners.

One-way agreements

50. Where an agreement has been listed under the BEPS MLI by only one of its treaty partners although both treaty partners have signed the BEPS MLI, the minimum standard would not be implemented

in the agreement. Where both partners have signed the BEPS MLI, but only one has listed the agreement, listing the agreement would be interpreted as a request to implement the minimum standard. The parties would have an obligation to implement the minimum standard in the agreement and agree bilaterally on the method to be used.

51. As of 31 May 2023, about 160 bilateral agreements, concluded between pairs of signatories to the BEPS MLI that are members of the Inclusive Framework, would not be modified by the BEPS MLI because, at this stage, only one jurisdiction had listed the agreement under the BEPS MLI ("one-way agreements").[5]

52. In some cases, the treaty partner that has not listed a "one-way agreement" to be covered under the BEPS MLI has formulated a plan to implement the minimum standard in that agreement by expanding its list of covered tax agreements under the BEPS MLI to include that agreement. In other cases, those "one-way agreements" have not been listed under the BEPS MLI because the treaty partner is pursuing bilateral renegotiations to implement the minimum standard. That treaty partner may also be intending to cover elements that go beyond the implementation of the minimum standard and other treaty-related BEPS measures. That said, while jurisdictions will understandably want to conserve resources and renegotiate different aspects of an agreement in the course of a single renegotiation process, agreeing to implement the minimum standard should not be made conditional upon any additional amendment being made to an agreement.

Waiting agreements

53. In addition to the one-way agreement, there are over 280 bilateral agreements concluded between pairs of jurisdictions that are members of the Inclusive Framework where only one of them has signed the BEPS MLI ("waiting agreements"). For that reason, none of these agreements would, at this stage, be modified by the BEPS MLI. Nearly all these agreements would become covered under the BEPS MLI if the treaty partner that has not yet signed the BEPS MLI would do so and would list the agreement.

54. The OECD Secretariat has been liaising with some of the jurisdictions that have been working towards signature of the BEPS MLI as part of their plan to implement the minimum standard (see Chapter 3 below). Those included Antigua and Barbuda, Benin, Mauritania, Montenegro and others, which between them have over 70 waiting agreements that would become covered agreements under the BEPS MLI following their signatures.

Notes

[1] One other jurisdiction that is not a member of the Inclusive Framework (Lesotho) also ratified the BEPS MLI in the past year.

[2] The BEPS MLI generally started to take effect as of 1 January 2023, with respect to agreements of jurisdictions that ratified it before the end of September 2022.

[3] Armenia, Côte d'Ivoire, Mexico, Papua New Guinea, Tunisia and Viet Nam deposited their instruments of ratification of the BEPS MLI after October 2022.

[4] Article 35 of the BEPS MLI provides for the rules on its entry into effect and divides modifications into two categories based on the type of taxation to which they apply. In general, under Article 35(1)(a), with respect to taxes withheld at source on amounts paid or credited to non-residents, the BEPS MLI enters into effect on or after the first day of the next calendar year that begins on or after the latest of the dates on which the Convention enters into force for each of the Contracting Jurisdictions to a Covered Tax Agreement. As for all the other taxes levied by a jurisdiction, Article 35(1)(b) provides that the BEPS MLI generally enters into effect with respect to taxable periods beginning on or after the expiration of a period of six calendar months from the latest of the dates on which the Convention enters into force for each of the Contracting Jurisdictions to a Covered Tax Agreement.

[5] The BEPS MLI can only modify bilateral agreements that have been listed by both treaty partners under the BEPS MLI.

3 Plans for the implementation of the minimum standard and support provided to jurisdictions

Framework for the development of plans to implement the minimum standard

55. A number of jurisdictions reported agreements, concluded with other members of the Inclusive Framework, that are not compliant, not subject to a complying instrument or to a general statement on the detailed LOB, and in respect of which no steps have been taken to implement the minimum standard. These agreements are included in the table titled 'Other agreements' in the jurisdictional sections.

56. Where a jurisdiction did not provide reasons why, for that jurisdiction, such agreements do not give rise to material treaty-shopping concerns, it was invited to develop a plan to implement the minimum standard in those agreements concluded with another member of the Inclusive Framework.[1]

57. Where a jurisdiction already formulated such a plan in the context of the 2021 or 2022 peer reviews, it was invited to provide an update on that plan if changes occurred. Jurisdictions facing any difficulty in implementing their plan were also able to report such difficulty to the Secretariat.

58. The information included in an implementation plan concerns the way in which the minimum standard will be implemented – for example, that the jurisdictions will:

- include the agreements in their list of covered tax agreements under the BEPS MLI;
- enter into bilateral negotiations for the implementation of the minimum standard; or
- sign and ratify the BEPS MLI and list the agreements as covered tax agreements.

59. Each year, jurisdictions will be invited to provide an update on their implementation plan if changes occur, and as applicable, to report any difficulty in implementing the plan to the Secretariat.

60. In cases where a jurisdiction did not make a plan (or provide an update on the plan) to implement the minimum standard where a plan was called for, a recommendation to provide one has been made. These recommendations are discussed in Chapter 4 below.

Status of plans to implement the minimum standard

61. As mentioned above, implementation plans can take a variety of forms. While some jurisdictions have developed the same implementation plan for all concerned agreements, others have developed tailored plans for each agreement. A small number of jurisdictions have also stated that their plan, which was discussed with the OECD Secretariat, at this stage, remains under internal deliberation and therefore detail has not been included in this report.

62. In total, 28 jurisdictions are currently working to give effect to their respective plans for the implementation of the minimum standard, covering around 260 non-compliant agreements.

63. The table below broadly sets out the different categories of implementation plans that are in place in 2023 for the concerned jurisdictions.

Table 3.1. Plans to implement the minimum standard

Jurisdiction	BEPS MLI		Other	Under internal deliberation
	Plan to join the BEPS MLI	Plan to expand list of covered tax agreements		
Albania			x	
Antigua and Barbuda	x			
Austria			x	
Benin	x			
Botswana	x			
Brunei Darussalam	x			
Cabo Verde			x	
Czechia		x	x	
Democratic Republic of the Congo	x			
Dominican Republic			x	
Faroe Islands			x	
Gabon		x		
Georgia		x		
Hungary		x		
Italy		x		
Kenya		x		
Mauritania	x			
Montenegro	x			
Norway			x	
Paraguay				x
Saint Kitts and Nevis				x
South Africa			x	
Sri Lanka			x	
Trinidad and Tobago			x	
Togo				x
United Arab Emirates		x		x
Uzbekistan				x
Zambia				x

Note: Detail on each jurisdiction's plan to implement the minimum standard is included in that jurisdiction's jurisdictional section.

64. Most of the plans that have been developed, since 2021, to implement the minimum standard involve the application of the provisions of the BEPS MLI. Such plans are also those that are implemented most rapidly. Indeed, four out of the six jurisdictions that have given effect to their implementation plans over the past year (Austria, Azerbaijan, Eswatini and Indonesia) did so by either joining the BEPS MLI, or expanding their lists of covered tax agreements. Moreover, most recent members of the Inclusive Framework (namely Azerbaijan and Mauritania) have chosen to implement the minimum standard in their agreements by joining the BEPS MLI and listing those agreements to be covered. Currently, 14 out of the 23 jurisdictions that have confirmed their plan intend to implement the minimum standard in the relevant agreements by way of an extension of their existing lists of covered tax agreements, or in the context of a plan to join the BEPS MLI. In the light of the experience gathered by many members of the Inclusive

Framework in signing, ratifying and implementing the BEPS MLI, the BEPS MLI evidently continues to be a key recourse for the implementation of the minimum standard. Many jurisdictions note that a majority or their agreements are, or would become, matched agreements under the BEPS MLI and seek out the efficiency, in terms of time and resources, offered by the BEPS MLI.

65. Jurisdictions choosing to implement the minimum standard by other means, such as bilateral discussions, do so for several reasons. Sometimes, this plan forms part of a wider effort to renegotiate different aspects of an agreement, beyond the implementation of the minimum standard. It may also be that their treaty partner has indicated that it does not intend to use the BEPS MLI to implement the minimum standard in that agreement. Jurisdictions with small treaty networks are also more likely to consider bilateral negotiations to implement the minimum standard.

66. An update will be provided in the next Action 6 peer review report on the status of each implementation plan.

Note

[1] The Secretariat contacted the jurisdictions that have agreements for which a plan for the implementation of the minimum standard had to be developed to offer its support in developing and giving effect to such a plan. Where a jurisdiction wants to implement the minimum standard through the PPT and some or all of its treaty partners are already signatories to the BEPS MLI, the Secretariat has encouraged the jurisdiction to sign and ratify the BEPS MLI. Where a jurisdiction has already joined the BEPS MLI, the Secretariat similarly encouraged the jurisdiction to expand its list of agreements to be covered under the BEPS MLI in order to include the concerned agreements. For tax treaties that would not become covered tax agreements under the BEPS MLI, the Secretariat encouraged the treaty partners to develop a plan, and where possible a joint plan, for the implementation of the minimum standard.

4 Recommendations

67. As part of the support provided to jurisdictions in the implementation of the minimum standard under the revised peer review methodology, recommendations are issued to members in two categories of cases. First, a member that is implementing the minimum standard by signing the BEPS MLI will be recommended to complete the steps to have it take effect with respect to its tax agreements. Second, where a jurisdiction has tax agreements for which a plan for the implementation of the minimum standard needs to be developed, if the jurisdiction does not make such a plan (or provide an update on the plan), a recommendation will be made to provide a plan with respect to the concerned tax agreements.

68. In the context of the 2022 peer review, 19 jurisdictions were recommended to take steps to have the BEPS MLI take effect with respect to their agreements listed to be covered.[1] Eight of these jurisdictions have since completed the steps in this regard: Armenia, Côte d'Ivoire, Mexico, Papua New Guinea, Romania, Tunisia and Viet Nam. Their agreements that will be modified by the BEPS MLI will come into compliance with the minimum standard once the provisions of the BEPS MLI take effect. This year, 12 jurisdictions have been recommended to complete the steps to have the BEPS MLI take effect.

69. Additional recommendations have been made this year to four jurisdictions to develop a plan, or provide an update on the plan, for the implementation of the minimum standard. Further detail on the recommendations made can be found in the jurisdictional sections in Chapter 8.

70. The Secretariat has contacted the concerned jurisdictions to offer its support, as applicable, in completing the steps to have the BEPS MLI take effect and to develop a plan for the implementation of the minimum standard. As discussed in Section 4 above, the information to be included in an implementation plan is the way in which the minimum standard will be implemented – for example, that the jurisdictions will:

- include the tax agreements in their list of covered tax agreements under the BEPS MLI;
- enter into bilateral negotiations for the implementation of the minimum standard; or
- sign and ratify the BEPS MLI and list the tax agreements as covered tax agreements.

71. Recommendations were issued to those jurisdictions that did not confirm an implementation plan in respect of the agreements for which a plan needs to be developed.

72. An update will be provided in the next Action 6 peer review report on the steps taken by each jurisdiction that has received a recommendation.

Note

[1] This type of recommendation mostly concerns jurisdictions that have signed the BEPS MLI but have not yet completed the steps to deposit the instrument of ratification of the BEPS MLI (until which time, in accordance with Articles 34 and 35 of the BEPS MLI, the provisions of the BEPS MLI cannot start to take effect). In some cases, a similar recommendation is made to jurisdictions that are Parties to the BEPS MLI but that have made a reservation under Article 35(7) BEPS MLI to delay the entry into effect of the provisions of the BEPS MLI until the completion of their internal procedures but have not yet notified the completion of such internal procedures for any of their covered tax agreements.

5 Difficulties in implementing the minimum standard

73. The peer review provides jurisdictions that encounter difficulties in reaching agreement with another jurisdiction to implement the Action 6 minimum standard with an opportunity to raise concerns with the OECD Secretariat. This process, which is set out in paragraph 35 of the Revised Peer Review Documents, has been in place since the 2017 Peer Review Documents (paragraph 19) to identify cases where a jurisdiction is facing a treaty partner that is a member of the Inclusive Framework that is unwilling to respect its commitment to implement the minimum standard.

74. No concern has been raised on the implementation of the minimum standard in the context of the 2023 Action 6 peer review process. Moreover, any such concerns raised in previous years have been addressed.

Previous concern regarding the CARICOM Agreement

75. The CARICOM Agreement was concluded in 1994 to encourage regional trade and investment within the CARICOM, and contains several unusual features,[1] not found in the OECD Model Tax Convention or UN Model Double Taxation Convention, which could lead to certain income flows escaping tax altogether. These departures from standard tax treaty provisions may have encouraged greater economic integration within the CARICOM at the time, but they may also have made the Agreement more vulnerable to treaty shopping and other forms of abuse.

76. At this stage, the CARICOM Agreement does not contain the elements required to satisfy the Action 6 minimum standard. Implementing the Action 6 minimum standard, or updating the CARICOM Agreement more broadly, requires agreement by all eleven jurisdictions that are parties to that agreement.

77. Discussions have now commenced among CARICOM Member States to bring the CARICOM Agreement up to date. Those talks follow previous Action 6 peer review processes where concerns had been raised on the CARICOM Agreement. In the course of the 2019 peer review, a jurisdiction raised a concern about the Agreement and called upon other treaty partners to launch talks to modernise it. In the 2020 and 2021 peer reviews, jurisdictions that are parties to the CARICOM Agreement were encouraged to bring that agreement up to date by commencing talks among all the treaty partners. In the 2022 peer review, it was acknowledged that discussions to bring the CARICOM Agreement up to date should be continued.

78. The Secretariat has offered its full support to the jurisdictions that are parties to the CARICOM Agreement and members of the Inclusive Framework in working towards bringing this agreement into compliance with the minimum standard.

Note

[1] The CARICOM Agreement provides for an almost exclusive source-based taxation of all income, gains and profits. Some income – for instance, dividends – is also entirely exempted from tax under the CARICOM Agreement.

6 Conclusion and next steps

79. In line with peer reviews in previous years, the 2023 peer review shows that in general, most jurisdictions that are members of the Inclusive Framework are respecting their commitment to implement the minimum standard. The 2023 peer review also highlights that the BEPS MLI, which has been the main tool used to implement the minimum standard, has continued to have a significant and increased effect and is strengthening the bilateral tax treaty network of jurisdictions that ratified it.

80. That said, as in previous years, this year's peer review shows that the Action 6 minimum standard is still being implemented unevenly and, in particular, important differences persist in the progress made on its implementation between jurisdictions that have ratified the BEPS MLI and other jurisdictions.

81. Indeed, the peer review shows that jurisdictions that have not signed or ratified the BEPS MLI have still generally made slower progress in implementing the minimum standard. The 2023 peer review thus highlights that ratification of the BEPS MLI is an effective tool for the implementation of the minimum standard.

82. That said, additional insight is gained regarding steps taken other than under the BEPS MLI to implement the minimum standard. Currently, such steps have been taken in respect of around 200 agreements (including around 120 agreements for which the treaty partner has taken concurrent steps under the BEPS MLI). An additional 53 agreements covering 55 bilateral relationships between members of the Inclusive Framework are the object of a general statement on one party's intention to use the detailed LOB as part of its commitment to implement the minimum standard. By comparison, steps to implement the minimum standard under the BEPS MLI have been taken in respect of over 430 agreements (including the 120 agreements, mentioned above, in respect of which the treaty partner has taken concurrent steps other than under the BEPS MLI).

83. This year, around 1,360 agreements concluded by members of the Inclusive Framework complied with the minimum standard. This represents an increase of around 30% as compared to 2022. In total, over 2,400 agreements concluded between members of the Inclusive Framework are compliant, subject to a complying instrument, subject to steps taken by at least one treaty partner to implement the minimum standard, or are the object of a general statement by one treaty partner that it intends to use the detailed LOB to implement the minimum standard in all its bilateral agreements.

84. Moreover, this year's peer review shows continued progress by jurisdictions to develop and give effect to plans to implement the minimum standard where one was called for (see Chapter 3 above). The majority of these plans involve the application of the BEPS MLI to the concerned agreements. Once all plans to implement the minimum standard are in effect, the minimum standard will be implemented, or on course to being implemented, in nearly all of the agreements concluded between members of the Inclusive Framework.

Next steps for certain members of the Inclusive Framework

85. Pursuant to the revised peer review methodology applicable since 2021, this year's peer review contains, in Chapter 8, recommendations to jurisdictions that have not yet completed the steps to have the BEPS MLI take effect, and to jurisdictions that have not made a plan (or provided an update on the plan)

to implement the minimum standard where needed, to ensure those jurisdictions can be provided with appropriate support in the implementation of the minimum standard. The immediate next steps for jurisdictions are to take note of these recommendations and follow them in their progress towards the implementation of the minimum standard.

86. When no recommendations are made, no other implementation issues are identified with respect to a jurisdiction and no other jurisdiction has raised any concerns regarding their agreements with that jurisdiction, no immediate next steps are indicated for that jurisdiction.[1]

Next steps for the Inclusive Framework

87. The implementation of the minimum standard – in particular the actions taken to follow the recommendations made, and the progress made to give effect to the implementation plans that have been developed – will continue to be monitored and reported in the context of the new peer review exercise.

Note

[1] The jurisdictional section of each such jurisdiction includes the mention that "No jurisdiction has raised any concerns about their agreements with the jurisdiction."

7 Background on the Action 6 minimum standard and peer review

Context of the peer review

88. Over the last decades, bilateral tax agreements, concluded by nearly every jurisdiction in the world, have served to prevent harmful double taxation and remove obstacles to cross-border trade in goods and services, and movements of capital, technology and persons. This extensive network of tax agreements has, however, also given rise to so-called "treaty-shopping" arrangements.

89. As set out in the Action 6 Final Report, treaty shopping typically involves the attempt by a person to indirectly access the benefits of a tax agreement between two jurisdictions without being a resident of one of those jurisdictions.[1]

90. Treaty shopping is undesirable for several reasons, including:

- Treaty benefits negotiated between the parties to an agreement are economically extended to residents of a third jurisdiction in a way the parties did not intend. The principle of reciprocity is therefore breached and the balance of concessions that the parties make is altered;
- Income may escape taxation altogether or be subject to inadequate taxation in a way the parties did not intend; and
- The jurisdiction of residence of the ultimate income beneficiary has less incentive to enter into a tax agreement with the jurisdiction of source, because residents of the jurisdiction of residence can indirectly receive treaty benefits from the jurisdiction of source without the need for the jurisdiction of residence to provide reciprocal benefits.

Some previous attempts to tackle treaty shopping

91. Concerns about treaty shopping are not new. For example, in 1977, the concept of "beneficial owner" was introduced into the dividends, interest, and royalties articles of the OECD Model Tax Convention to clarify the meaning of the words "paid to", and deal with simple treaty-shopping situations where income is paid to an intermediary resident of a treaty country who is not treated as the owner of that income for tax purposes (such as an agent or nominee).[2]

92. In 1977, the Commentary on Article 1 of the OECD Model Tax Convention was also updated to include a section on the improper use of tax agreements.[3] In 1986, the Committee on Fiscal Affairs (CFA) published two reports: *Double Taxation and the Use of Base Companies* and *Double Taxation and the Use of Conduit Companies*. In 2002, the Committee published the report, *Restricting the Entitlement to Treaty Benefits*. The Commentary on Article 1 of the OECD Model Tax Convention was expanded on several occasions, notably in 2003, with the inclusion of sample provisions that countries could use to counter treaty shopping.

93. A review of jurisdictions' practices shows that they have tried to address treaty shopping in the past and have used different approaches to do so. Some have relied on specific anti-abuse rules based

on the legal nature, ownership, and general activities of residents of a jurisdiction party to a tax agreement.[4] Others have favoured a general anti-abuse rule based on the purpose of transactions or arrangements.

BEPS and treaty shopping

94. The BEPS Action Plan[5], developed by the CFA and endorsed by the G20 Leaders in September 2013,[6] identified 15 actions to address base erosion and profit shifting (BEPS). It identified treaty abuse, and in particular treaty shopping, as one of the most important sources of BEPS concerns.

95. Action 6 (Prevent Treaty Abuse) of the BEPS Action Plan called for the development of treaty provisions to prevent the granting of treaty benefits in inappropriate circumstances. In parallel, Action 15 of the BEPS Action Plan called for an analysis of the possible development of a multilateral instrument "to enable jurisdictions that wish to do so to implement measures developed in the course of the work on BEPS and amend bilateral tax treaties".

96. After two years of work, the CFA including OECD and G20 countries working on an equal footing, produced the final BEPS Package,[7] which was endorsed by the OECD Council and the G20 Leaders in November 2015.

97. Jurisdictions agreed that four of the BEPS measures would be minimum standards that participating jurisdictions would commit to implement. The Action 6 Report sets out one of these minimum standards. The Action 6 minimum standard requires jurisdictions to commit to include in their tax treaties provisions dealing with treaty shopping to ensure a minimum level of protection against treaty abuse.

The Action 6 minimum standard

98. The minimum standard on treaty shopping requires jurisdictions to include two components in their tax agreements: an express statement on non-taxation (generally in the preamble) and one of three methods of addressing treaty shopping.

99. The minimum standard does not provide how these two components should be implemented (i.e. through the BEPS MLI or amending instruments). It recognises, however, that these provisions need to be agreed bilaterally and that a jurisdiction will be required to implement the minimum standard when requested to do so by another member of the Inclusive Framework.

The express statement

100. As set out in paragraphs 22 and 23 of the Final Report on Action 6, jurisdictions have agreed to include in their tax agreements an express statement that their common intention is to eliminate double taxation without creating opportunities for non-taxation or reduced taxation through tax evasion or avoidance, including through treaty-shopping arrangements. The following provision now appears in the 2017 OECD Model Tax Convention:

> *Intending to conclude a Convention for the elimination of double taxation with respect to taxes on income and on capital without creating opportunities for non-taxation or reduced taxation through tax evasion or avoidance (including through treaty-shopping arrangements aimed at obtaining reliefs provided in this Convention for the indirect benefit of residents of third States)*

Three methods of addressing treaty shopping

101. Jurisdictions have also committed to implement that "common intention" through the inclusion of treaty provisions in one of the following three forms:

- a principal purpose test (PPT) equivalent to paragraph 9 of Article 29 of the 2017 OECD Model Tax Convention together with either a simplified or a detailed version of the limitation on benefits (LOB) rule that appears in paragraphs 1 to 7 of the 2017 OECD Model Tax Convention; or
- the PPT alone; or
- a detailed version of the LOB rule together with a mechanism (such as a treaty rule that might take the form of a PPT rule restricted to conduit arrangements, or domestic anti-abuse rules or judicial doctrines that would achieve a similar result) that would deal with conduit arrangements not already dealt with in tax treaties.

The obligation to implement the minimum standard

102. The Action 6 Report recognised that "some flexibility in the implementation of the Action 6 minimum standard would be required, as these provisions need to be adapted to each country's specificities and to the circumstances of the negotiation of bilateral conventions." In particular:

- a jurisdiction is required to implement the minimum standard in a treaty only if asked to do so by another member of the Inclusive Framework;
- the way in which the minimum standard will be implemented in each bilateral treaty will need to be agreed to between the contracting jurisdictions.
- the commitment applies to existing and future treaties but since the conclusion of a new treaty and the modification of an existing treaty depend on the overall balance of the provisions of a treaty, this commitment should not be interpreted as a commitment to conclude new treaties or amend existing treaties within a specified period of time.
- if a jurisdiction is not itself concerned by the effect of treaty shopping on its own taxation rights as a jurisdiction of source, it will not be obliged to apply provisions such as the LOB or the PPT as long as it agrees to include in a treaty provisions that its treaty partner will be able to use for that purpose.

103. It is also understood from the Action 6 that, while the BEPS MLI provides an effective way for jurisdictions that choose to apply the PPT to implement the minimum standard swiftly, participation in the BEPS MLI is not mandatory and jurisdictions may have different preferences as to how the minimum standard should be met. However, jurisdictions that have signed the BEPS MLI are expected to take steps to ensure that it starts to take effect with respect to their Covered Tax Agreements. Where two parties to a tax treaty have signed the BEPS MLI but only one has listed the tax treaty, listing the tax treaty amounts to a request to implement the minimum standard.

104. In May 2017, the Inclusive Framework agreed the Terms of Reference for the peer review and its methodology (the 2017 Peer Review Documents) (OECD, 2017[1]) and decided that the methodology would be reviewed in 2020. In 2021, members of the Inclusive Framework on BEPS approved the 2021 Peer Review Document (OECD, 2021[2]) which is an updated version of the 2017 Peer Review Documents. The changes to the Peer Review Documents related to the methodology; changes to other sections of the Peer Review Documents were mostly conforming in nature. The Action 6 minimum standard and the way it is reflected in the Terms of Reference remained unchanged.

105. This 2021 Peer Review Document governs the conduct of the peer reviews of the Action 6 minimum standard as of 2021. It describes: the core output of the peer review and monitoring process; the process for the resolution of interpretation and application issues that might arise in the course of implementing the minimum standard on treaty-shopping; the process to be followed by jurisdictions that encounter difficulties in getting agreement from another jurisdiction member of the Inclusive Framework on BEPS in order to implement the Action 6 minimum standard; and the confidentiality of documents produced in the review process.

The 2018 peer review

106. The first peer review was conducted in 2018 and covered the 116 jurisdictions that were members of the Inclusive Framework on 30 June 2018. The Peer Review Report, which was adopted by the Inclusive Framework in January 2019, was published on 14 February 2019.

107. The 2018 peer review revealed that, as the provisions of the BEPS MLI had not taken effect at the time of the first peer review, nearly all of the agreements reviewed for this report did not at that time comply with the minimum standard. Substantial progress had, however, been made in 2017 and 2018 towards its implementation and a large majority of Inclusive Framework members had begun to translate their commitment on treaty shopping into actions and were in the process of modifying their treaty networks.

108. In total, on 30 June 2018, the peer review showed that 82 jurisdictions had some agreements that were already compliant with the minimum standard or were subject to a complying instrument that would bring their agreements into compliance.[8] The first Peer Review highlighted the effectiveness of the BEPS MLI in implementing the treaty-related BEPS measures. It was by far the preferred tool of Inclusive Framework members for implementing the minimum standard.

109. In the course of the first peer review, all concerns raised by jurisdictions on the implementation of the minimum standard in their agreements had been resolved when the Report was approved by the Inclusive Framework and therefore no recommendation was made under the first peer review.

The 2019 peer review

110. The Second peer review was conducted in 2019 and covered the 129 jurisdictions that were members of the Inclusive Framework on 30 June 2019. The Peer Review Report, which was adopted by the Inclusive Framework in January 2020, was published on 24 March 2020.

111. The 2019 peer review revealed that, by 30 June 2019, 91 Inclusive Framework members had begun to update their bilateral treaty network and were implementing the minimum standard. The data compiled for this peer review demonstrated that the BEPS MLI had been the tool used by the vast majority of jurisdictions that had begun to implement the minimum standard.

112. By 30 June 2019, the BEPS MLI had already modified around 60 bilateral agreements. The BEPS MLI's impact was expected to increase quickly as jurisdictions ratified it.

113. In the course of the Second peer review, a jurisdiction had raised a concern with respect to the CARICOM Agreement, a multilateral agreement concluded by eleven jurisdictions, ten of which were members of the Inclusive Framework. The CARICOM Agreement had been concluded in 1994 to encourage regional trade and investment within the Community, and contains several unusual features,9 not found in the OECD Model Tax Convention or the UN Model Double Taxation Convention, which could lead to certain income flows escaping tax altogether. These departures from standard tax treaty provisions may have encouraged greater economic integration within the CARICOM Community at the time. But they may also have made the CARICOM Agreement more vulnerable to treaty shopping and other forms of abuse. Previous renegotiation attempts of the CARICOM Agreement had proven to be difficult.

The 2020 peer review

114. The Third peer review was conducted in 2020 and covered the 137 jurisdictions that were members of the Inclusive Framework on 30 June 2020. The Peer Review Report, which was adopted by the Inclusive Framework in February 2021, was published on 1 April 2021.

115. The 2020 peer review revealed that, by 30 June 2020, 98 Inclusive Framework members jurisdictions of the Inclusive Framework had some agreements that already complied with the minimum standard or that were subject to a complying instrument and would therefore become compliant shortly.

The data compiled for this peer review demonstrated that the BEPS MLI had been the tool used by the vast majority of jurisdictions that had begun to implement the minimum standard.

116. By 30 June 2020, the BEPS MLI had already modified around 350 bilateral agreements. The BEPS MLI's impact was expected to increase quickly as jurisdictions ratified it.

117. Concerning the CARICOM Agreement, the concern raised in 2019 remained as the parties to the CARICOM Agreement have not yet modernised it. All Jurisdictions that are parties to the CARICOM Agreement were encouraged to bring that agreement up to date by commencing talks among all the treaty partners.

118. Moreover, encouragements were made to members of the Inclusive Framework that were signatories to the BEPS MLI but that had not yet ratified it, as the agreements listed under the BEPS MLI would only start to become compliant after their ratification.

119. The 2020 Action 6 peer review report also identified gaps in BEPS MLI coverage, or "non-covered agreements" under the BEPS MLI (agreements concluded between pairs of signatories to the BEPS MLI where one treaty partner has not listed the agreement under the BEPS MLI; and agreements concluded between jurisdictions only one of which has signed the BEPS MLI).

The 2021 peer review

120. The Fourth peer review was conducted in 2021 and covered the 139 jurisdictions that were members of the Inclusive Framework on 30 June 2021. The Peer Review Report, which was adopted by the Inclusive Framework in February 2022, was published on 21 March 2022.

121. The 2021 peer review was the first peer review to be governed by the revised peer review methodology in the 2021 Peer Review Document. In 2021, the BEPS MLI continued to significantly expand the implementation of the minimum standard for the jurisdictions that have ratified it. The number of compliant agreements concluded between members of the Inclusive Framework and covered by the BEPS MLI almost doubled, from approximately 350 to more than 650 (out of around 710 compliant agreements), between the 2020 and 2021 peer reviews.

122. In total, as at 30 June 2021, around 2,330 agreements concluded between members of the Inclusive Framework are either compliant, subject to a complying instrument, subject to steps taken by at least one treaty partner to implement the minimum standard, or the object of a general statement by one treaty partner that it intends to use the detailed LOB, together with a mechanism to address conduit arrangements, to implement the minimum standard in all its bilateral agreements.

123. The review further revealed jurisdictions' plans to implement the minimum standard in non-compliant agreements concluded with other members of the Inclusive Framework, that were not already subject to a complying instrument or general statement on the detailed LOB, and in respect of which no steps have been taken to implement the minimum standard (and where no reasons were provided why, for that member, the tax agreement does not give rise to material treaty-shopping concerns). The vast majority of these plans involved the application of the BEPS MLI to the concerned agreements. Once all plans to implement the minimum standard would be in effect, the minimum standard would be implemented, or on course to being implemented, in nearly all of the agreements concluded between members of the Inclusive Framework.

124. Finally, recommendations were made in the review to jurisdictions that had to formulate a plan for the implementation of the minimum standard, and to those that had signed the BEPS MLI but had not yet completed the steps for the entry into effect of its provisions.

The 2022 peer review

125. The Fifth peer review was conducted in 2022 and covered the 141 jurisdictions that were members of the Inclusive Framework on 31 May 2022. The Peer Review Report, which was adopted by the Inclusive Framework in February 2023, was published on 21 March 2023.

126. The 2022 peer review was the second peer review to be governed by the revised peer review methodology set out in the 2021 Peer Review Document. In 2022, the BEPS MLI continued to significantly expand the implementation of the minimum standard for the jurisdictions that have ratified it. As at 31 May 2022, over 850 out of the 975 of the compliant agreements concluded between members of the Inclusive Framework had been brought into compliance by application of the BEPS MLI.

127. In total, as at 31 May 2022, over 2 400 agreements concluded between members of the Inclusive Framework were either compliant, subject to a complying instrument, subject to steps taken by at least one treaty partner to implement the minimum standard, or the object of a general statement by one treaty partner that it intends to use the detailed LOB, together with a mechanism to address conduit arrangements, to implement the minimum standard in all its bilateral agreements.

128. The 2022 review further revealed jurisdictions' progress to give effect to their plans to implement the minimum standard in non-compliant agreements concluded with other members of the Inclusive Framework, that were not already subject to a complying instrument or general statement on the detailed LOB, and in respect of which no steps have been taken to implement the minimum standard (and where no reasons were provided why, for that member, the tax agreement does not give rise to material treaty-shopping concerns). The majority of these plans involved the application of the BEPS MLI to the concerned agreements. Once all plans to implement the minimum standard would be in effect, the minimum standard would be implemented, or on course to being implemented, in nearly all of the agreements concluded between members of the Inclusive Framework.

129. Finally, recommendations were made in the review to jurisdictions that had to formulate a plan for the implementation of the minimum standard, and to those that had signed the BEPS MLI but had not yet completed the steps for the entry into effect of its provisions.

Conduct of the 2023 peer review

130. The review started with a questionnaire sent to members of the Inclusive Framework in March 2023. This questionnaire was similar to the questionnaire issued for 2022, reflecting the revised methodology in the 2021 Peer Review Document. Similar to the questionnaires issued in previous years,[10] each jurisdiction was asked to list all of its comprehensive income tax agreements in force.

131. For each tax agreement listed, members indicate whether or not it complies with the minimum standard described in the Terms of Reference referred to above. A tax agreement complies with the minimum standard if it does so as originally signed, if an amending instrument that implements the minimum standard in that tax agreement is in force, or if the relevant provisions of the BEPS MLI have started to take effect for that tax agreement (in accordance with Article 35 of the BEPS MLI).

132. For each tax agreement listed that is non-compliant with the minimum standard, members indicate whether it is on course to become compliant with the minimum standard (i.e. whether it is subject to a complying instrument). This is satisfied if a member has signed the BEPS MLI and both jurisdictions have listed the agreement as one to be covered. It is also satisfied if an amending bilateral tax agreement implementing the minimum standard in the agreement has been signed or if a completely new treaty that complies with the Action 6 minimum standard and that would replace that treaty has been signed.

133. Members were requested to provide additional information for tax agreements that are not compliant and not subject to a complying instrument:

- *Plan to implement a detailed LOB provision*: If a member intends to use the detailed LOB as part of its commitment to implement the minimum standard in all of its bilateral tax agreements, the additional information to be provided would be a general statement that it intends to implement the minimum standard bilaterally by negotiating a detailed LOB provision and that the negotiation of its agreements will take place as time and resources permit.
- *Steps taken to enable the tax treaty to become subject to a complying instrument*: A member that does not intend to use the detailed LOB as part of its commitment to implement the minimum standard in all of its bilateral tax agreements to implement the minimum standard would provide information on the steps it has taken to implement the minimum standard for each tax agreement not compliant with the minimum standard or not subject to a complying instrument.
- *Other tax treaties*: For tax agreements not dealt with above and concluded with other members of the Inclusive Framework, a member would provide reasons why, for that member, the tax agreement does not give rise to material treaty-shopping concerns. Where, for a tax treaty, a jurisdiction does not provide such information, it would formulate a plan to include the minimum standard in that tax agreement. Where a jurisdiction had formulated such a plan in 2021 or 2022, it was invited to provide an update on this plan.

134. Each jurisdiction was invited to complete the questionnaire taking into account the agreements that were in force, or expected to be in force, by 31 May 2023.

135. Each jurisdiction was also asked to answer additional questions on ratification of complying instruments and issues described in Sections D and E of the Peer Review Document on difficulties encountered in getting agreement from another jurisdiction to implement the minimum standard. Jurisdictions were also free to add any further comments. The list of the 142 jurisdictions that were subject to the peer review[11] and full details by jurisdiction are contained in the Annex.

136. The Secretariat analysed jurisdictions' responses to verify and reconcile any divergent information and produced a first draft of this report.

References

OECD (2021), *BEPS Action 6 on Preventing the Granting of Treaty Benefits in Inappropriate Circumstances – Revised Peer Review Documents*, OECD/G20 Base Erosion and Profit Shifting Project, OECD, Paris, http://www.oecd.org/tax/beps/beps-action-6-preventing-the-granting-of-treaty-benefits-in-inappropriate-circumstances-revised-peer-review-documents.pdf. [2]

OECD (2017), *BEPS Action 6 on Preventing the Granting of Treaty Benefits in Inappropriate Circumstances – Peer Review Documents*, OECD/G20 Base Erosion and Profit Shifting Project, OECD, Paris, http://www.oecd.org/tax/beps/beps-action-6-preventing-the-granting-of-treaty-benefits-in-inappropriatecircumstance-peer-review-documents.pdf. [1]

Notes

1 See paragraph 17 of the BEPS Action 6 Final Report (2015). As the Report also notes, cases where a resident of the Contracting State in which income originates seeks to obtain treaty benefits (e.g. through a transfer of residence to the other Contracting State or through the use of an entity established in that other State) could also be considered a form of treaty shopping.

2 See paragraph 2 of Articles 10 and 11, and paragraph 1 of Article 12 of the OECD Model Tax Convention.

3 See paragraphs 7-10 of the Commentary on Article 1 of the 1977 Model Tax Convention.

4 “Limitation on benefits” provisions commonly found in agreements concluded by the United States are the best-known example.

5 https://www.oecd.org/ctp/BEPSActionPlan.pdf.

6 http://www.g20.utoronto.ca/2013/2013-0906-declaration.html.

7 In October 2015, the CFA, including OECD and G20 countries working on an equal footing, produced the Final BEPS Package, in the form of reports on each of the 15 actions accompanied by an Explanatory Statement. The Final BEPS Package gives countries and economies the tools they need to ensure that profits are taxed where economic activities generating the profits are performed and where value is created, while at the same time giving businesses greater certainty by reducing disputes over the application of international tax rules and standardising compliance requirements.

8 A further seven jurisdictions had no comprehensive tax agreements and were outside the scope of this exercise.

9 The CARICOM Agreement provides for an almost exclusive source-based taxation of all income, gains and profits. Some income – for instance dividends – are also entirely exempted from tax under the CARICOM Agreement.

[10] See, for example, the 2018 Action 6 peer review questionnaire (https://www.oecd.org/tax/treaties/beps-action-6-preventing-the-granting-of-treaty-benefits-in-inappropriate-circumstance-peer-review-documents.pdf).

[11] See also note 3.

8 Jurisdictional Sections

Inclusive Framework members on 31 May 2023

1	Albania	51	France	101	Oman
2	Andorra	52	Gabon	102	Pakistan
3	Angola	53	Georgia	103	Panama
4	Anguilla	54	Germany	104	Papua New Guinea
5	Antigua and Barbuda	55	Gibraltar	105	Paraguay
6	Argentina	56	Greece	106	Peru
7	Armenia	57	Greenland	107	Poland
8	Aruba	58	Grenada	108	Portugal
9	Australia	59	Guernsey	109	Qatar
10	Austria	60	Haiti	110	Romania
11	Azerbaijan	61	Honduras	111	Russian Federation
12	The Bahamas	62	Hong Kong, China	112	Saint Kitts and Nevis
13	Bahrain	63	Hungary	113	Saint Lucia
14	Barbados	64	Iceland	114	Saint Vincent and the Grenadines
15	Belarus	65	India	115	Samoa
16	Belgium	66	Indonesia	116	San Marino
17	Belize	67	Ireland	117	Saudi Arabia
18	Benin	68	Isle of Man	118	Senegal
19	Bermuda	69	Israel	119	Serbia
20	Bosnia-Herzegovina	70	Italy	120	Seychelles
21	Botswana	71	Jamaica	121	Sierra Leone
22	Brazil	72	Japan	122	Singapore
23	British Virgin Islands	73	Jersey	123	Slovak Republic
24	Brunei Darussalam	74	Jordan	124	Slovenia
25	Bulgaria	75	Kazakhstan	125	South Africa
26	Burkina Faso	76	Kenya	126	Spain
27	Cabo Verde	77	Korea	127	Sri Lanka
28	Cameroon	78	Latvia	128	Sweden
29	Canada	79	Liberia	129	Switzerland
30	Cayman Islands	80	Liechtenstein	130	Thailand
31	Chile	81	Lithuania	131	Togo
32	China (People's Republic of)	82	Luxembourg	132	Trinidad and Tobago
33	Colombia	83	Macau, China	133	Tunisia
34	Congo	84	Malaysia	134	Turks and Caicos Islands
35	Cook Islands	85	Maldives	135	Türkiye
36	Costa Rica	86	Malta	136	Ukraine
37	Côte d'Ivoire	87	Mauritius	137	United Arab Emirates
38	Croatia	88	Mauritania	138	United Kingdom
39	Curaçao	89	Mexico	139	United States
40	Czechia	90	Monaco	140	Uruguay
41	Democratic Republic of the Congo	91	Mongolia	141	Viet Nam

42	Denmark	92	Montenegro	142	Zambia
43	Djibouti	93	Montserrat		
44	Dominica	94	Morocco		
45	Dominican Republic	95	Namibia		
46	Egypt	96	Netherlands		
47	Estonia	97	New Zealand		
48	Eswatini	98	Nigeria		
49	Faroe Islands	99	North Macedonia		
50	Finland	100	Norway		

1. The jurisdictional sections include tax agreements with jurisdictions that are not members of the Inclusive Framework. Such agreements are indicated with an asterisk (*).
2. Chapter 8 includes a jurisdictional section for Uzbekistan. Noting that Uzbekistan became a member of the Inclusive Framework on 9 June 2023, which is after the reference date for this year's peer review exercise (31 May 2023), its treaty partners have not been expected to provide any additional information about their agreements with Uzbekistan.
3. Chapter 8 does not include a jurisdictional section for the Philippines and Kuwait. Noting that the Philippines and Kuwait became members of the Inclusive Framework on 10 November 2023 and 15 November 2023, respectively, which dates are after the reference date for this year's peer review exercise (31 May 2023), their treaty partners have not been expected to provide any additional information about their agreements with the Philippines or Kuwait.
4. Chapter 8 does not include jurisdictional sections for Belarus or the Russian Federation.

Albania

A. Progress in the implementation of the minimum standard

Albania has 43 tax agreements in force, as reported in its response to the Peer Review questionnaire. Twenty-seven of those agreements comply with the minimum standard.

Albania signed the MLI in 2019 and deposited its instrument of ratification on 22 September 2020. The MLI entered into force for Albania on 1 January 2021. The agreements modified by the MLI come into compliance with the minimum standard once the provisions of the MLI take effect.

Albania has not listed its agreement with Saudi Arabia under the MLI but indicated in its response to the Peer Review questionnaire that this agreement did not give rise to material treaty-shopping concerns for Albania. Saudi Arabia has listed its agreement with Albania to be covered under the MLI.

Albania is implementing the minimum standard through the inclusion of the preamble statement and the PPT.[1]

B. Conclusion

Saudi Arabia has listed its agreement with Albania under the MLI, which amounts to a request to implement the minimum standard in that agreement.

Albania indicated in its response to the Peer Review questionnaire that while this agreement did not give rise to material treaty-shopping concerns for Albania, Albania intends to implement the minimum standard in this agreement through bilateral negotiations.

Summary of the jurisdiction response – Albania

	1.Treaty partners	2. Compliance with the standard	3. Signature of a complying instrument	4. Minimum standard provision used
1	Austria	No	No	PPT
2	Belgium	Yes MLI		PPT
3	Bosnia-Herzegovina	Yes MLI		PPT
4	Bulgaria	Yes MLI		PPT
5	China (People's Republic of)	Yes MLI		PPT
6	Croatia	Yes MLI		PPT
7	Czechia	No	No	PPT
8	Egypt	Yes MLI		PPT
9	Estonia	No	Yes MLI	PPT
10	France	Yes MLI		PPT
11	Germany	No	No	PPT
12	Greece	Yes MLI		PPT
13	Hungary	Yes MLI		PPT

[1] For its agreements listed under the MLI, Albania is implementing the preamble statement (Article 6 of the MLI) and the PPT (Article 7 of the MLI).

14	Iceland	Yes MLI		PPT
15	India	Yes MLI		PPT
16	Ireland	Yes MLI		PPT
17	Israel	Yes other		
18	Italy	No	No	PPT
19	Korea	No	No	PPT
20	Kosovo*	Yes other		PPT
21	Kuwait	No	No	PPT
22	Latvia	Yes MLI		PPT
23	Malaysia	Yes MLI		PPT
24	Malta	Yes MLI		PPT
25	Moldova*	No	No	PPT
26	Montenegro	No	No	PPT
27	Netherlands	Yes MLI		PPT
28	North Macedonia	No	Yes MLI	PPT
29	Norway	No	No	PPT
30	Poland	Yes MLI		PPT
31	Qatar	Yes MLI		PPT
32	Romania	No	Yes MLI	PPT
33	Russian Federation	Yes MLI		PPT
34	Serbia	Yes MLI		PPT
35	Singapore	Yes MLI		PPT
36	Slovenia	Yes MLI		PPT
37	Spain	Yes MLI		PPT
38	Sweden	No	Yes MLI	PPT
39	Switzerland	No	No	PPT
40	Türkiye	No	Yes MLI	PPT
41	United Arab Emirates	Yes MLI		PPT
42	United Kingdom	Yes MLI		PPT

Other agreements

	1.Treaty partners	2. Inclusive Framework member
1	Saudi Arabia	Yes

Andorra

A. Progress in the implementation of the minimum standard

Andorra has ten tax agreements in force, as reported in its response to the Peer Review questionnaire. Each of those agreements complies with the minimum standard.

Andorra signed the MLI in 2017 and deposited its instrument of ratification on 29 September 2021, listing its non-compliant agreements. The MLI entered into force for Andorra on 1 January 2022. The agreements modified by the MLI came into compliance with the minimum standard once the provisions of the MLI take effect.

Andorra is implementing the minimum standard through the inclusion of the preamble statement and the PPT.[2]

B. Conclusion

No jurisdiction has raised any concerns about their agreements with Andorra.

Summary of the jurisdiction response – Andorra

	1.Treaty partners	2. Compliance with the standard	3. Signature of a complying instrument	4. Minimum standard provision used
1	Cyprus*	Yes other		PPT
2	France	Yes MLI		PPT
3	Hungary	Yes other		PPT
4	Liechtenstein	Yes MLI		PPT
5	Luxembourg	Yes MLI		PPT
6	Malta	Yes MLI		PPT
7	Portugal	Yes MLI		PPT
8	San Marino	Yes other		PPT
9	Spain	Yes MLI		PPT
10	United Arab Emirates	Yes MLI		PPT

[2] For its agreements listed under the MLI, Andorra is implementing the preamble statement (Article 6 of the MLI) and the PPT (Article 7 of the MLI). Andorra has made a reservation pursuant to Article 7(15)(b) of the MLI not to apply Article 7(1) of the MLI with respect to agreements that already contain a PPT (covering two agreements).

Angola

A. Progress in the implementation of the minimum standard

Angola has three tax agreements in force, as reported in its response to the Peer Review questionnaire. Each of those agreements complies with the minimum standard.

Angola is implementing the minimum standard through the inclusion of the preamble statement and the PPT.

B. Conclusion

No jurisdiction has raised any concerns about their agreements with Angola.

Summary of the jurisdiction response – Angola

	1.Treaty partners	2. Compliance with the standard	3. Signature of a complying instrument	4. Minimum standard provision used
1	China (People's Republic of)	Yes other		PPT
2	Portugal	Yes other		PPT
3	United Arab Emirates	Yes other		PPT

Anguilla

A. Progress in the implementation of the minimum standard

Anguilla has no tax agreements in force, as reported in its response to the Peer Review questionnaire.

B. Conclusion

No jurisdiction has raised any concerns about Anguilla.

Antigua and Barbuda

A. Progress in the implementation of the minimum standard

Antigua and Barbuda has four tax agreements in force as reported in its response to the Peer Review questionnaire, including the multilateral agreement among the members of the CARICOM concluded with ten treaty partners (the CARICOM Agreement).[3] None of those agreements comply with the minimum standard.

Antigua and Barbuda has not signed the MLI.

Antigua and Barbuda indicated in its response to the Peer Review questionnaire that steps have been taken (other than under the MLI) to implement the minimum standard in the CARICOM Agreement.

In its response to the Peer Review Questionnaire, Switzerland indicated that its agreement with Antigua and Barbuda did not give rise to material treaty shopping concerns for Switzerland.

B. Conclusion

Antigua and Barbuda has developed a plan for the implementation of the minimum standard in its agreements with the United Kingdom and the United Arab Emirates. Antigua and Barbuda indicated in its response to the Peer Review questionnaire that it intends to sign the MLI and list those agreements.

Summary of the jurisdiction response – Antigua and Barbuda

	1.Treaty partners	2. Compliance with the standard	3. Signature of a complying instrument	4. Minimum standard provision used
1	CARICOM Agreement treaty partners (Barbados, Belize, Dominica, Grenada, Guyana*, Jamaica, Saint Kitts and Nevis, Saint Lucia, Saint Vincent and the Grenadines, Trinidad and Tobago)	No	No	

Other agreements

	1.Treaty partners	2. Inclusive Framework member
1	Switzerland	Yes
2	United Kingdom	Yes
3	United Arab Emirates	Yes

[3] Agreement Among the Governments of the Member States of the Caribbean Community for the Avoidance of Double Taxation and the Prevention of Fiscal Evasion with Respect to Taxes on Income, Profits or Gains and Capital Gains and for the Encouragement of Regional Trade and Investment, St. Michael Barbados, 6 July 1994; between: Antigua and Barbuda (18 February 1998), Barbados (7 July 1995), Belize (30 November 1994), Dominica (19 June 1996), Grenada (1 March 1996), Guyana* (26 November 1997), Jamaica (16 February 1995), St. Kitts/Nevis (8 May 1997), St. Lucia (22 May 1995) St. Vincent (12 February 1998) and Trinidad & Tobago (29 November 1994).

Argentina

A. Progress in the implementation of the minimum standard

Argentina has 21 tax agreements in force, as reported in its response to the Peer Review questionnaire. Four of those agreements comply with the minimum standard.

Argentina signed the MLI in 2017. The agreements modified by the MLI will come into compliance with the minimum standard once the provisions of the MLI take effect.

Argentina has not listed its agreement with Germany under the MLI but indicated in its response to the Peer Review questionnaire that steps have been taken (other than under the MLI) to implement the minimum standard in this agreement.

Argentina is implementing the minimum standard through the inclusion of the preamble statement and the PPT combined with the LOB.[4]

B. Conclusion

Recommendation

It is recommended that Argentina completes the steps to have the MLI take effect with respect to its agreements listed under the MLI as those agreements will only be modified by the MLI (and come into compliance with the minimum standard) once the provisions of the MLI take effect.

Summary of the jurisdiction response – Argentina

	1.Treaty partners	2. Compliance with the standard	3. Signature of a complying instrument	4. Minimum standard provision used
1	Australia	No	Yes MLI	PPT
2	Belgium	No	Yes MLI	PPT
3	Brazil	Yes other		PPT
4	Canada	No	Yes MLI	PPT
5	Chile	Yes other		PPT+LOB
6	Denmark	No	Yes MLI	PPT+LOB
7	Finland	No	Yes MLI	PPT
8	France	No	Yes MLI	PPT
9	Germany	No	No	
10	Italy	No	Yes MLI	PPT

[4] For 15 of its agreements listed under the MLI, Argentina is implementing the preamble statement (Article 6 of the MLI) and the PPT (Article 7 of the MLI). Argentina has made a reservation pursuant to Article 6(4) of the MLI not to apply Article 6(1) of the MLI with respect to agreements that already contain the relevant preamble language (covering two agreements). Argentina has also made a reservation pursuant to Article 7(15)(b) of the MLI not to apply Article 7(1) of the MLI with respect to agreements that already contain a PPT (covering four agreements). Argentina has also adopted the simplified LOB under Article 7(6) of the MLI.

11	Mexico	Yes other		PPT+ LOB
12	Netherlands	No	Yes MLI	PPT
13	Norway	No	Yes MLI	PPT+ LOB
14	Qatar	Yes other		PPT
15	Russian Federation	No	Yes MLI	PPT+ LOB
16	Spain	No	Yes MLI	PPT
17	Sweden	No	Yes MLI	PPT
18	Switzerland	No	Yes MLI	PPT
19	United Arab Emirates	No	Yes MLI	PPT
20	United Kingdom	No	Yes MLI	PPT

Other agreements

	1.Treaty partners	2. Inclusive Framework member
1	Bolivia*	No

Armenia

A. Progress in the implementation of the minimum standard

Armenia has 52 tax agreements in force, as reported in its response to the Peer Review questionnaire. Three of those agreements comply with the minimum standard.

Armenia signed the MLI in 2017 and deposited its instrument of ratification on 25 September 2023. The MLI enters into force for Armenia on 1 January 2024. The agreements modified by the MLI will come into compliance with the minimum standard once the provisions of the MLI take effect.

Armenia has not listed its agreement with Japan under the MLI. This agreement will therefore not, at this stage, be modified under the MLI. In its response to the Peer Review Questionnaire, Japan indicated that its agreement with Armenia did not give rise to material treaty shopping concerns for Japan.

Armenia is implementing the minimum standard through the inclusion of the preamble statement and the PPT combined with the LOB.[5]

B. Conclusion

No jurisdiction has raised any concerns about their agreements with Armenia.

Summary of the jurisdiction response – Armenia

	1.Treaty partners	2. Compliance with the standard	3. Signature of a complying instrument	4. Minimum standard provision used
1	Austria	No	No	PPT
2	Belarus	No	No	PPT
3	Belgium	No	Yes MLI	PPT
4	Bulgaria	No	Yes MLI	PPT
5	Canada	No	Yes MLI	PPT
6	China (People's Republic of)	No	Yes MLI	PPT
7	Croatia	No	Yes MLI	PPT
8	Cyprus*	No	Yes MLI	PPT
9	Czechia	No	Yes MLI	PPT
10	Denmark	No	No	PPT
11	Estonia	No	Yes MLI	PPT
12	Finland	No	Yes MLI	PPT
13	France	No	Yes MLI	PPT
14	Georgia	No	No	PPT
15	Germany	No	No	PPT
16	Greece	No	Yes MLI	PPT
17	Hungary	No	Yes MLI	PPT
18	India	No	Yes MLI	PPT
19	Indonesia	No	Yes MLI	PPT
20	Iran*	No	No	PPT

5 For its agreements listed under the MLI, Armenia is implementing the preamble statement (Article 6 of the MLI) and the PPT (Article 7 of the MLI). Armenia has also adopted the simplified LOB under Article 7(6) of the MLI.

21	Ireland	No	Yes MLI	PPT
22	Israel	No	Yes MLI	PPT
23	Italy	No	Yes MLI	PPT
24	Kazakhstan	No	Yes MLI	PPT
25	Kuwait	No	Yes MLI	PPT
26	Kyrgyzstan*	No	No	
27	Latvia	No	Yes MLI	PPT
28	Lebanon*	No	No	PPT
29	Lithuania	No	Yes MLI	PPT
30	Luxembourg	No	Yes MLI	PPT
31	Malta	Yes other		PPT
32	Moldova*	No	No	PPT
33	Netherlands	No	Yes MLI	PPT
34	Poland	No	Yes MLI	PPT
35	Qatar	No	Yes MLI	PPT
36	Romania	No	Yes MLI	PPT
37	Russian Federation	No	Yes MLI	PPT
38	Serbia	No	Yes MLI	PPT
39	Singapore	Yes other		PPT
40	Slovak Republic	No	No	PPT
41	Slovenia	No	Yes MLI	PPT
42	Spain	No	Yes MLI	PPT
43	Sweden	No	Yes MLI	PPT
44	Switzerland	Yes other		PPT
45	Syrian Arab Republic*	No	No	PPT
46	Tajikistan*	No	No	PPT
47	Thailand	No	Yes MLI	PPT
48	Turkmenistan*	No	No	PPT
49	Ukraine	No	Yes MLI	PPT
50	United Arab Emirates	No	Yes MLI	PPT
51	United Kingdom	No	Yes MLI	PPT

Other agreements

	1.Treaty partners	2. Inclusive Framework member
1	Japan	Yes

Aruba

A. Progress in the implementation of the minimum standard

Aruba has one tax agreement in force, the agreement with the Netherlands, as reported in its response to the Peer Review questionnaire. The agreement does not comply with the minimum standard.

Aruba has not joined the MLI.

Aruba's agreement with Netherlands is an arrangement governed by the domestic law of the Kingdom of the Netherlands.[6] Aruba indicated in its response to the Peer Review questionnaire that steps have been taken (other than under the MLI) to implement the minimum standard in its agreement with the Netherlands.

B. Conclusion

No jurisdiction has raised any concerns about Aruba.

Summary of the jurisdiction response – Aruba

	1.Treaty partners	2. Compliance with the standard	3. Signature of a complying instrument	4. Minimum standard provision used
1	Netherlands	No	No	

[6] Aruba indicated in its response that the current tax arrangement for the Kingdom of the Netherlands applies between Aruba and the Netherlands (including the Caribbean part of the Netherlands), Curaçao and Sint Maarten*. In light of the implementation of the minimum standards a tax arrangement has been drafted separately with the Netherlands to implement the minimum standard. Steps have been taken (other than under the MLI) to implement the minimum standard in the tax arrangement with Curaçao and Sint Maarten*.

Australia

A. Progress in the implementation of the minimum standard

Australia has 45 tax agreements in force, as reported in its response to the Peer Review questionnaire. Twenty-nine of those agreements comply with the minimum standard.

Australia signed the MLI in 2017 and deposited its instrument of ratification on 26 September 2018, listing its non-compliant agreements concluded with other members of the Inclusive Framework. The MLI entered into force for Australia on 1 January 2019. The agreements modified by the MLI come into compliance with the minimum standard once the provisions of the MLI take effect.

Australia is implementing the minimum standard through the inclusion of the preamble statement and the PPT.[7]

B. Conclusion

No jurisdiction has raised any concerns about their agreements with Australia.

Summary of the jurisdiction response – Australia

	1.Treaty partners	2. Compliance with the standard	3. Signature of a complying instrument	4. Minimum standard provision used
1	Argentina	No	Yes MLI	PPT alone
2	Austria	No	No	
3	Belgium	Yes MLI		PPT alone
4	Canada	Yes MLI		PPT alone
5	Chile	Yes MLI		PPT alone
6	China (People's Republic of)	Yes MLI		PPT alone
7	Czechia	Yes MLI		PPT alone
8	Denmark	Yes MLI		PPT alone
9	Fiji*	No	Yes MLI	PPT alone
10	Finland	Yes MLI		PPT alone
11	France	Yes MLI		PPT alone
12	Germany	Yes other		PPT alone
13	Hungary	Yes MLI		PPT alone
14	India	Yes MLI		PPT alone
15	Indonesia	Yes MLI		PPT alone
16	Ireland	Yes MLI		PPT alone
17	Israel	Yes other		PPT alone
18	Italy	No	Yes MLI	PPT alone
19	Japan	Yes MLI		PPT+LOB
20	Kiribati*	No	No	
21	Korea	Yes MLI		PPT alone
22	Malaysia	Yes MLI		PPT alone

[7] For its agreements listed under the MLI, Australia is implementing the preamble statement (Article 6 of the MLI) and the PPT (Article 7 of the MLI). In the case of the agreement concluded with Japan, Australia has supplemented the PPT with an LOB.

23	Malta	Yes MLI		PPT alone
24	Mexico	No	Yes MLI	PPT alone
25	Netherlands	Yes MLI		PPT alone
26	New Zealand	Yes MLI		PPT alone
27	Norway	Yes MLI		PPT alone
28	Papua New Guinea	No	Yes MLI	PPT alone
29	Philippines	No	No	
30	Poland	Yes MLI		PPT alone
31	Romania	No	Yes MLI	PPT alone
32	Russian Federation	Yes MLI		PPT alone
33	Singapore	Yes MLI		PPT alone
34	Slovak Republic	Yes MLI		PPT alone
35	South Africa	Yes MLI		PPT alone
36	Spain	Yes MLI		PPT alone
37	Sri Lanka	No	No	
38	Sweden	No	No	
39	Switzerland	No	No	
40	Thailand	Yes MLI		PPT alone
41	Türkiye	No	Yes MLI	PPT alone
42	United Kingdom	Yes MLI		PPT alone
43	United States	No	No	
44	Viet Nam	No	Yes MLI	PPT alone

Other agreements

	1.Treaty partners	2. Inclusive Framework member
1	Chinese Taipei*	No

Austria

A. Progress in the implementation of the minimum standard

Austria has 89 tax agreements in force, as reported in its response to the Peer Review questionnaire[8]. Forty of those agreements comply with the minimum standard.[9]

Austria signed the MLI in 2017 and deposited its instrument of ratification on 22 September 2017. The MLI entered into force for Austria on 1 July 2018. On 28 August 2023, Austria made an additional notification to expand its list of agreements to be covered under the MLI. The agreements modified by the MLI come into compliance with the minimum standard once the provisions of the MLI take effect.[10]

Austria has not listed its agreements with Australia, Bahrain, Brazil, Indonesia, Kuwait, New Zealand, Qatar, Sweden, the United States and Uzbekistan, but indicated in its response to the Peer Review questionnaire that steps have been taken (other than under the MLI) to implement the minimum standard in those agreements as well as in the agreements with Germany and Switzerland.

Austria is implementing the minimum standard through the inclusion of the preamble statement and the PPT. [11]

B. Conclusion

No jurisdiction has raised any concerns about their agreements with Austria.

Australia, Bahrain, and New Zealand have listed their agreements with Austria under the MLI, which amount to requests to implement the minimum standard in those agreements.

Summary of the jurisdiction response – Austria

	1.Treaty partners	2. Compliance with the standard	3. Signature of a complying instrument	4. Minimum standard provision used
1	Albania	No	Yes MLI	PPT
2	Algeria*	No	No	PPT
3	Armenia	No	Yes MLI	PPT
4	Australia	No	No	
5	Azerbaijan	No	No	PPT
6	Bahrain	No	No	
7	Barbados	Yes MLI		PPT

[8] Austria indicated in its response that the agreement with Chinese Taipei* is an Arrangement for the Avoidance of Double Taxation and the Prevention of Fiscal Evasion with Respect to Taxes on Income between the Austrian Chamber of Commerce and the Taipei Chamber of Commerce.

[9] Austria has also concluded an agreement with Argentina, which, once it enters into force, will comply with the minimum standard.

[10] Austria has made a reservation under Article 35(3) of the MLI (Entry into Effect).

[11] For its agreements listed under the MLI, Austria is implementing the preamble statement (Article 6 of the MLI) and the PPT (Article 7 of the MLI). In the case of the agreement concluded with Japan, Austria has supplemented the PPT with an LOB.

8	Belarus	No	No	PPT
9	Belgium	Yes MLI		PPT
10	Belize	No	Yes MLI	PPT
11	Bosnia-Herzegovina	No	Yes MLI	PPT
12	Brazil	No	No	
13	Bulgaria	Yes MLI		PPT
14	Canada	Yes MLI		PPT
15	Chile	Yes MLI		PPT
16	China (People's Republic of)	Yes MLI		PPT
17	Croatia	Yes MLI		PPT
18	Cuba*	No	No	PPT
19	Cyprus*	Yes MLI		PPT
20	Czechia	Yes MLI		PPT
21	Denmark	No	Yes MLI	PPT
22	Egypt	No	Yes MLI	PPT
23	Estonia	Yes MLI		PPT
24	Finland	Yes MLI		PPT
25	France	Yes MLI		PPT
26	Georgia	No	No	PPT
27	Germany	No	Yes MLI	PPT
28	Greece	Yes MLI		PPT
29	Hong Kong (China)	Yes MLI		PPT
30	Hungary	Yes MLI		PPT
31	Iceland	No	Yes MLI	PPT
32	India	Yes MLI		PPT
33	Indonesia	No	No	
34	Iran*	No	No	PPT
35	Ireland	Yes MLI		PPT
36	Israel	Yes MLI		PPT
37	Italy	No	Yes MLI	PPT
38	Japan	Yes other		PPT+LOB
39	Kazakhstan	No	Yes MLI	PPT
40	Korea	Yes other		PPT
41	Kosovo*	Yes other		PPT
42	Kuwait	No	No	
43	Kyrgyzstan*	No	No	PPT
44	Latvia	Yes MLI		PPT
45	Liechtenstein	Yes other		PPT
46	Lithuania	Yes MLI		PPT
47	Luxembourg	Yes MLI		PPT
48	Malaysia	No	Yes MLI	PPT
49	Malta	Yes MLI		PPT
50	Mexico	No	Yes MLI	PPT
51	Moldova*	No	No	PPT
52	Mongolia	No	Yes MLI	PPT
53	Montenegro	No	No	PPT
54	Morocco	No	Yes MLI	PPT
55	Nepal*	No	No	PPT
56	Netherlands	Yes MLI		PPT
57	New Zealand	No	No	
58	North Macedonia	No	Yes MLI	PPT
59	Norway	No	No	PPT
60	Pakistan	Yes MLI		PPT

61	Philippines	No	No	PPT
62	Poland	Yes MLI		PPT
63	Portugal	Yes MLI		PPT
64	Qatar	No	No	
65	Romania	No	Yes MLI	PPT
66	Russian Federation	Yes MLI		PPT
67	San Marino	No	Yes MLI	PPT
68	Saudi Arabia	No	Yes MLI	PPT
69	Serbia	Yes MLI		PPT
70	Singapore	Yes MLI		PPT
71	Slovak Republic	Yes MLI		PPT
72	Slovenia	Yes MLI		PPT
73	South Africa	Yes MLI		PPT
74	Spain	Yes MLI		PPT
75	Sweden	No	No	
76	Switzerland	No	Yes MLI	PPT
77	Tajikistan*	No	No	PPT
78	Thailand	No	Yes MLI	PPT
79	Tunisia	No	No	PPT
80	Türkiye	No	Yes MLI	PPT
81	Turkmenistan*	No	No	PPT
82	Ukraine	Yes other		PPT
83	United Arab Emirates	Yes other		PPT
84	United Kingdom	Yes other		PPT
85	United States	No	No	
86	Uzbekistan	No	No	
87	Venezuela*	No	No	PPT
88	Viet Nam	No	Yes MLI	PPT

Other agreements

	1.Treaty partners	2. Inclusive Framework member
1	Chinese Taipei*	No

Azerbaijan

A. Progress in the implementation of the minimum standard

Azerbaijan has 54 tax agreements in force, as reported in its response to the Peer Review questionnaire. None of those agreements comply with the minimum standard.

Azerbaijan signed the MLI on 20 November 2023, listing its non-compliant agreements. The agreements modified by the MLI will come into compliance with the minimum standard once the provisions of the MLI take effect.

Azerbaijan has signed a bilateral complying instrument with respect to its agreement with Japan.

Azerbaijan indicated in its response to the Peer Review questionnaire that steps have been taken (other than under the MLI) to implement the minimum standard in its agreement with Türkiye.

Azerbaijan is implementing the minimum standard through the inclusion of the preamble statement and the PPT.[12]

In their responses to the Peer Review Questionnaire, Germany, Norway and Switzerland indicated that their agreements with Azerbaijan did not give rise to material treaty shopping concerns for their respective jurisdictions.

B. Conclusion

Azerbaijan has given effect to its plan for the implementation of the minimum standard in its agreements with Austria, Belarus, Belgium, Bosnia and Herzegovina, Bulgaria, Croatia, China (People's Republic of), Canada, Czechia, Denmark, Estonia, Finland, France, Germany, Greece, Georgia, Hungary, Iran, Israel, Italy, Jordan, Kazakhstan, Korea, Latvia, Lithuania, Luxembourg, Malta, Moldova/, Montenegro, Netherlands, Norway, North Macedonia, Pakistan, Poland, Qatar, Romania, the Russian Federation, San Marino, Saudi Arabia, Slovenia, Sweden, Switzerland, Spain, Serbia, Ukraine, the United Arab Emirates, the United Kingdom, Uzbekistan and Viet Nam, by signing the MLI in November 2023 and listing those agreements to be covered.

Summary of the jurisdiction response – Azerbaijan

	1.Treaty partners	2. Compliance with the standard	3. Signature of a complying instrument	4. Minimum standard provision used
1	Austria	No	Yes MLI	PPT
2	Belarus	No	No	
3	Belgium	No	Yes MLI	PPT
4	Bosnia and Herzegovina	No	Yes MLI	PPT
5	Bulgaria	No	Yes MLI	PPT
6	Canada	No	Yes MLI	PPT
7	China (People's Republic of)	No	Yes MLI	PPT
8	Croatia	No	Yes MLI	PPT
9	Czechia	No	No	

[12] For its agreements listed under the MLI, Azerbaijan is implementing the preamble statement (Article 6 of the MLI) and the PPT (Article 7 of the MLI).

10	Denmark	No	Yes MLI	PPT
11	Estonia	No	Yes MLI	PPT
12	Finland	No	Yes MLI	PPT
13	France	No	Yes MLI	PPT
14	Georgia	No	Yes MLI	PPT
15	Germany	No	No	
16	Greece	No	Yes MLI	PPT
17	Hungary	No	Yes MLI	PPT
18	Iran*	No	No	
19	Israel	No	Yes MLI	PPT
20	Italy	No	Yes MLI	PPT
21	Japan	No	Yes other	PPT
22	Jordan	No	Yes MLI	PPT
23	Kazakhstan	No	Yes MLI	PPT
24	Korea	No	Yes MLI	PPT
25	Kuwait	No	No	
26	Latvia	No	Yes MLI	PPT
27	Lithuania	No	Yes MLI	PPT
28	Luxembourg	No	Yes MLI	PPT
29	Malta	No	Yes MLI	PPT
30	Moldova*	No	No	
31	Montenegro	No	No	
32	Netherlands	No	Yes MLI	PPT
33	North Macedonia	No	Yes MLI	PPT
34	Norway	No	No	
35	Pakistan	No	Yes MLI	PPT
36	Poland	No	Yes MLI	PPT
37	Qatar	No	Yes MLI	PPT
38	Romania	No	Yes MLI	PPT
39	Russian Federation	No	Yes MLI	PPT
40	San Marino	No	Yes MLI	PPT
41	Saudi Arabia	No	Yes MLI	PPT
42	Serbia	No	Yes MLI	PPT
43	Slovenia	No	Yes MLI	PPT
44	Spain	No	Yes MLI	PPT
45	Sweden	No	Yes MLI	PPT
46	Switzerland	No	No	
47	Tajikistan*	No	No	
48	Türkiye	No	No	
49	Turkmenistan*	No	No	PPT
50	Ukraine	No	Yes	PPT
51	United Arab Emirates	No	Yes MLI	PPT
52	United Kingdom	No	Yes MLI	PPT
53	Uzbekistan	No	No	
54	Viet Nam	No	Yes MLI	PPT

The Bahamas

A. Progress in the implementation of the minimum standard

The Bahamas has no tax agreements in force, as reported in its response to the Peer Review questionnaire.

B. Conclusion

No jurisdiction has raised any concerns about the Bahamas.

Bahrain

A. Progress in the implementation of the minimum standard

Bahrain has 45 tax agreements in force, as reported in its response to the Peer Review questionnaire. Twenty-three of those agreements comply with the minimum standard.

Bahrain signed the MLI in 2020 and deposited its instrument of ratification on 23 February 2022, listing all its agreements. The MLI entered into force for Bahrain on 1 June 2022. The agreements modified by the MLI will come into compliance with the minimum standard once the provisions of the MLI take effect.

Bahrain indicated in its response to the Peer Review questionnaire that steps have also been taken (other than under the MLI) to implement the minimum standard in its agreements with Austria and Bermuda.

Bahrain is implementing the minimum standard through the inclusion of the preamble statement and the PPT.[13]

B. Conclusion

No jurisdiction has raised any concerns about their agreements with Bahrain.

Summary of the jurisdiction response – Bahrain

	1.Treaty partners	2. Compliance with the standard	3. Signature of a complying instrument	4. Minimum standard provision used
1	Algeria*	No	No	PPT
2	Austria	No	No	PPT
3	Bangladesh*	No	No	PPT
4	Barbados	Yes MLI		PPT
5	Belarus	No	No	PPT
6	Belgium	Yes MLI		PPT
7	Bermuda	No	No	PPT
8	Brunei Darussalam	No	No	PPT
9	Bulgaria	Yes MLI		PPT
10	China (People's Republic of)	Yes MLI		PPT
11	Cyprus*	Yes MLI		PPT
12	Czechia	No	No	PPT
13	Egypt	Yes MLI		PPT
14	Estonia	No	Yes MLI	PPT
15	France	Yes MLI		PPT
16	Georgia	No	No	PPT
17	Hungary	Yes MLI		PPT
18	Iran*	No	No	PPT
19	Ireland	Yes MLI		PPT
20	Isle of Man	Yes MLI		PPT
21	Jordan	Yes MLI		PPT

13 For its agreements listed under the MLI, Bahrain is implementing the preamble statement (Article 6 of the MLI) and the PPT (Article 7 of the MLI).

22	Korea	Yes MLI		PPT
23	Lebanon*	No	No	PPT
24	Luxembourg	Yes MLI		PPT
25	Malaysia	Yes MLI		PPT
26	Malta	Yes MLI		PPT
27	Mexico	No	Yes MLI	PPT
28	Morocco	No	Yes MLI	PPT
29	Netherlands	Yes MLI		PPT
30	Pakistan	Yes MLI		PPT
31	Philippines	No	No	PPT
32	Portugal	Yes MLI		PPT
33	Seychelles	Yes MLI		PPT
34	Singapore	Yes MLI		PPT
35	Sri Lanka	No	No	PPT
36	Sudan*	No	No	PPT
37	Switzerland	Yes other		PPT
38	Syrian Arab Republic*	No	No	PPT
39	Tajikistan*	No	No	PPT
40	Thailand	Yes MLI		PPT
41	Türkiye	No	Yes MLI	PPT
42	Turkmenistan*	No	No	PPT
43	United Kingdom	Yes MLI		PPT
44	Uzbekistan	No	No	PPT
45	Yemen*	No	No	PPT

Barbados

A. Progress in the implementation of the minimum standard

Barbados has 31 tax agreements in force as reported in its response to the Peer Review questionnaire, including the multilateral agreement among the members of the CARICOM concluded with ten treaty partners (the CARICOM Agreement).[14] Nineteen of those agreements comply with the minimum standard.

Barbados signed the MLI in 2018 and deposited its instrument of ratification on 21 December 2020, listing its non-compliant bilateral agreements concluded with other members of the Inclusive Framework. The MLI entered into force for Barbados on 1 April 2021. The agreements modified by the MLI come into compliance with the minimum standard once the provisions of the MLI take effect.

Barbados indicated in its response to the Peer Review questionnaire that steps have been taken (other than under the MLI) to implement the minimum standard in the CARICOM Agreement.

Barbados is implementing the minimum standard through the inclusion of the preamble statement and the PPT.[15]

B. Conclusion

No jurisdiction has raised any concerns about their agreements with Barbados.

Summary of the jurisdiction response – Barbados

	1.Treaty partners	2. Compliance with the standard	3. Signature of a complying instrument	4. Minimum standard provision used
1	Austria	No	No	PPT
2	Bahrain	Yes MLI		PPT
3	Botswana	No	No	PPT
4	Canada	Yes MLI		PPT
5	CARICOM Agreement treaty partners (Antigua and Barbuda, Belize, Dominica, Grenada, Guyana*, Jamaica, Saint Kitts and Nevis, Saint Lucia, Saint Vincent and the Grenadines, Trinidad and Tobago)	No	No	PPT
6	China (People's Republic of)	Yes MLI		PPT
7	Cyprus*	Yes MLI		PPT

14 Agreement Among the Governments of the Member States of the Caribbean Community for the Avoidance of Double Taxation and the Prevention of Fiscal Evasion with Respect to Taxes on Income, Profits or Gains and Capital Gains and for the Encouragement of Regional Trade and Investment, St. Michael Barbados, 6 July 1994; between: Antigua and Barbuda (18 February 1998), Barbados (7 July 1995), Belize (30 November 1994), Dominica (19 June 1996), Grenada (1 March 1996), Guyana* (26 November 1997), Jamaica (16 February 1995), St. Kitts/Nevis (8 May 1997), St. Lucia (22 May 1995) St. Vincent (12 February 1998) and Trinidad & Tobago (29 November 1994).

15 For its agreements listed under the MLI, Barbados is implementing the preamble statement (Article 6 of the MLI) and the PPT (Article 7 of the MLI).

8	Czechia	No	No	PPT
9	Finland	Yes MLI		PPT
10	Iceland	Yes MLI		PPT
11	Italy	No	Yes MLI	PPT
12	Luxembourg	Yes MLI		PPT
13	Malta	Yes MLI		PPT
14	Mauritius	Yes MLI		PPT
15	Mexico	No	Yes MLI	PPT
16	Netherlands	Yes MLI		PPT
17	Norway	No	No	PPT
18	Panama	Yes MLI		PPT
19	Portugal	Yes MLI		PPT
20	Qatar	Yes MLI		PPT
21	San Marino	Yes MLI		PPT
22	Seychelles	Yes MLI		PPT
23	Singapore	Yes MLI		PPT
24	Spain	Yes MLI		PPT
25	Sweden	No	Yes MLI	PPT
26	Switzerland	No	No	PPT
27	United Arab Emirates	Yes MLI		PPT
28	United Kingdom	Yes MLI		PPT
29	United States	No	No	
30	Venezuela*	No	No	PPT

Other agreements

	1.Treaty partners	2. Inclusive Framework member
1	Cuba*	No

Belgium

A. Progress in the implementation of the minimum standard

Belgium has 95 tax agreements in force, as reported in its response to the Peer Review questionnaire. Fifty-five of those agreements comply with the minimum standard.

Belgium signed the MLI in 2017 and deposited its instrument of ratification on 26 June 2019. The MLI entered into force for Belgium on 1 October 2019. The agreements modified by the MLI come into compliance with the minimum standard once the provisions of the MLI take effect.

Belgium has not listed its agreements with Germany and Switzerland under the MLI but indicated in its response to the Peer Review questionnaire that steps have been taken (other than under the MLI) to implement the minimum standard in those agreements.

Belgium has signed a bilateral complying instrument with respect to its agreement with Norway.

Belgium is implementing the minimum standard through the inclusion of the preamble statement and the PPT.[16]

B. Conclusion

No jurisdiction has raised any concerns about their agreements with Belgium.

Summary of the jurisdiction response – Belgium

	1.Treaty partners	2. Compliance with the standard	3. Signature of a complying instrument	4. Minimum standard provision used
1	Albania	Yes MLI		PPT
2	Algeria*	No	No	PPT
3	Argentina	No	Yes MLI	PPT
4	Armenia	No	Yes MLI	PPT
5	Australia	Yes MLI		PPT
6	Austria	Yes MLI		PPT
7	Azerbaijan	No	No	PPT
8	Bahrain	Yes MLI		PPT
9	Bangladesh*	No	No	PPT
10	Belarus	No	No	PPT
11	Bosnia-Herzegovina	Yes MLI		PPT
12	Brazil	No	No	PPT
13	Bulgaria	Yes MLI		PPT
14	Canada	Yes MLI		PPT
15	Chile	Yes MLI		PPT
16	China (People's Republic of)	Yes MLI		PPT
17	Côte d'Ivoire	No	Yes MLI	PPT
18	Croatia	Yes MLI		PPT

[16] For its agreements listed under the MLI, Belgium is implementing the preamble statement (Article 6 of the MLI) and the PPT (Article 7 of the MLI). In the case of the agreement concluded with Japan, Belgium has supplemented the PPT with an LOB.

19	Cyprus*	Yes MLI		PPT
20	Czechia	Yes MLI		PPT
21	Democratic Republic of the Congo	No	No	PPT
22	Denmark	Yes MLI		PPT
23	Ecuador*	No	No	PPT
24	Egypt	Yes MLI		PPT
25	Estonia	Yes MLI		PPT
26	Finland	Yes MLI		PPT
27	France	Yes MLI		PPT
28	Gabon	No	Yes MLI	PPT
29	Georgia	Yes MLI		PPT
30	Germany	No	No	PPT
31	Ghana*	No	No	PPT
32	Greece	Yes MLI		PPT
33	Hong Kong (China)	Yes MLI		PPT
34	Hungary	Yes MLI		PPT
35	Iceland	Yes MLI		PPT
36	India	Yes MLI		PPT
37	Indonesia	Yes MLI		PPT
38	Ireland	Yes MLI		PPT
39	Israel	Yes MLI		PPT
40	Italy	No	Yes MLI	PPT
41	Japan	Yes other		PPT+LOB
42	Kazakhstan	Yes MLI		PPT
43	Korea	Yes MLI		PPT
44	Kosovo*	No	No	PPT
45	Kuwait	No	Yes MLI	PPT
46	Kyrgyzstan*	No	No	PPT
47	Latvia	Yes MLI		PPT
48	Lithuania	Yes MLI		PPT
49	Luxembourg	Yes MLI		PPT
50	Malaysia	Yes MLI		PPT
51	Malta	Yes MLI		PPT
52	Mauritius	Yes MLI		PPT
53	Mexico	No	Yes MLI	PPT
54	Moldova*	No	No	PPT
55	Mongolia	No	Yes MLI	PPT
56	Montenegro	No	No	PPT
57	Morocco	No	Yes MLI	PPT
58	Netherlands	Yes MLI		PPT
59	New Zealand	Yes MLI		PPT
60	Nigeria	No	Yes MLI	PPT
61	North Macedonia	No	Yes MLI	PPT
62	Norway	No	Yes other	PPT
63	Pakistan	Yes MLI		PPT
64	Philippines	No	No	PPT
65	Poland	Yes MLI		PPT
66	Portugal	Yes MLI		PPT
67	Romania	No	Yes MLI	PPT
68	Russian Federation	Yes MLI		PPT
69	Rwanda*	No	No	PPT
70	San Marino	Yes MLI		PPT
71	Senegal	Yes MLI		PPT

72	Serbia	Yes MLI		PPT
73	Seychelles	Yes MLI		PPT
74	Singapore	Yes MLI		PPT
75	Slovak Republic	Yes MLI		PPT
76	Slovenia	Yes MLI		PPT
77	South Africa	Yes MLI		PPT
78	Spain	Yes MLI		PPT
79	Sri Lanka	No	No	PPT
80	Sweden	No	Yes MLI	PPT
81	Switzerland	No	No	PPT
82	Tajikistan*	No	No	PPT
83	Thailand	Yes MLI		PPT
84	Tunisia	No	Yes MLI	PPT
85	Türkiye	No	Yes MLI	PPT
86	Turkmenistan*	No	No	PPT
87	Ukraine	Yes MLI		PPT
88	United Arab Emirates	Yes MLI		PPT
89	United Kingdom	Yes MLI		PPT
90	United States	No	No	
91	Uruguay	Yes MLI		PPT
92	Uzbekistan	No	No	PPT
93	Venezuela*	No	No	PPT
94	Viet Nam	No	Yes MLI	PPT

Other agreements

	1.Treaty partners	2. Inclusive Framework member
1	Chinese Taipei*	No

Belize

A. Progress in the implementation of the minimum standard

Belize has five tax agreements in force as reported in its response to the Peer Review questionnaire, including the multilateral agreement among the members of the CARICOM concluded with ten treaty partners (the CARICOM Agreement).[17] Two of those agreements comply with the minimum standard.

Belize signed the MLI in 2019 and deposited its instrument of ratification on 7 April 2022, listing its non-compliant bilateral agreements. The MLI entered into force for Belize on 1 August 2022. The agreements modified by the MLI come into compliance with the minimum standard once the provisions of the MLI take effect.

Belize indicated in its response to the Peer Review questionnaire that steps have been taken (other than under the MLI) to implement the minimum standard in the CARICOM Agreement.

Belize is implementing the minimum standard through the inclusion of the preamble statement and the PPT.[18]

B. Conclusion

No jurisdiction has raised any concerns about their agreements with Belize.

Summary of the jurisdiction response – Belize

	1.Treaty partners	2. Compliance with the standard	3. Signature of a complying instrument	4. Minimum standard provision used
1	Austria	No	No	PPT
2	CARICOM Agreement treaty partners (Antigua and Barbuda, Barbados, Dominica, Grenada, Guyana*, Jamaica, Saint Kitts and Nevis, Saint Lucia, Saint Vincent and the Grenadines, Trinidad and Tobago)	No	No	PPT
3	Switzerland	No	No	PPT
4	United Arab Emirates	Yes MLI		PPT
5	United Kingdom	Yes MLI		PPT

[17] Agreement Among the Governments of the Member States of the Caribbean Community for the Avoidance of Double Taxation and the Prevention of Fiscal Evasion with Respect to Taxes on Income, Profits or Gains and Capital Gains and for the Encouragement of Regional Trade and Investment, St. Michael Barbados, 6 July 1994; between: Antigua and Barbuda (18 February 1998), Barbados (7 July 1995), Belize (30 November 1994), Dominica (19 June 1996), Grenada (1 March 1996), Guyana* (26 November 1997), Jamaica (16 February 1995), St. Kitts/Nevis (8 May 1997), St. Lucia (22 May 1995) St. Vincent (12 February 1998) and Trinidad & Tobago (29 November 1994).

[18] For its agreements listed under the MLI, Belize is implementing the preamble statement (Article 6 of the MLI) and the PPT (Article 7 of the MLI).

Benin

A. Progress in the implementation of the minimum standard

Benin has four tax agreements in force, as reported in its response to the Peer Review questionnaire, including the multilateral Regulation 08/2008/COM adopting the rules for the avoidance of double taxation within the West African Economic and Monetary Union and the rule for assistance in tax matters (the UEMOA) concluded with seven treaty partners,[19] and the multilateral Supplementary Act A/SA, 5/12/18 adopting community rules for the elimination of double taxation with respect to taxes on income, capital and inheritance and the prevention of tax evasion and avoidance within the ECOWAS Member States (the ECOWAS Supplementary Act) concluded with fourteen treaty partners. Two of those agreements, including the ECOWAS Supplementary Act, comply with the minimum standard.

Benin has not signed the MLI.

Benin is implementing the minimum standard through the inclusion of the preamble statement and the PPT.

B. Conclusion

Benin has developed a plan for the implementation of the minimum standard in its agreements with France and Norway. Benin indicated in its response to the Peer Review questionnaire that it intends to sign the MLI and list those agreements to be covered.

The UEMOA does not at this stage comply with the minimum standard and discussions to bring this agreement up to date should be contemplated.[20]

Summary of the jurisdiction response – Benin

	1.Treaty partners	2. Compliance with the standard	3. Signature of a complying instrument	4. Minimum standard provision used
1	Morocco	Yes other		PPT
2	ECOWAS Supplementary Act treaty partners (Burkina Faso, Cabo Verde, Côte d'Ivoire, The Gambia*, Ghana*, Guinea-Bissau*, Guinea Conakry*, Liberia, Mali*, Niger*, Nigeria, Senegal, Sierra Leone, Togo)	Yes other		PPT

[19] Règlement n°08/2008/CM des pays de l'Union économique et monétaire Ouest Africaine (UEMOA) du 26 septembre 2008 portant adoption des règles visant à éviter la double imposition au sein de l'UEMOA et des règles d'assistance en matière fiscale.

[20] Revisions to the UEMOA require an agreement from its eight treaty partners.

Other agreements

	1.Treaty partners	2. Inclusive Framework member
1	France	Yes
2	Norway	Yes
3	UEMOA treaty partners (Burkina Faso, Côte d'Ivoire, Guinea-Bissau*, Mali*, Niger*, Senegal, Togo)	Yes (Burkina Faso, Côte d'Ivoire, Sénégal, Togo) No (Guinea-Bissau*, Mali*, Niger*).

Bermuda

A. Progress in the implementation of the minimum standard

Bermuda has four tax agreements in force, as reported in its response to the Peer Review questionnaire. None of those agreements comply with the minimum standard.

Bermuda concluded a bilateral complying instrument with respect to its agreements with Bahrain and Qatar.

Bermuda indicated in its response to the Peer Review questionnaire that steps have been taken (other than under the MLI) to implement the minimum standard in its agreement with the Seychelles and the United Arab Emirates.

B. Conclusion

No jurisdiction has raised any concerns about their agreements with Bermuda.

Summary of the jurisdiction response – Bermuda

	1.Treaty partners	2. Compliance with the standard	3. Signature of a complying instrument	4. Minimum standard provision used
1	Bahrain	No	Yes other	PPT
2	Qatar	No	Yes other	PPT
3	Seychelles	No	No	PPT
4	United Arab Emirates	No	No	PPT

Bosnia-Herzegovina

A. Progress in the implementation of the minimum standard

Bosnia-Herzegovina has 38 tax agreements in force, as reported in its response to the Peer Review questionnaire. Twenty-two of those agreements comply with the minimum standard.

Bosnia-Herzegovina signed the MLI in 2019 and deposited its instrument of ratification on 16 September 2020, listing its non-compliant agreements concluded with other members of the Inclusive Framework. The MLI entered into force for Bosnia-Herzegovina on 1 January 2021. The agreements modified by the MLI come into compliance with the minimum standard once the provisions of the MLI take effect.

Bosnia-Herzegovina is implementing the minimum standard through the inclusion of the preamble statement and the PPT.[21]

B. Conclusion

No jurisdiction has raised any concerns about their agreements with Bosnia-Herzegovina.

Summary of the jurisdiction response – Bosnia-Herzegovina

	1.Treaty partners	2. Compliance with the standard	3. Signature of a complying instrument	4. Minimum standard provision used
1	Albania	Yes MLI		PPT
2	Algeria*	No	No	PPT
3	Austria	No	No	PPT
4	Azerbaijan	No	No	PPT
5	Belgium	Yes MLI		PPT
6	China (People's Republic of)	Yes MLI		PPT
7	Croatia	Yes MLI		PPT
8	Cyprus*	Yes MLI		PPT
9	Czechia	No	No	PPT
10	Finland	Yes MLI		PPT
11	France	Yes MLI		PPT
12	Germany	No	No	PPT
13	Greece	Yes MLI		PPT
14	Hungary	Yes MLI		PPT
15	Ireland	Yes MLI		PPT
16	Italy	No	Yes MLI	PPT
17	Jordan	Yes MLI		PPT
18	Kuwait	No	Yes MLI	PPT
19	Malaysia	Yes MLI		PPT
20	Moldova*	No	No	PPT
21	Montenegro	No	No	PPT
22	Netherlands	Yes MLI		PPT
23	North Macedonia	No	Yes MLI	PPT

[21] For its agreements listed under the MLI, Bosnia-Herzegovina is implementing the preamble statement (Article 6 of the MLI) and the PPT (Article 7 of the MLI).

24	Norway	No	No	PPT
25	Pakistan	Yes MLI		PPT
26	Poland	Yes MLI		PPT
27	Qatar	Yes MLI		PPT
28	Romania	No	Yes MLI	PPT
29	Serbia	Yes MLI		PPT
30	Slovak Republic	Yes MLI		PPT
31	Slovenia	Yes MLI		PPT
32	Spain	Yes MLI		PPT
33	Sri Lanka	No	No	PPT
34	Sweden	No	No	PPT
35	Türkiye	No	Yes MLI	PPT
36	United Arab Emirates	Yes MLI		PPT
37	United Kingdom	Yes MLI		PPT

Other agreements

	1.Treaty partners	2. Inclusive Framework member
1	Iran*	No

Botswana

A. Progress in the implementation of the minimum standard

Botswana has 20 tax agreements in force, as reported in its response to the Peer Review questionnaire. Two of those agreements comply with the minimum standard.

Botswana has not signed the MLI.

Botswana indicated in its response to the peer review questionnaire that steps have been taken (other than under the MLI) to implement the minimum standard in its agreement with Mauritius.

Botswana is implementing the minimum standard through the inclusion of the preamble statement and the PPT.

B. Conclusion

Botswana has developed a plan for the implementation of the minimum standard in its agreements with Barbados, China (People's Republic of), Czechia, Eswatini, France, India, Ireland, Malta, Namibia, the Russian Federation, the Seychelles, Sweden, the United Kingdom, and Zambia. Botswana indicated in its response to the Peer Review questionnaire that it intends to sign the MLI and list those agreements to be covered.

Summary of the jurisdiction response – Botswana

	1.Treaty partners	2. Compliance with the standard	3. Signature of a complying instrument	4. Minimum standard provision used
1	Luxembourg	Yes other		PPT
2	Mauritius	No	No	
3	United Arab Emirates	Yes other		PPT

Other agreements

	1.Treaty partners	2. Inclusive Framework member
1	Barbados	Yes
2	China (People's Republic of)	Yes
3	Czechia	Yes
4	Eswatini	Yes
5	France	Yes
6	India	Yes
7	Ireland	Yes
8	Malta	Yes
9	Mozambique*	No
10	Namibia	Yes
11	Russian Federation	Yes
12	Seychelles	Yes
13	South Africa	Yes
14	Sweden	Yes
15	United Kingdom	Yes
16	Zambia	Yes
17	Zimbabwe*	No

Brazil

A. Progress in the implementation of the minimum standard

Brazil has 36 tax agreements in force, as reported in its response to the Peer Review questionnaire. Four of those agreements comply with the minimum standard.

Brazil has not signed the MLI.

Brazil has signed a bilateral complying instrument with respect to its agreements with Chile, China (People's Republic of), India, Norway and Sweden.

Brazil indicated in its response to the Peer Review questionnaire that steps have been taken (other than under the MLI) to implement the minimum standard in its agreements with Austria, Belgium, Canada, Czechia, Denmark, Ecuador*, Finland, France, Hungary, Israel, Italy, Japan, Korea, Luxembourg, Mexico, the Netherlands, Peru, Philippines, Portugal, the Russian Federation, Slovak Republic, South Africa, Spain, Trinidad and Tobago, Türkiye and Ukraine.

Brazil is implementing the minimum standard through the inclusion of the preamble statement and the PPT combined with the LOB.

B. Conclusion

No jurisdiction has raised any concerns about their agreements with Brazil.

Summary of the jurisdiction response – Brazil

	1.Treaty partners	2. Compliance with the standard	3. Signature of a complying instrument	4. Minimum standard provision used
1	Argentina	Yes other		PPT+LOB
2	Austria	No	No	
3	Belgium	No	No	
4	Canada	No	No	
5	Chile	No	Yes other	PPT+LOB
6	China (People's Republic of)	No	Yes other	PPT+LOB
7	Czechia	No	No	
8	Denmark	No	No	
9	Ecuador*	No	No	
10	Finland	No	No	
11	France	No	No	
12	Hungary	No	No	
13	India	No	Yes other	
14	Israel	No	No	
15	Italy	No	No	
16	Japan	No	No	
17	Korea	No	No	
18	Luxembourg	No	No	
19	Mexico	No	No	
20	Netherlands	No	No	
21	Norway	No	Yes other	

22	Peru	No	No	
23	Philippines	No	No	
24	Portugal	No	No	
25	Russian Federation	No	No	
26	Singapore	Yes other		PPT+LOB
27	Slovak Republic	No	No	
28	South Africa	No	No	
29	Spain	No	No	
30	Sweden	No	Yes other	PPT+LOB
31	Switzerland	Yes other		PPT+LOB
32	Trinidad and Tobago	No	No	
33	Türkiye	No	No	
34	Ukraine	No	No	
35	United Arab Emirates	Yes other		PPT+LOB

Other agreements

	1.Treaty partners	2. Inclusive Framework member
1	Venezuela*	No

British Virgin Islands

A. Progress in the implementation of the minimum standard

British Virgin Islands has one tax agreement in force, the agreement with Switzerland, as reported in its response to the Peer Review questionnaire. The agreement does not comply with the minimum standard.

British Virgin Islands has not signed the MLI.

In its response to the Peer Review questionnaire, Switzerland indicated that its agreement with the British Virgin Islands did not give rise to material treaty shopping concern for Switzerland.

B. Conclusion

No jurisdiction has raised any concerns about the British Virgin Islands.

Other agreements

This Table shows the agreements that are not compliant, not subject to a complying instrument, not covered by a general statement on the implementation of the detailed LOB and for which no steps have been taken to implement the minimum standard.

	1.Treaty partners	2. Inclusive Framework member
1	Switzerland	Yes

Brunei Darussalam

A. Progress in the implementation of the minimum standard

Brunei Darussalam has 18 tax agreements in force, as reported in its response to the Peer Review questionnaire. None of those agreements comply with the minimum standard.

Brunei Darussalam has not signed the MLI.

B. Conclusion

Brunei Darussalam has developed a plan for the implementation of the minimum standard in its agreements with Bahrain, China (People's Republic of), Hong Kong (China), Indonesia, Japan, Korea, Luxembourg, Malaysia, Oman, Pakistan, Qatar, Singapore, the United Arab Emirates, the United Kingdom, and Viet Nam. Brunei Darussalam indicated in its response to the Peer Review questionnaire that it is currently amending its legal framework in order to join the MLI.

Other agreements

This Table shows the agreements that are not compliant, not subject to a complying instrument, not covered by a general statement on the implementation of the detailed LOB and for which no steps have been taken to implement the minimum standard.

	1.Treaty partners	2. Inclusive Framework member
1	Bahrain	Yes
2	Cambodia*	No
3	China (People's Republic of)	Yes
4	Hong Kong (China)	Yes
5	Indonesia	Yes
6	Japan	Yes
7	Korea	Yes
8	Kuwait	Yes
9	Lao People's Democratic Republic*	No
10	Luxembourg	Yes
11	Malaysia	Yes
12	Oman	Yes
13	Pakistan	Yes
14	Qatar	Yes
15	Singapore	Yes
16	United Arab Emirates	Yes
17	United Kingdom	Yes
18	Viet Nam	Yes

Bulgaria

A. Progress in the implementation of the minimum standard

Bulgaria has 71 tax agreements in force, as reported in its response to the Peer Review questionnaire. Forty-one of those agreements comply with the minimum standard.

Bulgaria signed the MLI in 2017 and deposited its instrument of ratification on 16 September 2022, listing 64 of its agreements. The MLI entered into force for Bulgaria on 1 January 2023. The agreements modified by the MLI come into compliance with the minimum standard once the provisions of the MLI take effect.

Bulgaria has not listed its agreements with Finland, Germany, Malta, Switzerland and Uzbekistan under the MLI, but indicated in its response to the Peer Review questionnaire that steps have been taken (other than under the MLI) to implement the minimum standard in those agreements.

Bulgaria is implementing the minimum standard through the inclusion of the preamble statement and the PPT.

B. Conclusion

No jurisdiction has raised any concerns about their agreements with Bulgaria.

Summary of the jurisdiction response – Bulgaria

	1.Treaty partners	2. Compliance with the standard	3. Signature of a complying instrument	4. Minimum standard provision used
1	Albania	Yes MLI		PPT
2	Algeria*	No	No	PPT
3	Armenia	No	Yes MLI	PPT
4	Austria	Yes MLI		PPT
5	Azerbaijan	No	No	PPT
6	Bahrain	Yes MLI		PPT
7	Belarus	No	No	PPT
8	Belgium	Yes MLI		PPT
9	Canada	Yes MLI		PPT
10	China (People's Republic of)	Yes MLI		PPT
11	Croatia	Yes MLI		PPT
12	Cyprus*	Yes MLI		PPT
13	Czechia	Yes MLI		PPT
14	Democratic People's Republic of Korea	No	No	PPT
15	Denmark	Yes MLI		PPT
16	Egypt	Yes MLI		PPT
17	Estonia	No	Yes MLI	PPT
18	Finland	No	No	
19	France	Yes MLI		PPT
20	Georgia	Yes MLI		PPT
21	Germany	No	Yes other	PPT
22	Greece	Yes MLI		PPT
23	Hungary	Yes MLI		PPT

24	India	Yes MLI		PPT
25	Indonesia	No	Yes MLI	PPT
26	Iran*	No	No	PPT
27	Ireland	Yes MLI		PPT
28	Israel	Yes MLI		PPT
29	Italy	No	Yes MLI	PPT
30	Japan	Yes MLI		PPT
31	Jordan	Yes MLI		PPT
32	Kazakhstan	Yes MLI		PPT
33	Korea	Yes MLI		PPT
34	Kuwait	No	Yes MLI	PPT
35	Latvia	Yes MLI		PPT
36	Lebanon*	No	No	PPT
37	Lithuania	Yes MLI		PPT
38	Luxembourg	Yes MLI		PPT
39	Malta	No	No	
40	Moldova*	No	No	PPT
41	Mongolia	No	Yes MLI	PPT
42	Montenegro	No	No	PPT
43	Morocco	No	Yes MLI	PPT
44	Netherlands	Yes other		PPT
45	North Macedonia	No	Yes MLI	PPT
46	Norway	Yes MLI		PPT
47	Pakistan	Yes other		PPT
48	Poland	Yes MLI		PPT
49	Portugal	Yes MLI		PPT
50	Qatar	Yes MLI		PPT
51	Romania	No	Yes MLI	PPT
52	Russian Federation	No	Yes MLI	PPT
53	Saudi Arabia	Yes other		PPT
54	Serbia	Yes MLI		PPT
55	Singapore	Yes MLI		PPT
56	Slovak Republic	Yes MLI		PPT
57	Slovenia	Yes MLI		PPT
58	South Africa	Yes MLI		PPT
59	Spain	No	Yes MLI	PPT
60	Sweden	No	Yes MLI	PPT
61	Switzerland	No	No	
62	Syrian Arab Republic*	No	No	PPT
63	Thailand	Yes MLI		PPT
64	Türkiye	No	Yes MLI	PPT
65	Ukraine	Yes MLI		PPT
66	United Arab Emirates	Yes MLI		PPT
67	United Kingdom	Yes MLI		PPT
68	United States	No	No	PPT+D-LOB
69	Uzbekistan	No	No	
70	Viet Nam	No	Yes MLI	PPT
71	Zimbabwe*	No	No	PPT

Burkina Faso

A. Progress in the implementation of the minimum standard

Burkina Faso has four tax agreements in force, as reported in its response to the Peer Review questionnaire, including the multilateral Regulation 08/2008/COM adopting the rules for the avoidance of double taxation within the West African Economic and Monetary Union and the rule for assistance in tax matters (the UEMOA) concluded with seven treaty partners,[22] and the multilateral Supplementary Act A/SA, 5/12/18 adopting community rules for the elimination of double taxation with respect to taxes on income, capital and inheritance and the prevention of tax evasion and avoidance within the ECOWAS Member States (the ECOWAS Supplementary Act) concluded with fourteen treaty partners. Two of those agreements, including the ECOWAS Supplementary Act, comply with the minimum standard.

Burkina Faso signed the MLI in 2017 and deposited its instrument of ratification on 30 October 2020, listing its non-compliant bilateral agreements. The MLI entered into force for Burkina Faso on 1 February 2021. The agreements modified by the MLI come into compliance with the minimum standard once the provisions of the MLI take effect.

Burkina Faso is implementing the minimum standard through the inclusion of the preamble statement and the PPT.[23]

B. Conclusion

The UEMOA does not at this stage comply with the minimum standard and discussions to bring this agreement up to date should be contemplated.[24]

Summary of the jurisdiction response – Burkina Faso

	1.Treaty partners	2. Compliance with the standard	3. Signature of a complying instrument	4. Minimum standard provision used
1	France	Yes MLI		PPT
2	ECOWAS Supplementary Act treaty partners (Benin, Cabo Verde, Côte d'Ivoire, Gambia*, Ghana*, Guinea-Bissau*, Guinea Conakry*, Liberia, Mali*, Niger*, Nigeria, Senegal, Sierra Leone, Togo)	Yes other		PPT
3	Tunisia	No	Yes MLI	PPT

[22] Règlement n°08/2008/CM des pays de l'Union économique et monétaire Ouest Africaine (UEMOA) du 26 septembre 2008 portant adoption des règles visant à éviter la double imposition au sein de l'UEMOA et des règles d'assistance en matière fiscale.

[23] For its agreements listed under the MLI, Burkina Faso is implementing the preamble statement (Article 6 of the MLI) and the PPT (Article 7 of the MLI).

[24] Revisions to the UEMOA require an agreement from its eight treaty partners.

Other agreements

	1.Treaty partners	2. Inclusive Framework member
1	UEMOA treaty partners (Benin, Côte d'Ivoire, Guinea-Bissau*, Mali*, Niger*, Senegal, Togo)	Yes (Benin, Côte d'Ivoire, Senegal, Togo) No (Guinea-Bissau*, Mali*, Niger*).

Cabo Verde

A. Progress in the implementation of the minimum standard

Cabo Verde has six tax agreements in force, as reported in its response to the Peer Review questionnaire, including the multilateral Supplementary Act A/SA, 5/12/18 adopting community rules for the elimination of double taxation with respect to taxes on income, capital and inheritance and the prevention of tax evasion and avoidance within the ECOWAS Member States (the ECOWAS Supplementary Act) concluded with fourteen treaty partners. Two of those agreements, including the ECOWAS Supplementary Act, comply with the minimum standard.

Cabo Verde has not signed the MLI.

Cabo Verde indicated in its response to the Peer Review questionnaire that steps have been taken (other than under the MLI) to implement the minimum standard in its agreements with Macau (China), Mauritius and Portugal.

Cabo Verde is implementing the minimum standard through the inclusion of the preamble statement and the PPT.

B. Conclusion

Cabo Verde has developed a plan for the implementation of the minimum standard in its agreement with Spain. Cabo Verde indicated in its response to the Peer Review questionnaire that bilateral negotiations would be pursued with respect to that agreement.

Summary of the jurisdiction response – Cabo Verde

	1.Treaty partners	2. Compliance with the standard	3. Signature of a complying instrument	4. Minimum standard provision used
1	ECOWAS Supplementary Act treaty partners (Benin, Burkina Faso, Côte d'Ivoire, The Gambia*, Ghana*, Guinea-Bissau*, Guinea Conakry*, Liberia, Mali*, Niger*, Nigeria, Senegal, Sierra Leone, Togo)	Yes other		PPT
2	Macau (China)	No	No	PPT
3	Mauritius	No	No	PPT
4	Portugal	No	No	PPT
5	Senegal	Yes other		PPT

Other agreements

	1.Treaty partners	2. Inclusive Framework member
1	Spain	Yes

Cameroon

A. Progress in the implementation of the minimum standard

Cameroon has six tax agreements in force, as reported in its response to the Peer Review questionnaire. Four of those agreements comply with the minimum standard.

Cameroon signed the MLI in 2017 and deposited its instrument of ratification on 21 April 2022, listing its non-compliant agreements. The MLI entered into force for Cameroon on 1 August 2022. The agreements modified by the MLI come into compliance with the minimum standard once the provisions of the MLI take effect.

Cameroon is implementing the minimum standard through the inclusion of the preamble statement and the PPT.[25]

B. Conclusion

No jurisdiction has raised any concerns about their agreements with Cameroon.

Summary of the jurisdiction response – Cameroon

	1.Treaty partners	2. Compliance with the standard	3. Signature of a complying instrument	4. Minimum standard provision used
1	Canada	Yes MLI		PPT
2	France	Yes MLI		PPT
3	Morocco	No	Yes MLI	PPT
4	South Africa	Yes MLI		PPT
5	Tunisia	No	Yes MLI	PPT
6	United Arab Emirates	Yes MLI		PPT

[25] For its agreements listed under the MLI, Cameroon is implementing the preamble statement (Article 6 of the MLI) and the PPT (Article 7 of the MLI).

Canada

A. Progress in the implementation of the minimum standard

Canada has 94 tax agreements in force,[26] as reported in its response to the Peer Review questionnaire. Fifty of those agreements comply with the minimum standard.

Canada signed the MLI in 2017 and deposited its instrument of ratification on 29 August 2019. The MLI entered into force for Canada on 1 December 2019. The agreements modified by the MLI come into compliance with the minimum standard once the provisions of the MLI take effect.

Canada indicated in its response to the Peer Review questionnaire that steps have been taken (other than under the MLI) to implement the minimum standard in the agreements with Brazil, Germany, Norway, Switzerland and the United States.

Canada is implementing the minimum standard through the inclusion of the preamble statement and the PPT.[27]

B. Conclusion

No jurisdiction has raised any concerns about their agreements with Canada.

Summary of the jurisdiction response – Canada

	1.Treaty partners	2. Compliance with the standard	3. Signature of a complying instrument	4. Minimum standard provision used
1	Algeria*	No	No	PPT
2	Argentina	No	Yes MLI	PPT
3	Armenia	No	Yes MLI	PPT
4	Australia	Yes MLI		PPT
5	Austria	Yes MLI		PPT
6	Azerbaijan	No	No	PPT
7	Bangladesh*	No	No	PPT
8	Barbados	Yes MLI		PPT
9	Belgium	Yes MLI		PPT
10	Brazil	No	No	
11	Bulgaria	Yes MLI		PPT
12	Cameroon	Yes MLI		PPT
13	Chile	Yes MLI		PPT
14	China (People's Republic of)	Yes MLI		PPT
15	Colombia	No	Yes MLI	PPT

[26] This includes an Arrangement for the Avoidance of Double Taxation and the Prevention of Fiscal Evasion with Respect to Taxes on Income between the Canadian Trade Office in Taipei and the Taipei Economic and Cultural Office in Canada.

[27] For its agreements listed under the MLI, Canada is implementing the preamble statement (Article 6 of the MLI) and the PPT (Article 7 of the MLI). Canada expressed a statement, in accordance with Article 7(17)(a) of the MLI, that while it accepts the application of PPT alone as an interim measure, it intends where possible to adopt an LOB provision in addition to or in replacement of the PPT through bilateral negotiation.

16	Côte d'Ivoire	No	Yes MLI	PPT
17	Croatia	Yes MLI		PPT
18	Cyprus*	Yes MLI		PPT
19	Czechia	Yes MLI		PPT
20	Denmark	Yes MLI		PPT
21	Dominican Republic	No	No	PPT
22	Egypt	Yes MLI		PPT
23	Estonia	No	Yes MLI	PPT
24	Finland	Yes MLI		PPT
25	France	Yes MLI		PPT
26	Gabon	No	Yes MLI	PPT
27	Germany	No	No	
28	Greece	Yes MLI		PPT
29	Hong Kong (China)	Yes MLI		PPT
30	Hungary	Yes MLI		PPT
31	Iceland	Yes MLI		PPT
32	India	Yes MLI		PPT
33	Indonesia	Yes MLI		PPT
34	Ireland	Yes MLI		PPT
35	Israel	Yes MLI		PPT
36	Italy	No	Yes MLI	PPT
37	Jamaica	No	Yes MLI	PPT
38	Japan	Yes MLI		PPT
39	Jordan	Yes MLI		PPT
40	Kazakhstan	Yes MLI		PPT
41	Kenya	No	Yes MLI	PPT
42	Korea	Yes MLI		PPT
43	Kuwait	No	Yes MLI	PPT
44	Latvia	Yes MLI		PPT
45	Lithuania	Yes MLI		PPT
46	Luxembourg	Yes MLI		PPT
47	Malaysia	Yes MLI		PPT
48	Malta	Yes MLI		PPT
49	Mexico	No	Yes MLI	PPT
50	Moldova*	No	No	PPT
51	Mongolia	No	Yes MLI	PPT
52	Morocco	No	Yes MLI	PPT
53	Netherlands	Yes MLI		PPT
54	New Zealand	Yes MLI		PPT
55	Nigeria	No	Yes MLI	PPT
56	Norway	No	No	
57	Oman	Yes MLI		PPT
58	Pakistan	Yes MLI		PPT
59	Papua New Guinea	No	Yes MLI	PPT
60	Peru	No	Yes MLI	PPT
61	Philippines	No	No	PPT
62	Poland	Yes MLI		PPT
63	Portugal	Yes MLI		PPT
64	Romania	No	Yes MLI	PPT
65	Russian Federation	Yes MLI		PPT
66	Senegal	Yes MLI		PPT
67	Serbia	Yes MLI		PPT
68	Singapore	Yes MLI		PPT

69	Slovak Republic	Yes MLI		PPT
70	Slovenia	Yes MLI		PPT
71	South Africa	Yes MLI		PPT
72	Spain	Yes MLI		PPT
73	Sri Lanka	No	No	PPT
74	Sweden	No	Yes MLI	PPT
75	Switzerland	No	No	
76	Tanzania*	No	No	PPT
77	Thailand	Yes MLI		PPT
78	Trinidad and Tobago	No	No	PPT
79	Tunisia	No	Yes MLI	PPT
80	Türkiye	No	Yes MLI	PPT
81	Ukraine	Yes MLI		PPT
82	United Arab Emirates	Yes MLI		PPT
83	United Kingdom	Yes MLI		PPT
84	United States	No	No	
85	Viet Nam	No	Yes MLI	PPT
86	Zambia	No	No	PPT
87	Zimbabwe*	No	No	PPT

Other agreements

	1.Treaty partners	2. Inclusive Framework member
1	Chinese Taipei*	No
2	Ecuador*	No
3	Guyana*	No
4	Kyrgyzstan*	No
5	Madagascar*	No
6	Uzbekistan	Yes
7	Venezuela*	No

Cayman Islands

A. Progress in the implementation of the minimum standard

The Cayman Islands has no tax agreements in force, as reported in its response to the Peer Review questionnaire.

B. Conclusion

No jurisdiction has raised any concerns about the Cayman Islands.

Chile

A. Progress in the implementation of the minimum standard

Chile has 36 tax agreements in force, as reported in its response to the Peer Review questionnaire. Twenty-eight of those agreements comply with the minimum standard.

Chile signed the MLI in 2017 and deposited its instrument of ratification on 26 November 2020, listing its non-compliant agreements. The MLI entered into force for Chile on 1 March 2021. The agreements modified by the MLI come into compliance with the minimum standard once the provisions of the MLI take effect.

Chile has signed a bilateral complying instrument with respect to its agreement with Brazil.

Chile indicated in its response to the Peer Review questionnaire that steps have been taken (other than under the MLI) to implement the minimum standard in the agreements with Ecuador* and Paraguay.

Chile is generally implementing the minimum standard through the inclusion of the preamble statement and the PPT combined with the LOB. [28]

B. Conclusion

No jurisdiction has raised any concerns about their agreements with Chile.

Summary of the jurisdiction response – Chile

	1.Treaty partners	2. Compliance with the standard	3. Signature of a complying instrument	4. Minimum standard provision used
1	Argentina	Yes other		PPT+LOB
2	Australia	Yes MLI		PPT
3	Austria	Yes MLI		PPT
4	Belgium	Yes MLI		PPT
5	Brazil	No	Yes other	PPT+LOB
6	Canada	Yes MLI		PPT
7	China (People's Republic of)	Yes other		PPT+LOB
8	Colombia	No	Yes MLI	PPT+LOB
9	Croatia	Yes MLI		PPT
10	Czechia	Yes MLI		PPT
11	Denmark	Yes MLI		PPT+LOB
12	Ecuador*	No	No	PPT+LOB
13	France	Yes MLI		PPT
14	India	Yes other		PPT+LOB

[28] For its agreements listed under the MLI, Chile is implementing the preamble statement (Article 6 of the MLI) and the PPT (Article 7 of the MLI). Chile has also adopted the simplified LOB under Article 7(6) of the MLI and expressed a statement, in accordance with Article 7(17)(a) of the MLI, that while Chile accepts the application of the PPT under the MLI, it intends where possible to adopt an LOB provision through bilateral negotiation. Chile has made a reservation pursuant to Article 6(4) of the MLI not to apply Article 6(1) of the MLI with respect to agreements, which already contain the relevant preamble language (covering four agreements). Chile has also made a reservation pursuant to Article 7(15)(b) of the MLI not to apply Article 7(1) of the MLI with respect to agreements which already contain a PPT (covering four agreements).

15	Ireland	Yes MLI		PPT
16	Italy	Yes other		PPT
17	Japan	Yes other		PPT
18	Korea	Yes MLI		PPT
19	Malaysia	Yes MLI		PPT
20	Mexico	No	Yes MLI	PPT+LOB
21	Netherlands	Yes other		PPT+LOB
22	New Zealand	Yes MLI		PPT
23	Norway	Yes MLI		PPT+LOB
24	Paraguay	No	No	PPT+LOB
25	Peru	No	Yes MLI	PPT
26	Poland	Yes MLI		PPT
27	Portugal	Yes MLI		PPT
28	Russian Federation	Yes MLI		PPT+LOB
29	South Africa	Yes MLI		PPT
30	Spain	Yes MLI		PPT
31	Sweden	No	Yes MLI	PPT
32	Switzerland	No	Yes MLI	PPT
33	Thailand	Yes MLI		PPT
34	United Arab Emirates	Yes other		PPT
35	United Kingdom	Yes MLI		PPT
36	Uruguay	Yes other		PPT+LOB

China (People's Republic of)

A. Progress in the implementation of the minimum standard

China has 105 tax agreements in force as reported in its response to the Peer Review questionnaire. Sixty of those agreements comply with the minimum standard.

China signed the MLI in 2017 and deposited its instrument of ratification on 25 May 2022, listing its non-compliant agreements. The MLI entered into force for China on 1 September 2022. The agreements modified by the MLI come into compliance with the minimum standard once the provisions of the MLI take effect.

China has signed a bilateral complying instrument with respect to its agreements with Brazil and Italy.

China indicated in its response to the Peer Review questionnaire that steps have been taken (other than under the MLI) to implement the minimum standard in its agreements with Germany and Switzerland.

China is generally implementing the minimum standard through the inclusion of the preamble statement and PPT.[29]

B. Conclusion

No jurisdiction has raised any concerns about their agreements with China.

Summary of the jurisdiction response – China (People's Republic of)

	1.Treaty partners	2. Compliance with the standard	3. Signature of a complying instrument	4. Minimum standard provision used
1	Albania	Yes MLI		PPT
2	Algeria*	No	No	PPT
3	Angola	Yes other		PPT
4	Armenia	No	Yes MLI	PPT
5	Australia	Yes MLI		PPT
6	Austria	Yes MLI		PPT
7	Azerbaijan	No	No	PPT
8	Bahrain	Yes MLI		PPT
9	Bangladesh*	No	No	PPT
10	Barbados	Yes MLI		PPT
11	Belarus	No	No	PPT
12	Belgium	Yes MLI		PPT
13	Bosnia-Herzegovina	Yes MLI		PPT
14	Botswana	No	No	PPT
15	Brazil	No	Yes other	PPT+LOB
16	Brunei Darussalam	No	No	PPT
17	Bulgaria	Yes MLI		PPT
18	Cambodia*	No	No	PPT
19	Canada	Yes MLI		PPT

29 For its agreements listed under the MLI, China is implementing the preamble statement (Article 6 of the MLI) and the PPT (Article 7 of the MLI).

20	Chile	Yes other		PPT+LOB
21	Congo	Yes other		PPT
22	Croatia	Yes MLI		PPT
23	Cuba*	No	No	PPT
24	Cyprus*	Yes MLI		PPT
25	Czechia	Yes MLI		PPT
26	Denmark	Yes MLI		PPT
27	Ecuador*	No	No	PPT+LOB
28	Egypt	Yes MLI		PPT
29	Estonia	No	Yes MLI	PPT
30	Ethiopia*	No	No	PPT
31	Finland	Yes MLI		PPT
32	France	Yes MLI		PPT
33	Georgia	Yes MLI		PPT
34	Germany	No	No	PPT
35	Greece	Yes MLI		PPT
36	Hungary	Yes MLI		PPT
37	Iceland	Yes MLI		PPT
38	India	Yes other		PPT
39	Indonesia	Yes MLI		PPT
40	Iran*	No	No	PPT
41	Ireland	Yes MLI		PPT
42	Israel	Yes MLI		PPT
43	Italy	No	Yes MLI	PPT
44	Jamaica	No	Yes MLI	PPT
45	Japan	Yes MLI		PPT
46	Kazakhstan	Yes MLI		PPT
47	Korea	Yes MLI		PPT
48	Kuwait	No	Yes MLI	PPT
49	Kyrgyzstan*	No	No	PPT
50	Lao People's Democratic Republic*	No	No	PPT
51	Latvia	Yes MLI		PPT
52	Lithuania	Yes MLI		PPT
53	Luxembourg	Yes MLI		PPT
54	Malaysia	Yes MLI		PPT
55	Malta	Yes MLI		PPT
56	Mauritius	Yes MLI		PPT
57	Mexico	No	Yes MLI	PPT
58	Moldova*	No	No	PPT
59	Mongolia	No	No	PPT
60	Montenegro	No	No	PPT
61	Morocco	No	Yes MLI	PPT
62	Nepal*	No	No	PPT
63	Netherlands	Yes MLI		PPT
64	New Zealand	Yes other		PPT
65	Nigeria	No	Yes MLI	PPT
66	North Macedonia	No	Yes MLI	PPT
67	Norway	Yes MLI		PPT
68	Oman	Yes MLI		PPT
69	Pakistan	Yes MLI		PPT
70	Papua New Guinea	No	Yes MLI	PPT
71	Philippines	No	No	PPT
72	Poland	Yes MLI		PPT

73	Portugal	Yes MLI		PPT
74	Qatar	Yes MLI		PPT
75	Romania	No	Yes MLI	PPT
76	Russian Federation	No	Yes MLI	PPT+LOB
77	Rwanda*	Yes other		PPT
78	Saudi Arabia	Yes MLI		PPT
79	Serbia	Yes MLI		PPT
80	Seychelles	Yes MLI		PPT
81	Singapore	Yes MLI		PPT
82	Slovak Republic	Yes MLI		PPT
83	Slovenia	Yes MLI		PPT
84	South Africa	Yes MLI		PPT
85	Spain	Yes other		PPT
86	Sri Lanka	No	No	PPT
87	Sudan*	No	No	PPT
88	Sweden	No	Yes MLI	PPT
89	Switzerland	No	No	PPT
90	Syrian Arab Republic*	No	No	PPT
91	Tajikistan*	No	No	PPT
92	Thailand	Yes MLI		PPT
93	Trinidad and Tobago	No	No	PPT
94	Tunisia	No	Yes MLI	PPT
95	Türkiye	No	Yes MLI	PPT
96	Turkmenistan*	No	No	PPT
97	Ukraine	Yes MLI		PPT
98	United Arab Emirates	Yes MLI		PPT
99	United Kingdom	Yes MLI		PPT
100	United States	No	No	
101	Uzbekistan	No	No	PPT
102	Venezuela*	No	No	PPT
103	Viet Nam	No	Yes MLI	PPT
104	Zambia	No	No	PPT
105	Zimbabwe*	No	No	PPT

Colombia

A. Progress in the implementation of the minimum standard

Colombia has 14 tax agreements in force as reported in its response to the Peer Review questionnaire, including the Decision 578 of the Andean Community Commission (Decision 578) for the members of the Andean Community (the Andean Community Agreement).[30] Four of those agreements comply with the minimum standard.

Colombia signed the MLI in 2017 and listed its non-compliant bilateral agreements. The agreements modified by the MLI come into compliance with the minimum standard once the provisions of the MLI take effect.

Colombia indicated in its response to the Peer Review questionnaire that steps have been taken (other than under the MLI) to implement the minimum standard in the Andean Community Agreement and the agreement with Switzerland.

Colombia is implementing the minimum standard through the inclusion of the preamble statement and the PPT combined with the LOB.[31]

B. Conclusion

Recommendation

It is recommended that Colombia completes the steps to have the MLI take effect with respect to its agreements listed under the MLI as those agreements will only be modified by the MLI (and come into compliance with the minimum standard) once the provisions of the MLI take effect.

---

[30] The Decision of the Commission of the Andean Community 578 on the regime for the avoidance of double taxation and the prevention of fiscal evasion, adopted on 4 May 2004. The current members of the Andean Community are Bolivia*, Colombia, Ecuador* and Peru.

[31] For its agreements listed under the MLI, Colombia is implementing the preamble statement (Article 6 of the MLI) and the PPT (Article 7 of the MLI). Colombia has also adopted the simplified LOB under Article 7(6) of the MLI and expressed a statement, in accordance with Article 7(17)(a) of the MLI, that while it accepts the application of PPT alone as an interim measure, it intends where possible to adopt an LOB provision in addition to or in replacement of the PPT through bilateral negotiation. Colombia has made a reservation pursuant to Article 6(4) of the MLI not to apply Article 6(1) of the MLI with respect to agreements that already contain the relevant preamble language (covering one agreement).

Summary of the jurisdiction response – Colombia

	1.Treaty partners	2. Compliance with the standard	3. Signature of a complying instrument	4. Minimum standard provision used
1	Andean Community Agreement treaty partners (Bolivia*, Ecuador*, Peru)	No	No	
2	Canada	No	Yes MLI	PPT+LOB
3	Chile	No	Yes MLI	PPT+LOB
4	Czechia	No	Yes MLI	PPT
5	France	Yes other		PPT
6	India	No	Yes MLI	PPT+LOB
7	Italy	Yes other		PPT
8	Japan	Yes other		PPT+LOB
9	Korea	No	Yes MLI	PPT+LOB
10	Mexico	No	Yes MLI	PPT+LOB
11	Portugal	No	Yes MLI	PPT+LOB
12	Spain	No	Yes MLI	PPT+LOB
13	Switzerland	No	No	PPT+LOB
14	United Kingdom	Yes other		PPT

Congo

A. Progress in the implementation of the minimum standard

Congo has four tax agreements in force as reported in its response to the Peer Review questionnaire. One of those agreements, the agreement with China (People's Republic of), complies with the minimum standard.

Congo has not signed the MLI.

In its response to the Peer Review Questionnaire, Italy indicated that its agreement with Congo did not give rise to material treaty shopping concerns for Italy.

B. Conclusion

Recommendation

It is recommended that Congo formulates a plan for the implementation of the minimum standard in its agreements for which no steps have yet been taken and that were concluded with members of the BEPS Inclusive Framework (France and Mauritius).

Summary of jurisdiction response – Congo

	1.Treaty partners	2. Compliance with the standard	3. Signature of a complying instrument	4. Minimum standard provision used
1	China (People's Republic of)	Yes other		PPT

Other agreements

	1.Treaty partners	2. Inclusive Framework member
1	France	Yes
2	Italy	Yes
3	Mauritius	Yes

Cook Islands

A. Progress in the implementation of the minimum standard

The Cook Islands has no tax agreements in force, as reported in its response to the Peer Review questionnaire.

B. Conclusion

No jurisdiction has raised any concerns about the Cook Islands.

Costa Rica

A. Progress in the implementation of the minimum standard

Costa Rica has four tax agreements in force as reported in its response to the Peer Review questionnaire. One of those agreements, the agreement with Spain, complies with the minimum standard.

Costa Rica signed the MLI in 2017 and deposited its instrument of ratification on 22 September 2020.[32] The MLI entered into force for Costa Rica on 1 January 2021. The agreements modified by the MLI come into compliance with the minimum standard once the provisions of the MLI take effect.

Costa Rica has not listed its agreement with Germany under the MLI but indicated in its response to the Peer Review questionnaire that steps have been taken (other than under the MLI) to implement the minimum standard in that agreement.

Costa Rica is implementing the minimum standard through the inclusion of the preamble statement and the PPT.[33]

B. Conclusion

No jurisdiction has raised any concerns about their agreements with Costa Rica.

Summary of the jurisdiction response – Costa Rica

	1.Treaty partners	2. Compliance with the standard	3. Signature of a complying instrument	4. Minimum standard provision used
1	Germany	No	No	PPT
2	Mexico	No	Yes MLI	PPT
3	Spain	Yes MLI		PPT
4	United Arab Emirates	No	No	PPT

[32] While Costa Rica has not listed its agreement with the United Arab Emirates in its definitive list of reservations and notifications under the MLI (MLI Position) deposited upon ratification, Costa Rica has included this agreement to be covered under the MLI in its draft consolidated MLI Position, for deposit subsequent to ratification. Costa Rica indicated that it will deposit this consolidated MLI Position following the completion of its domestic procedures.

[33] For its agreements listed under the MLI, Costa Rica is implementing the preamble statement (Article 6 of the MLI) and the PPT (Article 7 of the MLI).

Côte d'Ivoire

A. Progress in the implementation of the minimum standard

Côte d'Ivoire has thirteen tax agreements in force as reported in its response to the Peer Review questionnaire, including the multilateral Regulation 08/2008/COM adopting the rules for the avoidance of double taxation within the West African Economic and Monetary Union and the rule for assistance in tax matters (the UEMOA) concluded with seven treaty partners,[34] and the multilateral Supplementary Act A/SA, 5/12/18 adopting community rules for the elimination of double taxation with respect to taxes on income, capital and inheritance and the prevention of tax evasion and avoidance within the ECOWAS Member States (the ECOWAS Supplementary Act) concluded with fourteen treaty partners. One of those agreements, the ECOWAS Supplementary Act, complies with the minimum standard.

Côte d'Ivoire signed the MLI in 2018 and deposited its instrument of ratification on 25 September 2023. The MLI enters into force for Côte d'Ivoire on 1 January 2024. The agreements modified by the MLI come into compliance with the minimum standard once the provisions of the MLI take effect.

Côte d'Ivoire has not listed its agreement with Switzerland under the MLI but indicated in its response to the Peer Review questionnaire that steps have been taken (other than under the MLI) to implement the minimum standard in that agreement.

Côte d'Ivoire is implementing the minimum standard through the inclusion of the preamble statement and the PPT.[35]

B. Conclusion

The UEMOA does not at this stage comply with the minimum standard and discussions to bring this agreement up to date should be contemplated.[36]

Summary of the jurisdiction response – Côte d'Ivoire

	1.Treaty partners	2. Compliance with the standard	3. Signature of a complying instrument	4. Minimum standard provision used
1	Belgium	No	Yes MLI	PPT
2	Canada	No	Yes MLI	PPT
3	France	No	Yes MLI	PPT

[34] Règlement n°08/2008/CM des pays de l'Union économique et monétaire Ouest Africaine (UEMOA) du 26 septembre 2008 portant adoption des règles visant à éviter la double imposition au sein de l'UEMOA et des règles d'assistance en matière fiscale.

[35] For its agreements listed under the MLI, Côte d'Ivoire is implementing the preamble statement (Article 6 of the MLI) and the PPT (Article 7 of the MLI). Côte d'Ivoire has also adopted the asymmetrical application of the simplified LOB under Article 7(7)(b) of the MLI.

[36] Revisions to the UEMOA require an agreement from its eight treaty partners.

4	Germany	No	No	PPT
5	Italy	No	Yes MLI	PPT
6	Morocco	No	Yes MLI	PPT
7	Norway	No	No	PPT
8	ECOWAS Supplementary Act treaty partners (Benin, Burkina Faso, Cabo Verde, The Gambia*, Ghana*, Guinea-Bissau*, Guinea Conakry*, Liberia, Mali*, Niger*, Nigeria, Senegal, Sierra Leone, Togo)	Yes other		PPT
9	Portugal	No	Yes MLI	PPT
10	Switzerland	No	No	PPT
11	Tunisia	No	Yes MLI	PPT
12	United Kingdom	No	Yes MLI	PPT

Other agreements

	1.Treaty partners	2. Inclusive Framework member
1	UEMOA treaty partners (Benin, Burkina Faso, Guinea-Bissau*, Mali*, Niger*, Senegal, Togo)	Yes (Benin, Burkina Faso, Senegal, Togo) No (Guinea-Bissau*, Mali*, Niger*).

Croatia

A. Progress in the implementation of the minimum standard

Croatia has 66 tax agreements in force as reported in its response to the Peer Review questionnaire. Forty-five of those agreements comply with the minimum standard.

Croatia signed the MLI in 2017 and deposited its instrument of ratification on 18 February 2021, listing its non-compliant agreements. The MLI entered into force for Croatia on 1 June 2021. The agreements modified by the MLI come into compliance with the minimum standard once the provisions of the MLI take effect.

Croatia indicated in its response to the Peer Review questionnaire that steps have been taken (other than under the MLI) to implement the minimum standard in the agreements with Sweden and Switzerland.

Croatia is implementing the minimum standard through the inclusion of the preamble statement and the PPT.[37]

B. Conclusion

No jurisdiction has raised any concerns about their agreements with Croatia.

Summary of the jurisdiction response – Croatia

	1.Treaty partners	2. Compliance with the standard	3. Signature of a complying instrument	4. Minimum standard provision used
1	Albania	Yes MLI		PPT
2	Armenia	No	Yes MLI	PPT
3	Austria	Yes MLI		PPT
4	Azerbaijan	No	No	PPT
5	Belarus	No	No	PPT
6	Belgium	Yes MLI		PPT
7	Bosnia-Herzegovina	Yes MLI		PPT
8	Bulgaria	Yes MLI		PPT
9	Canada	Yes MLI		PPT
10	Chile	Yes MLI		PPT
11	China (People's Republic of)	Yes MLI		PPT
12	Czechia	Yes MLI		PPT
13	Denmark	Yes MLI		PPT
14	Estonia	No	Yes MLI	PPT
15	Finland	Yes MLI		PPT
16	France	Yes MLI		PPT
17	Georgia	Yes MLI		PPT
18	Germany	No	Yes MLI	PPT
19	Greece	Yes MLI		PPT
20	Hungary	Yes MLI		PPT

[37] For its agreements listed under the MLI, Croatia is implementing the preamble statement (Article 6 of the MLI) and the PPT (Article 7 of the MLI).

21	Iceland	Yes MLI		PPT
22	India	Yes MLI		PPT
23	Indonesia	Yes MLI		PPT
24	Iran*	No	No	PPT
25	Ireland	Yes MLI		PPT
26	Israel	Yes MLI		PPT
27	Italy	No	Yes MLI	PPT
28	Japan	Yes other		PPT+LOB
29	Jordan	Yes MLI		PPT
30	Kazakhstan	Yes MLI		PPT
31	Korea	Yes MLI		PPT
32	Kosovo*	No	No	PPT
33	Kuwait	No	Yes MLI	PPT
34	Latvia	Yes MLI		PPT
35	Lithuania	Yes MLI		PPT
36	Luxembourg	Yes MLI		PPT
37	Malaysia	Yes MLI		PPT
38	Malta	Yes MLI		PPT
39	Mauritius	Yes MLI		PPT
40	Moldova*	No	No	PPT
41	Montenegro	No	No	PPT
42	Morocco	No	Yes MLI	PPT
43	Netherlands	Yes MLI		PPT
44	North Macedonia	No	Yes MLI	PPT
45	Norway	No	No	PPT
46	Oman	Yes MLI		PPT
47	Poland	Yes MLI		PPT
48	Portugal	Yes MLI		PPT
49	Qatar	Yes MLI		PPT
50	Romania	No	Yes MLI	PPT
51	Russian Federation	Yes MLI		PPT
52	San Marino	Yes MLI		PPT
53	Serbia	Yes MLI		PPT
54	Slovak Republic	Yes MLI		PPT
55	Slovenia	Yes MLI		PPT
56	South Africa	Yes MLI		PPT
57	Spain	Yes MLI		PPT
58	Sweden	No	No	PPT
59	Switzerland	No	No	PPT
60	Syrian Arab Republic*	No	No	PPT
61	Türkiye	No	Yes MLI	PPT
62	Turkmenistan*	No	No	PPT
63	Ukraine	Yes MLI		PPT
64	United Arab Emirates	Yes MLI		PPT
65	United Kingdom	Yes MLI		PPT
66	Viet Nam	No	Yes MLI	PPT

Curaçao

A. Progress in the implementation of the minimum standard

Curaçao has four tax agreements in force as reported in its response to the Peer Review Questionnaire. One of those agreements, the agreement with Malta, complies with the minimum standard.

Curaçao joined the MLI in 2017 and the Kingdom of the Netherlands deposited its instrument of acceptance on 29 March 2019, listing its non-compliant agreements. The MLI entered into force for Curaçao on 1 July 2019. The agreements modified by the MLI come into compliance with the minimum standard once the provisions of the MLI take effect.

Curaçao indicated in its response to the Peer Review questionnaire that steps have been taken (other than under the MLI) to implement the minimum standard in the arrangement for the Kingdom of the Netherlands (applicable between Curaçao, Aruba and Sint Maarten*) and the arrangement between Curaçao and the Netherlands, that are governed by the domestic law of the Kingdom of the Netherlands.[38]

Curaçao is implementing the minimum standard through the inclusion of the preamble statement and the PPT.[39]

B. Conclusion

No jurisdiction has raised any concerns about their agreements with Curaçao.

Summary of the jurisdiction response – Curaçao

	1.Treaty partners	2. Compliance with the standard	3. Signature of a complying instrument	4. Minimum standard provision used
1	Aruba / Sint Maarten*	No	No	
2	Malta	Yes MLI		PPT
3	Netherlands	No	No	PPT
4	Norway	No	No	PPT

[38] Curaçao indicated in its response that the tax arrangement for the Kingdom of the Netherlands governs the relationship between Aruba, Curaçao, Sint Maarten* and the Netherlands. This arrangement is similar to the agreement Curaçao has with the Netherlands. The MLI cannot be applicable to those arrangements, since they are arrangements governed by the domestic law of the Kingdom of the Netherlands.

[39] For its agreements listed under the MLI, Curaçao is implementing the preamble statement (Article 6 of the MLI) and the PPT (Article 7 of the MLI).

Czechia

A. Progress in the implementation of the minimum standard

Czechia has 95 tax agreements in force[40] as reported in its response to the Peer Review questionnaire. Forty-eight of those agreements[41] comply with the minimum standard.

Czechia signed the MLI in 2017 and deposited its instrument of ratification on 13 May 2020. The MLI entered into force for Czechia on 1 September 2020. The agreements modified by the MLI come into compliance with the minimum standard once the provisions of the MLI take effect.

Czechia has not listed its non-compliant agreements with Albania, Bahrain, Barbados, Belarus, Bosnia-Herzegovina, Botswana, Brazil, Estonia, Indonesia, Jordan, Kazakhstan, Malaysia, Mongolia, Montenegro[42], Morocco, North Macedonia, Panama, Saudi Arabia, Thailand, Tunisia, Ukraine, the United States, Uzbekistan and Viet Nam. These agreements will therefore not, at this stage, be modified by the MLI. Albania, Bahrain, Barbados, Bosnia-Herzegovina, Estonia, Indonesia, Jordan, Kazakhstan, Malaysia, Mongolia, Morocco, North Macedonia, Panama, Saudi Arabia, Thailand, Tunisia, Ukraine and Viet Nam have listed their agreements with Czechia under the MLI.

Czechia has signed a bilateral complying instrument in respect of its agreements with Sri Lanka and the United Arab Emirates.

Czechia indicated in its response to the Peer Review questionnaire that steps have been taken (other than under the MLI) to implement the minimum standard in its agreements with Brazil, Montenegro[43] and North Macedonia.

Czechia is implementing the minimum standard through the inclusion of the preamble statement and the PPT.[44]

B. Conclusion

Albania, Bahrain, Barbados, Bosnia-Herzegovina, Estonia, Indonesia, Jordan, Kazakhstan, Malaysia, Mongolia, Morocco, North Macedonia, Panama, Saudi Arabia, Thailand, Tunisia, Ukraine and Viet Nam have listed their agreements with Czechia under the MLI, which amount to requests to implement the minimum standard.

Czechia has developed a plan for the implementation of the minimum standard in its agreements with Albania, Bahrain, Barbados, Belarus, Bosnia-Herzegovina, Botswana, Estonia, Indonesia, Jordan,

---

[40] Czechia has 95 agreements in force. These 95 agreements relate to 96 jurisdictions, because Czechia continues to apply the agreement with former Serbia and Montenegro to both Serbia and Montenegro.

[41] One of these agreements, the agreement with former Serbia and Montenegro, complies with the minimum standard only in relation to Serbia. Czechia has indicated that domestic procedures are ongoing in preparation for signature of a new agreement that has been negotiated with Montenegro.

[42] Czechia has listed the agreement with former Serbia and Montenegro under the MLI only in relation to Serbia.

[43] Czechia indicated in its response to the Peer Review questionnaire that a new agreement with Montenegro has been negotiated.

[44] For its agreements listed under the MLI, Czechia is implementing the preamble statement (Article 6 of the MLI) and the PPT (Article 7 of the MLI).

Kazakhstan, Malaysia, Mongolia, Morocco, Panama, Saudi Arabia, Thailand, Tunisia, Ukraine, the United States, Uzbekistan and Viet Nam.

Czechia indicated in its response to the Peer Review questionnaire that this year, it intends to expand its list of agreements to be covered under the MLI to include the agreements concluded with jurisdictions that have signed the MLI and have listed their agreements with Czechia. Czechia has indicated that to avoid doubts and misunderstandings in the future, Czechia will list only the agreements with such jurisdictions with which it bilaterally confirms the changes that the MLI would bring to the treaty. After finishing this procedure, Czechia indicated that it would pursue bilateral renegotiations or negotiations of amending protocols to implement the minimum standard in its remaining agreements.

Summary of the jurisdiction response – Czechia

	1.Treaty partners	2. Compliance with the standard	3. Signature of a complying instrument	4. Minimum standard provision used
1	Armenia	No	Yes MLI	PPT
2	Australia	Yes MLI		PPT
3	Austria	Yes MLI		PPT
4	Bangladesh*	Yes other		PPT
5	Belgium	Yes MLI		PPT
6	Brazil	No	No	
7	Bulgaria	Yes MLI		PPT
8	Canada	Yes MLI		PPT
9	Chile	Yes MLI		PPT
10	China (People's Republic of)	Yes MLI		PPT
11	Colombia	No	Yes MLI	PPT
12	Croatia	Yes MLI		PPT
13	Cyprus*	Yes MLI		PPT
14	Denmark	Yes MLI		PPT
15	Egypt	Yes MLI		PPT
16	Finland	Yes MLI		PPT
17	France	Yes MLI		PPT
18	Georgia	Yes MLI		PPT
19	Germany	No	Yes MLI	PPT
20	Greece	Yes MLI		PPT
21	Hong Kong (China)	Yes MLI		PPT
22	Hungary	Yes MLI		PPT
23	Iceland	Yes MLI		PPT
24	India	Yes MLI		PPT
25	Ireland	Yes MLI		PPT
26	Israel	Yes MLI		PPT
27	Italy	No	Yes MLI	PPT
28	Japan	Yes MLI		PPT
29	Korea	Yes other		PPT
30	Kuwait	No	Yes MLI	PPT
31	Kyrgyzstan*	Yes other		PPT
32	Latvia	Yes MLI		PPT
33	Liechtenstein	Yes MLI		PPT
34	Lithuania	Yes MLI		PPT
35	Luxembourg	Yes MLI		PPT
36	Malta	Yes MLI		PPT
37	Mexico	No	Yes MLI	PPT

38	Montenegro	No	No	
39	Netherlands	Yes MLI		PPT
40	New Zealand	Yes MLI		PPT
41	Nigeria	No	Yes MLI	PPT
42	North Macedonia	No	No	
43	Norway	Yes MLI		PPT
44	Pakistan	Yes MLI		PPT
45	Poland	Yes MLI		PPT
46	Portugal	Yes MLI		PPT
47	Qatar	Yes other		PPT
48	Romania	No	Yes MLI	PPT
49	Russian Federation	Yes MLI		PPT
50	San Marino	Yes other		PPT
51	Senegal	Yes other		PPT
52	Serbia	Yes MLI		PPT
53	Singapore	Yes MLI		PPT
54	Slovak Republic	Yes MLI		PPT
55	Slovenia	Yes MLI		PPT
56	South Africa	Yes MLI		PPT
57	Spain	Yes MLI		PPT
58	Sri Lanka	No	Yes other	PPT
59	Sweden	No	Yes MLI	PPT
60	Switzerland	Yes MLI		PPT
61	Türkiye	No	Yes MLI	PPT
62	United Arab Emirates	No	Yes other	PPT
63	United Kingdom	Yes MLI		PPT
64	United States	No	No	

Other agreements

	1.Treaty partners	2. Inclusive Framework member
1	Albania	Yes
2	Azerbaijan	Yes
3	Bahrain	Yes
4	Barbados	Yes
5	Belarus	Yes
6	Bosnia-Herzegovina	Yes
7	Botswana	Yes
8	Democratic People's Republic of Korea*	No
9	Estonia	Yes
10	Ethiopia*	No
11	Ghana*	No
12	Indonesia	Yes
13	Iran*	No
14	Jordan	Yes
15	Kazakhstan	Yes
16	Lebanon*	No
17	Malaysia	Yes
18	Moldova*	No
19	Mongolia	Yes
20	Morocco	Yes
21	Panama	Yes

22	Philippines	Yes
23	Saudi Arabia	Yes
24	Syrian Arab Republic*	No
25	Tajikistan*	No
26	Thailand	Yes
27	Tunisia	Yes
28	Turkmenistan*	No
29	Ukraine	Yes
30	Uzbekistan	Yes
31	Venezuela*	No
32	Viet Nam	Yes

Democratic Republic of the Congo

A. Progress in the implementation of the minimum standard

The Democratic Republic of the Congo has two tax agreements in force as reported in its response to the Peer Review questionnaire. Neither of those agreements comply with the minimum standard.

The Democratic Republic of the Congo has not signed the MLI.

B. Conclusion

Recommendation

It is recommended that the Democratic Republic of the Congo formulates a plan for the implementation of the minimum standard in its agreements for which no steps have yet been taken and that were concluded with members of the BEPS Inclusive Framework (Belgium and South Africa).[45]

Other agreements

This Table shows the agreements that are not compliant, not subject to a complying instrument, not covered by a general statement on the implementation of the detailed LOB and for which no steps have been taken to implement the minimum standard.

	1.Treaty partners	2. Inclusive Framework member
1	Belgium	Yes
2	South Africa	Yes

[45] It is noted that the Democratic Republic of Congo has worked with the Secretariat towards signature of the MLI and has prepared a draft list of reservations and notifications under the MLI.

Denmark

A. Progress in the implementation of the minimum standard

Denmark has 71 tax agreements in force as reported in its response to the Peer Review questionnaire, including the multilateral Nordic Convention concluded with the Faroe Islands, Finland, Iceland, Norway and Sweden (the Nordic Convention).[46] Forty-one of those agreements, including the Nordic Convention, comply with the minimum standard.

Denmark signed the MLI in 2017 and deposited its instrument of ratification on 30 September 2019. The MLI entered into force for Denmark on 1 January 2020. The agreements modified by the MLI come into compliance with the minimum standard once the provisions of the MLI take effect.

Denmark has not listed its agreement with Switzerland under the MLI but indicated in its response to the Peer Review questionnaire that steps have been taken (other than under the MLI) to implement the minimum standard in that agreement, as well as in the agreements with Greenland and Sri Lanka.

Denmark is implementing the minimum standard through the inclusion of the preamble statement and the PPT.[47]

B. Conclusion

No jurisdiction has raised any concerns about their agreements with Denmark.

Summary of the jurisdiction response – Denmark

	1.Treaty partners	2. Compliance with the standard	3. Signature of a complying instrument	4. Minimum standard provision used
1	Argentina	No	Yes MLI	PPT+LOB
2	Armenia	Yes other		PPT
3	Australia	Yes MLI		PPT
4	Austria	No	No	PPT+LOB
5	Azerbaijan	No	No	PPT+LOB
6	Bangladesh*	No	No	PPT+LOB
7	Belgium	Yes MLI		PPT
8	Brazil	No	No	PPT+LOB
9	Bulgaria	Yes MLI		PPT
10	Canada	Yes MLI		PPT
11	Chile	Yes MLI		PPT+LOB
12	China (People's Republic of)	Yes MLI		PPT
13	Chinese Taipei*	No	No	PPT+LOB
14	Croatia	Yes MLI		PPT
15	Cyprus*	Yes MLI		PPT

46 See the Multilateral convention concluded by Denmark, Finland, the Faroe Islands, Iceland, Norway and Sweden: for the avoidance of double taxation with respect to taxes on income and on capital (1996, 1997, 2008 and 2018).

47 For its agreements listed under the MLI, Denmark is implementing the preamble statement (Article 6 of the MLI) and the PPT (Article 7 of the MLI). Under Article 7(7)(a) of the MLI, Denmark is also implementing the simplified LOB (Article 7(8 to 13) of the MLI) in agreements concluded with treaty partners that have adopted the simplified LOB.

16	Czechia	Yes MLI		PPT
17	Egypt	Yes MLI		PPT
18	Estonia	Yes MLI		PPT
19	Georgia	No	No	PPT+LOB
20	Germany	Yes other		PPT
21	Ghana*	No	No	PPT+LOB
22	Greece	Yes MLI		
23	Greenland	No	No	
24	Hungary	Yes MLI		
25	India	Yes MLI		PPT+LOB
26	Indonesia	Yes MLI		PPT
27	Ireland	Yes MLI		PPT
28	Israel	Yes MLI		PPT
29	Italy	No	Yes MLI	PPT
30	Jamaica	No	Yes MLI	PPT
31	Japan	Yes other		PPT+LOB
32	Kenya	No	Yes MLI	PPT+LOB
33	Korea	Yes MLI		PPT
34	Kuwait	No	Yes MLI	PPT
35	Latvia	Yes MLI		PPT
36	Lithuania	Yes MLI		PPT
37	Luxembourg	Yes MLI		PPT
38	Malaysia	Yes MLI		PPT
39	Malta	Yes MLI		PPT
40	Mexico	No	Yes MLI	PPT+LOB
41	Montenegro	No	No	PPT+LOB
42	Morocco	No	Yes MLI	PPT
43	Netherlands	Yes other		PPT
44	New Zealand	Yes MLI		PPT
45	Nordic Convention treaty partners (Faroe Islands, Finland, Iceland, Norway, Sweden)	Yes other		PPT
46	North Macedonia	No	Yes MLI	PPT
47	Pakistan	Yes MLI		PPT+LOB
48	Philippines	No	No	PPT+LOB
49	Poland	Yes MLI		PPT
50	Portugal	Yes MLI		PPT
51	Romania	No	Yes MLI	PPT
52	Russian Federation	Yes MLI		PPT+LOB
53	Serbia	Yes MLI		PPT
54	Singapore	Yes MLI		PPT
55	Slovak Republic	Yes MLI		PPT+LOB
56	Slovenia	Yes MLI		PPT
57	South Africa	Yes MLI		PPT
58	Sri Lanka	No	No	PPT
59	Switzerland	No	No	PPT
60	Tanzania*	No	No	PPT+LOB
61	Thailand	Yes MLI		PPT
62	Tunisia	No	Yes MLI	PPT
63	Türkiye	No	Yes MLI	PPT
64	Uganda*	No	No	PPT+LOB
65	Ukraine	Yes MLI		PPT
66	United Kingdom	Yes MLI		PPT

67	United States	No	No	
68	Venezuela*	No	No	PPT+LOB
69	Viet Nam	No	Yes MLI	PPT+LOB
70	Zambia	No	No	PPT+LOB

Other agreements

	1.Treaty partners	2. Inclusive Framework member
1	Belarus	Yes

Djibouti

A. Progress in the implementation of the minimum standard

Djibouti has no tax agreements in force, as reported in its response to the Peer Review questionnaire.

B. Conclusion

No jurisdiction has raised any concerns about Djibouti.

Dominica

A. Progress in the implementation of the minimum standard

Dominica has two tax agreements in force as reported in its response to the Peer Review questionnaire, including the multilateral agreement among the members of the CARICOM concluded with ten treaty partners (the CARICOM Agreement).[48] Neither of those agreements comply with the minimum standard.

Dominica has not signed the MLI.

Dominica indicated in its response to the Peer Review questionnaire that steps have been taken (other than under the MLI) to implement the minimum standard in the CARICOM Agreement.

In its response to the Peer Review questionnaire, Switzerland indicated that its agreement with Dominica did not give rise to material treaty shopping concerns for Switzerland.

B. Conclusion

No jurisdiction has raised any concerns about their agreements with Dominica.

Summary of the jurisdiction response – Dominica

	1.Treaty partners	2. Compliance with the standard	3. Signature of a complying instrument	4. Minimum standard provision used
1	CARICOM Agreement treaty partners (Antigua and Barbuda, Barbados, Belize, Grenada, Guyana*, Jamaica, Saint Kitts and Nevis, Saint Lucia, Saint Vincent and the Grenadines, Trinidad and Tobago)	No	No	

Other agreements

	1.Treaty partners	2. Inclusive Framework member
1	Switzerland	Yes

[48] Agreement Among the Governments of the Member States of the Caribbean Community for the Avoidance of Double Taxation and the Prevention of Fiscal Evasion with Respect to Taxes on Income, Profits or Gains and Capital Gains and for the Encouragement of Regional Trade and Investment, St. Michael Barbados, 6 July 1994; between: Antigua and Barbuda (18 February 1998), Barbados (7 July 1995), Belize (30 November 1994), Dominica (19 June 1996), Grenada (1 March 1996), Guyana* (26 November 1997), Jamaica (16 February 1995), St. Kitts/Nevis (8 May 1997), St. Lucia (22 May 1995) St. Vincent (12 February 1998) and Trinidad & Tobago (29 November 1994).

Dominican Republic

A. Progress in the implementation of the minimum standard

The Dominican Republic has two tax agreements in force as reported in its response to the Peer Review questionnaire. Neither of those agreements comply with the minimum standard.

The Dominican Republic has not signed the MLI.

B. Conclusion

The Dominican Republic has developed a plan for the implementation of the minimum standard in its agreements with Canada and Spain. The Dominican Republic indicated in its response to the Peer Review questionnaire that bilateral negotiations would be pursued with respect to those agreements.

Other agreements

This Table shows the agreements that are not compliant, not subject to a complying instrument, not covered by a general statement on the implementation of the detailed LOB and for which no steps have been taken to implement the minimum standard.

	1.Treaty partners	2. Inclusive Framework member
1	Canada	Yes
2	Spain	Yes

Egypt

A. Progress in the implementation of the minimum standard

Egypt has 59[49] tax agreements in force as reported in its response to the Peer Review questionnaire. Thirty-four of those agreements comply with the minimum standard.

Egypt signed the MLI in 2017 and deposited its instrument of ratification on 30 September 2020, listing its non-compliant agreements concluded with other members of the Inclusive Framework. The MLI entered into force for Egypt on 1 January 2021. The agreements modified by the MLI come into compliance with the minimum standard once the provisions of the MLI take effect.

Egypt is implementing the minimum standard through the inclusion of the preamble statement and the PPT.[50]

B. Conclusion

No jurisdiction has raised any concerns about their agreements with Egypt.

Summary of the jurisdiction response – Egypt

	1.Treaty partners	2. Compliance with the standard	3. Signature of a complying instrument	4. Minimum standard provision used
1	Albania	Yes MLI		PPT
2	Algeria*	No	No	PPT
3	Austria	No	No	PPT
4	Bahrain	Yes MLI		PPT
5	Belarus	No	No	PPT
6	Belgium	Yes MLI		PPT
7	Bulgaria	Yes MLI		PPT
8	Canada	Yes MLI		PPT
9	China (People's Republic of)	Yes MLI		PPT
10	Cyprus*	Yes other		PPT
11	Czechia	Yes MLI		PPT
12	Denmark	Yes MLI		PPT
13	Ethiopia*	No	No	PPT
14	Finland	Yes MLI		PPT
15	France	Yes MLI		PPT
16	Georgia	No	No	PPT
17	Germany	No	No	PPT
18	Greece	Yes MLI		PPT
19	Hungary	Yes MLI		PPT

49 Egypt indicated in its response to the Peer Review questionnaire that the agreement between the Arab Republic of Egypt and the Council of Ministers of Serbia and Montenegro was inherited between Serbia and has been counted as two separate agreements.

50 For its agreements listed under the MLI, Egypt is implementing the preamble statement (Article 6 of the MLI) and the PPT (Article 7 of the MLI).

20	India	Yes MLI		PPT
21	Indonesia	Yes MLI		PPT
22	Iraq*	No	No	PPT
23	Ireland	Yes MLI		PPT
24	Italy	No	Yes MLI	PPT
25	Japan	Yes MLI		PPT
26	Jordan	Yes MLI		PPT
27	Korea	Yes MLI		PPT
28	Kuwait	No	Yes MLI	PPT
29	Lebanon*	No	No	PPT
30	Libya*	No	No	PPT
31	Malaysia	Yes MLI		PPT
32	Malta	Yes MLI		PPT
33	Mauritius	Yes MLI		PPT
34	Montenegro	No	No	PPT
35	Morocco	No	Yes MLI	PPT
36	Netherlands	Yes MLI		PPT
37	Norway	No	No	PPT
38	Pakistan	Yes MLI		PPT
39	Palestine*	No	No	PPT
40	Poland	Yes MLI		PPT
41	Romania	No	Yes MLI	PPT
42	Russian Federation	Yes MLI		PPT
43	Saudi Arabia	Yes MLI		PPT
44	Serbia	Yes MLI		PPT
45	Singapore	Yes MLI		PPT
46	South Africa	Yes MLI		PPT
47	Spain	Yes MLI		PPT
48	Sudan*	No	No	PPT
49	Sweden	No	Yes MLI	PPT
50	Switzerland	No	No	PPT
51	Syria*	No	No	PPT
52	Tunisia	No	Yes MLI	PPT
53	Türkiye	No	Yes MLI	PPT
54	Ukraine	Yes MLI		PPT
55	United Arab Emirates	Yes other		PPT
56	United Kingdom	Yes MLI		PPT
57	United States	No	No	D-LOB
58	Yemen*	No	No	PPT

Other agreements

	1.Treaty partners	2. Inclusive Framework member
1	Uzbekistan	Yes

Estonia

A. Progress in the implementation of the minimum standard

Estonia has 62 tax agreements in force as reported in its response to the Peer Review questionnaire. Nineteen of those agreements comply with the minimum standard.

Estonia signed the MLI in 2018 and deposited its instrument of ratification on 15 January 2021. The MLI entered into force for Estonia on 1 May 2021. The agreements modified by the MLI come into compliance with the minimum standard once the provisions of the MLI take effect.

Estonia reserved the right to delay the entry into effect of the provisions of the MLI until Estonia has completed its internal procedures for this purpose with respect to each of its listed agreements.[51] Estonia notified that it completed its internal procedures for the entry into effect of the MLI with respect to its agreements with Austria, Cyprus*, Finland, Latvia, Poland, the Slovak Republic and Ukraine on 25 November 2021 and with respect to its agreements with Belgium, Georgia, India, Isle of Man, Lithuania, Norway and Spain on 1 June 2022.

Estonia has not listed its agreements with Switzerland under the MLI but indicated in its response to the Peer Review questionnaire that steps have been taken (other than under the MLI) to implement the minimum standard in that agreement.

Estonia is generally implementing the minimum standard through the inclusion of the preamble statement and the PPT.[52]

B. Conclusion

Estonia is encouraged to complete (and notify that is has completed) its internal procedures for the entry into effect of the MLI with respect to its agreements that are covered tax agreements under the MLI and for which no such notification has yet been made.

Summary of the jurisdiction response – Estonia

	1.Treaty partners	2. Compliance with the standard	3. Signature of a complying instrument	4. Minimum standard provision used
1	Albania	No	Yes MLI	PPT
2	Armenia	No	Yes MLI	PPT
3	Austria	Yes MLI		PPT
4	Azerbaijan	No	No	PPT
5	Bahrain	No	Yes MLI	PPT
6	Belarus	No	No	PPT
7	Belgium	Yes MLI		PPT
8	Bulgaria	No	Yes MLI	PPT
9	Canada	No	Yes MLI	PPT
10	China (People's Republic of)	No	Yes MLI	PPT

[51] The reservation was made under Article 35(7)(a) of the MLI.

[52] For its agreements listed under the MLI, Estonia is implementing the preamble statement (Article 6 of the MLI) and the PPT (Article 7 of the MLI).

11	Croatia	No	Yes MLI	PPT
12	Cyprus*	Yes MLI		PPT
13	Czechia	No	No	PPT
14	Denmark	No	Yes MLI	PPT
15	Finland	Yes MLI		PPT
16	France	No	Yes MLI	PPT
17	Georgia	Yes MLI		PPT
18	Germany	Yes other		PPT
19	Greece	No	Yes MLI	PPT
20	Guernsey	Yes other		PPT
21	Hong Kong (China)	Yes other		PPT
22	Hungary	No	Yes MLI	PPT
23	Iceland	No	Yes MLI	PPT
24	India	Yes MLI		PPT
25	Ireland	No	Yes MLI	PPT
26	Isle of Man	Yes MLI		PPT
27	Israel	No	Yes MLI	PPT
28	Italy	No	Yes MLI	PPT
29	Japan	Yes other		PPT+LOB
30	Jersey	No	Yes MLI	PPT
31	Kazakhstan	No	Yes MLI	PPT
32	Korea	No	Yes MLI	PPT
33	Kyrgyzstan*	No	No	PPT
34	Latvia	Yes MLI		PPT
35	Lithuania	Yes MLI		PPT
36	Luxembourg	No	Yes MLI	PPT
37	Malta	No	Yes MLI	PPT
38	Mauritius	Yes other		PPT
39	Mexico	No	Yes MLI	PPT
40	Moldova*	No	No	PPT
41	Netherlands	No	Yes MLI	PPT
42	North Macedonia	No	Yes MLI	PPT
43	Norway	Yes MLI		PPT
44	Poland	Yes MLI		PPT
45	Portugal	No	Yes MLI	PPT
46	Romania	No	Yes MLI	PPT
47	Serbia	No	Yes MLI	PPT
48	Singapore	No	Yes MLI	PPT
49	Slovak Republic	Yes MLI		PPT
50	Slovenia	No	Yes MLI	PPT
51	Spain	Yes MLI		PPT
52	Sweden	No	Yes MLI	PPT
53	Switzerland	No	No	PPT
54	Thailand	No	Yes MLI	PPT
55	Türkiye	No	Yes MLI	PPT
56	Turkmenistan*	No	No	PPT
57	Ukraine	Yes MLI		PPT
58	United Arab Emirates	No	Yes MLI	PPT
59	United Kingdom	No	Yes MLI	PPT
60	United States	No	No	
61	Uzbekistan	No	No	PPT
62	Viet Nam	No	Yes MLI	PPT

Eswatini

A. Progress in the implementation of the minimum standard

Eswatini has seven tax agreements in force as reported in its response to the Peer Review questionnaire. One of those agreements, the agreement with Lesotho*, complies with the minimum standard.

Eswatini signed the MLI on 27 September 2023, listing its non-compliant agreement concluded with other members of the Inclusive Framework. The agreements modified by the MLI come into compliance with the minimum standard once the provisions of the MLI take effect.

Eswatini is implementing the minimum standard through the inclusion of the preamble statement and the PPT combined with the LOB.[53]

B. Conclusion

Eswatini has given effect to its plan for the implementation of the minimum standard in its agreements with Botswana, Mauritius, Seychelles, South Africa and the United Kingdom. Eswatini signed the MLI in September 2023 and listed those agreements to be covered.

Acknowledging that Eswatini signed the MLI in September 2023, no recommendation is made that Eswatini ratifies the MLI in 2023. However, it is expected that Eswatini will swiftly start the process to complete the steps to have the MLI take effect with respect to its agreements listed under the MLI, as those agreement will only be modified by the MLI (and come into compliance with the minimum standard) once the provisions of the MLI take effect.

Summary of the jurisdiction response – Eswatini

	1.Treaty partners	2. Compliance with the standard	3. Signature of a complying instrument	4. Minimum standard provision used
1	Botswana	No	No	
2	Lesotho*	Yes other		PPT
3	Mauritius	No	Yes MLI	
4	Seychelles	No	Yes MLI	
5	South Africa	No	Yes MLI	
6	United Kingdom	No	Yes MLI	

Other agreements

	1.Treaty partners	2. Inclusive Framework member
1	Chinese Taipei*	No

[53] For its agreements listed under the MLI, Eswatini is implementing the preamble statement (Article 6 of the MLI) and the PPT (Article 7 of the MLI) and the simplified LOB (Article 7(6) of the MLI).

Faroe Islands

A. Progress in the implementation of the minimum standard

The Faroe Islands has three tax agreements in force as reported in its response to the Peer Review questionnaire, including the multilateral Nordic Convention concluded with Denmark, Finland, Iceland, Norway and Sweden (the Nordic Convention).[54] One of those agreements, the Nordic Convention, complies with the minimum standard.

The Faroe Islands has not joined the MLI.

The Faroe Islands indicated in its response to the Peer Review questionnaire that steps have been taken (other than under the MLI) to implement the minimum standard in its agreements with Switzerland.

The Faroe Islands is implementing the minimum standard through the inclusion of the preamble statement and the PPT.

B. Conclusion

The Faroe Islands has developed a plan for the implementation of the minimum standard in its agreement with the United Kingdom. The Faroe Islands indicated in its response to the Peer Review questionnaire that bilateral negotiations would be pursued with respect to that agreement.

Summary of the jurisdiction response – Faroe Islands

	1.Treaty partners	2. Compliance with the standard	3. Signature of a complying instrument	4. Minimum standard provision used
1	Nordic Convention treaty partners (Denmark, Finland, Iceland, Norway, Sweden)	Yes other		PPT
2	Switzerland	No	No	

Other agreements

	1.Treaty partners	2. Inclusive Framework member
1	United Kingdom	Yes

[54] See the Multilateral convention concluded by Denmark, Finland, the Faroe Islands, Iceland, Norway and Sweden: for the avoidance of double taxation with respect to taxes on income and on capital (1996, 1997, 2008 and 2018).

Finland

A. Progress in the implementation of the minimum standard

Finland has 74 tax agreements in force as reported in its response to the Peer Review questionnaire, including the multilateral Nordic Convention concluded with Denmark, the Faroe Islands, Iceland, Norway and Sweden (the Nordic Convention).[55] Forty-eight of those agreements, including the Nordic Convention, comply with the minimum standard.

Finland signed the MLI in 2017 and deposited its instrument of ratification on 25 February 2019. The MLI entered into force for Finland on 1 June 2019. The agreements modified by the MLI come into compliance with the minimum standard once the provisions of the MLI take effect.

Finland has not listed its agreement with Bulgaria under the MLI but indicated in its response to the Peer Review questionnaire that steps have been taken (other than under the MLI) to implement the minimum standard in that agreement.

Finland is implementing the minimum standard through the inclusion of the preamble statement and the PPT.[56]

B. Conclusion

No jurisdiction has raised any concerns about their agreements with Finland.

Summary of the jurisdiction response – Finland

	1.Treaty partners	2. Compliance with the standard	3. Signature of a complying instrument	4. Minimum standard provision used
1	Albania	Yes other		PPT
2	Argentina	No	Yes MLI	PPT
3	Armenia	No	Yes MLI	PPT
4	Australia	Yes MLI		PPT
5	Austria	Yes MLI		PPT
6	Azerbaijan	No	No	PPT
7	Barbados	Yes MLI		PPT
8	Belarus	No	No	PPT
9	Belgium	Yes MLI		PPT
10	Bosnia-Herzegovina	Yes MLI		PPT
11	Brazil	No	No	
12	Bulgaria	No	No	
13	Canada	Yes MLI		PPT
14	China (People's Republic of)	Yes MLI		PPT
15	Croatia	Yes MLI		PPT
16	Cyprus*	Yes MLI		PPT

[55] See the Multilateral convention concluded by Denmark, Finland, the Faroe Islands, Iceland, Norway and Sweden: for the avoidance of double taxation with respect to taxes on income and on capital (1996, 1997, 2008 and 2018).

[56] For its agreements listed under the MLI, Finland is implementing the preamble statement (Article 6 of the MLI) and the PPT (Article 7 of the MLI).

17	Czechia	Yes MLI		PPT
18	Egypt	Yes MLI		PPT
19	Estonia	Yes MLI		PPT
20	France	Yes MLI		PPT
21	Georgia	Yes MLI		PPT
22	Germany	Yes other		PPT
23	Greece	Yes MLI		PPT
24	Hong Kong (China)	Yes other		PPT
25	Hungary	Yes MLI		PPT
26	India	Yes MLI		PPT
27	Indonesia	Yes MLI		PPT
28	Ireland	Yes MLI		PPT
29	Israel	Yes MLI		PPT
30	Italy	No	Yes MLI	PPT
31	Japan	Yes MLI		PPT
32	Kazakhstan	Yes MLI		PPT
33	Korea	Yes MLI		PPT
34	Kosovo*	No	No	PPT
35	Kyrgyzstan*	No	No	PPT
36	Latvia	Yes MLI		PPT
37	Lithuania	Yes MLI		PPT
38	Luxembourg	Yes MLI		PPT
39	Malaysia	Yes MLI		PPT
40	Malta	Yes MLI		PPT
41	Mexico	No	Yes MLI	PPT
42	Moldova*	No	No	PPT
43	Montenegro	No	No	PPT
44	Morocco	No	Yes MLI	PPT
45	Netherlands	Yes MLI		PPT
46	New Zealand	Yes MLI		PPT
47	Nordic Convention treaty partners (Denmark, Faroe Islands, Iceland, Norway, Sweden)	Yes other		PPT
48	North Macedonia	No	Yes MLI	PPT
49	Pakistan	Yes MLI		PPT
50	Philippines	No	No	PPT
51	Poland	Yes MLI		PPT
52	Romania	No	Yes MLI	PPT
53	Russian Federation	Yes MLI		PPT
54	Serbia	Yes MLI		PPT
55	Singapore	Yes MLI		PPT
56	Slovak Republic	Yes MLI		PPT
57	Slovenia	Yes MLI		PPT
58	South Africa	Yes MLI		PPT
59	Spain	Yes MLI		PPT
60	Sri Lanka	No	No	PPT
61	Switzerland	No	No	PPT
62	Tajikistan*	No	No	PPT
63	Tanzania*	No	No	PPT
64	Thailand	Yes MLI		PPT
65	Türkiye	No	Yes MLI	PPT
66	Turkmenistan*	No	No	PPT
67	Ukraine	Yes MLI		PPT

68	United Arab Emirates	Yes MLI		PPT
69	United Kingdom	Yes MLI		PPT
70	United States	No	No	
71	Uruguay	Yes MLI		PPT
72	Uzbekistan	No	No	PPT
73	Viet Nam	No	Yes MLI	PPT
74	Zambia	No	No	PPT

France

A. Progress in the implementation of the minimum standard

France has 120 tax agreements in force as reported in its response to the Peer Review questionnaire. Fifty-nine of those agreements comply with the minimum standard.

France signed the MLI in 2017 and deposited its instrument of ratification on 26 September 2018. The MLI entered into force for France on 1 January 2019. On 22 September 2020, France made an additional notification to expand its list of agreements to be covered under the MLI. The agreements modified by the MLI come into compliance with the minimum standard once the provisions of the MLI take effect.

France has signed a bilateral complying instrument with respect to its agreement with Sweden.

France is implementing the minimum standard through the inclusion of the preamble statement and the PPT.[57]

B. Conclusion

No jurisdiction has raised any concerns about their agreements with France.

Summary of the jurisdiction response – France

	1.Treaty partners	2. Compliance with the standard	3. Signature of a complying instrument	4. Minimum standard provision used
1	Albania	Yes MLI		PPT
2	Algeria*	No	No	PPT
3	Andorra	Yes MLI		PPT
4	Argentina	No	Yes MLI	PPT
5	Armenia	No	Yes MLI	PPT
6	Australia	Yes MLI		PPT
7	Austria	Yes MLI		PPT
8	Azerbaijan	No	No	PPT
9	Bahrain	Yes MLI		PPT
10	Bangladesh*	No	No	PPT
11	Belarus	No	No	PPT
12	Belgium	Yes MLI		PPT
13	Benin	No	No	PPT
14	Bolivia*	No	No	PPT
15	Bosnia-Herzegovina	Yes MLI		PPT
16	Botswana	No	No	PPT
17	Brazil	No	No	PPT
18	Bulgaria	Yes MLI		PPT
19	Burkina Faso	Yes MLI		PPT
20	Cameroon	Yes MLI		PPT
21	Canada	Yes MLI		PPT

[57] For its agreements listed under the MLI, France is implementing the preamble statement (Article 6 of the MLI) and the PPT (Article 7 of the MLI).

22	Central African Republic*	No	No	PPT
23	Chile	Yes MLI		PPT
24	China (People's Republic of)	Yes MLI		PPT
25	Colombia	Yes other		PPT
26	Congo	No	No	PPT
27	Côte d'Ivoire	No	Yes MLI	PPT
28	Croatia	Yes MLI		PPT
29	Cyprus*	Yes MLI		PPT
30	Czechia	Yes MLI		PPT
31	Ecuador*	No	No	PPT
32	Egypt	Yes MLI		PPT
33	Estonia	No	Yes MLI	PPT
34	Ethiopia*	No	No	PPT
35	Finland	Yes MLI		PPT
36	Gabon	No	Yes MLI	PPT
37	Georgia	Yes MLI		PPT
38	Germany	No	Yes MLI	PPT
39	Ghana*	No	No	PPT
40	Greece	Yes MLI		PPT
41	Guinea*	No	No	PPT
42	Hong Kong (China)	No	Yes MLI	PPT
43	Hungary	Yes MLI		PPT
44	Iceland	Yes MLI		PPT
45	India	Yes MLI		PPT
46	Indonesia	Yes MLI		PPT
47	Iran*	No	No	PPT
48	Ireland	Yes MLI		PPT
49	Israel	Yes MLI		PPT
50	Italy	No	Yes MLI	PPT
51	Jamaica	No	Yes MLI	PPT
52	Japan	Yes MLI		PPT+LOB
53	Jordan	Yes MLI		PPT
54	Kazakhstan	Yes MLI		PPT
55	Kenya	No	Yes MLI	PPT
56	Korea	Yes MLI		PPT
57	Kosovo*	No	No	PPT
58	Kuwait	No	Yes MLI	PPT
59	Kyrgyzstan*	No	No	PPT
60	Latvia	Yes MLI		PPT
61	Lebanon*	No	No	PPT
62	Libya*	No	No	PPT
63	Lithuania	Yes MLI		PPT
64	Luxembourg	Yes other		PPT
65	Madagascar*	No	No	PPT
66	Malawi*	No	No	PPT
67	Malaysia	Yes MLI		PPT
68	Mali*	No	No	PPT
69	Malta	Yes MLI		PPT
70	Mauritania	No	No	PPT
71	Mauritius	Yes MLI		PPT
72	Mexico	No	Yes MLI	PPT
73	Monaco	Yes MLI		PPT
74	Mongolia	No	Yes MLI	PPT

75	Montenegro	No	No	PPT
76	Morocco	No	Yes MLI	PPT
77	Namibia	No	Yes MLI	PPT
78	Netherlands	Yes MLI		PPT
79	New Zealand	Yes MLI		PPT
80	Niger*	No	No	PPT
81	Nigeria	No	Yes MLI	PPT
82	North Macedonia	No	Yes MLI	PPT
83	Norway	No	No	PPT
84	Oman	Yes MLI		PPT
85	Pakistan	Yes MLI		PPT
86	Panama	Yes MLI		PPT
87	Philippines	No	No	PPT
88	Poland	Yes MLI		PPT
89	Portugal	Yes MLI		PPT
90	Qatar	Yes MLI		PPT
91	Quebec*	No	No	PPT
92	Romania	No	Yes MLI	PPT
93	Russian Federation	Yes MLI		PPT
94	Saudi Arabia	Yes MLI		PPT
95	Senegal	Yes MLI		PPT
96	Serbia	Yes MLI		PPT
97	Singapore	Yes MLI		PPT
98	Slovak Republic	Yes MLI		PPT
99	Slovenia	Yes MLI		PPT
100	South Africa	Yes MLI		PPT
101	Spain	Yes MLI		PPT
102	Sri Lanka	No	No	PPT
103	Sweden	No	Yes other	PPT
104	Switzerland	No	No	PPT
105	Syrian Arab Republic*	No	No	PPT
106	Thailand	Yes MLI		PPT
107	Togo	No	No	PPT
108	Trinidad and Tobago	No	No	PPT
109	Tunisia	No	Yes MLI	PPT
110	Türkiye	No	Yes MLI	PPT
111	Turkmenistan*	No	No	PPT
112	Ukraine	Yes MLI		PPT
113	United Arab Emirates	Yes MLI		PPT
114	United Kingdom	Yes MLI		PPT
115	United States	No	No	PPT
116	Uzbekistan	No	No	PPT
117	Venezuela*	No	No	PPT
118	Viet Nam	No	Yes MLI	PPT
119	Zambia	No	No	PPT
120	Zimbabwe*	No	No	PPT

Gabon

A. Progress in the implementation of the minimum standard

Gabon has six tax agreements in force as reported in its response to the Peer Review questionnaire. None of those agreements comply with the minimum standard.

Gabon signed the MLI in 2017. The agreements modified by the MLI come into compliance with the minimum standard once the provisions of the MLI take effect.

Gabon has not listed its agreements with Korea and Saudi Arabia. These agreements will therefore not, at this stage, be modified under the MLI. Korea and Saudi Arabia have both listed their agreements with Gabon under the MLI.

Gabon is implementing the minimum standard through the inclusion of the preamble statement and the PPT.[58]

B. Conclusion

Korea and Saudi Arabia have both listed their agreements with Gabon under the MLI, which amount to requests to implement the minimum standard.

Gabon has developed a plan for the implementation of the minimum standard in its agreements with Korea and Saudi Arabia. Gabon indicated in its response to the Peer Review questionnaire that it intends expand its list of agreements to be covered under the MLI in to include those agreements.

Recommendation

It is recommended that Gabon completes the steps to have the MLI take effect with respect to its agreements listed under the MLI as those agreements will only be modified by the MLI (and come into compliance with the minimum standard) once the provisions of the MLI take effect.

Summary of the jurisdiction response – Gabon

	1.Treaty partners	2. Compliance with the standard	3. Signature of a complying instrument	4. Minimum standard provision used
1	Belgium	No	Yes MLI	PPT
2	Canada	No	Yes MLI	PPT
3	France	No	Yes MLI	PPT
4	Morocco	No	Yes MLI	PPT

[58] For its agreements listed under the MLI, Gabon is implementing the preamble statement (Article 6 of the MLI) and the PPT (Article 7 of the MLI).

Other agreements

	1.Treaty partners	2. Inclusive Framework member
1	Korea	Yes
2	Saudi Arabia	Yes

Georgia

A. Progress in the implementation of the minimum standard

Georgia has 57 tax agreements in force as reported in its response to the Peer Review questionnaire. Thirty-three of those agreements, comply with the minimum standard.

Georgia signed the MLI in 2017 and deposited its instrument of ratification on 29 March 2019, listing 34 of its agreements in force at that time. The MLI entered into force for Georgia on 1 July 2019. The agreements modified by the MLI come into compliance with the minimum standard once the provisions of the MLI take effect.

Georgia has not listed its agreements with Armenia, Austria, Bahrain, Belarus, Denmark, Egypt, Germany, Kazakhstan, Malta, Qatar, Saudi Arabia, Switzerland, Ukraine and the United Arab Emirates, but indicated in its response to the Peer Review questionnaire that steps have been taken (other than under the MLI) to implement the minimum standard in its agreement with Malta. Armenia, Bahrain, Denmark, Egypt, Kazakhstan, Malta, Qatar, Saudi Arabia, Ukraine and the United Arab Emirates have listed their agreements with Georgia under the MLI.

Georgia is implementing the minimum standard through the inclusion of the preamble statement and the PPT.[59]

In its response to the Peer Review questionnaire, Germany indicated that its agreement with Georgia did not give rise to material treaty shopping concerns for Germany.

B. Conclusion

Armenia, Bahrain, Denmark, Egypt, Kazakhstan, Malta, Qatar, Saudi Arabia, Ukraine and the United Arab Emirates have listed their agreements with Georgia under the MLI, which amount to requests to implement the minimum standard.

Georgia is preparing to give effect to its plan for the implementation of the minimum standard in its agreements with Armenia, Austria, Bahrain, Belarus, Denmark, Egypt, Germany, Kazakhstan, Qatar, Saudi Arabia, Switzerland, Ukraine and the United Arab Emirates. Georgia indicated in its response to the Peer Review questionnaire that it intends to expand its list of agreements to be covered under the MLI to include these agreements and has provided the revised list of agreements under the MLI in preparation for deposit subsequent to ratification.

Georgia also indicated that bilateral negotiations would be pursued to implement the minimum standard in its agreements with Azerbaijan, Iran*, Kuwait, Moldova*, Turkmenistan* and Uzbekistan.

Summary of the jurisdiction response – Georgia

	1.Treaty partners	2. Compliance with the standard	3. Signature of a complying instrument	4. Minimum standard provision used
1	Belgium	Yes MLI		PPT
2	Bulgaria	Yes MLI		PPT

59 For its agreements listed under the MLI, Georgia is implementing the preamble statement (Article 6 of the MLI) and the PPT (Article 7 of the MLI).

3	China (People's Republic of)	Yes MLI		PPT
4	Croatia	Yes MLI		PPT
5	Cyprus*	Yes MLI		PPT
6	Czechia	Yes MLI		PPT
7	Estonia	Yes MLI		PPT
8	Finland	Yes MLI		PPT
9	France	Yes MLI		PPT
10	Greece	Yes MLI		PPT
11	Hong Kong (China)	Yes other		PPT
12	Hungary	Yes MLI		PPT
13	Iceland	Yes MLI		PPT
14	India	Yes MLI		PPT
15	Ireland	Yes MLI		PPT
16	Israel	Yes MLI		PPT
17	Italy	No	Yes MLI	PPT
18	Japan	Yes other		PPT+LOB
19	Korea	Yes MLI		PPT
20	Latvia	Yes MLI		PPT
21	Liechtenstein	Yes MLI		PPT
22	Lithuania	Yes MLI		PPT
23	Luxembourg	Yes MLI		PPT
24	Malta	No	No	
25	Netherlands	Yes MLI		PPT
26	Norway	Yes MLI		PPT
27	Poland	Yes other		PPT
28	Portugal	Yes MLI		PPT
29	Romania	No	Yes MLI	
30	San Marino	Yes MLI		PPT
31	Serbia	Yes MLI		PPT
32	Singapore	Yes MLI		PPT
33	Slovak Republic	Yes MLI		PPT
34	Slovenia	Yes MLI		PPT
35	Spain	Yes MLI		PPT
36	Sweden	No	Yes MLI	PPT
37	Türkiye	No	Yes MLI	PPT
38	United Kingdom	Yes MLI		PPT

Other agreements

	1.Treaty partners	2. Inclusive Framework member
1	Armenia	Yes
2	Austria	Yes
3	Azerbaijan	Yes
4	Bahrain	Yes
5	Belarus	Yes
6	Denmark	Yes
7	Egypt	Yes
8	Germany	Yes
9	Iran*	No
10	Kazakhstan	Yes
11	Kuwait	Yes
12	Moldova*	No

13	Qatar	Yes
14	Saudi Arabia	Yes
15	Switzerland	Yes
16	Turkmenistan*	No
17	Ukraine	Yes
18	United Arab Emirates	Yes
19	Uzbekistan	Yes

Germany

A. Progress in the implementation of the minimum standard

Germany has 94 tax agreements in force as reported in its response to the Peer Review questionnaire. Twelve of those agreements, comply with the minimum standard.

Germany signed the MLI in 2017 and deposited its instrument of ratification on 18 December 2020, listing 14 of its agreements in force at that time. The MLI entered into force for Germany on 1 April 2021. The agreements modified by the MLI come into compliance with the minimum standard once the provisions of the MLI take effect.

Germany reserved the right to delay the entry into effect of the provisions of the MLI until Germany has completed its internal procedures for this purpose with respect to each of its listed agreements.[60] Germany has not yet notified that it completed its internal procedures for the entry into effect of the MLI with respect to any of its agreements.

Germany has not listed its agreements under the MLI with Albania, Argentina, Armenia, Belgium, Belarus, Bosnia-Herzegovina, Canada, China (People's Republic of), Costa Rica, Côte d'Ivoire, Egypt, Georgia, Iceland, India, Indonesia, Israel, Jamaica, Kazakhstan, Kenya, Korea, Liberia, Malaysia, Mongolia, Montenegro, Morocco, Namibia, New Zealand, North Macedonia, Norway, Pakistan, Poland, Portugal, the Russian Federation, Serbia, Slovenia, South Africa, Sri Lanka, Switzerland, Thailand, Tunisia, Ukraine, Uruguay, Viet Nam and Zambia. These agreements will therefore not, at this stage, be modified under the MLI. Albania, Armenia, Bosnia-Herzegovina, China (People's Republic of), Côte d'Ivoire, Egypt, India, Jamaica, Kazakhstan, Malaysia, Morocco, Mongolia, Namibia, New Zealand, North Macedonia, Pakistan, Portugal, Serbia, Thailand, Tunisia, Ukraine, Uruguay and Viet Nam have listed their agreements with Germany under the MLI.

Germany indicated in its response to the Peer Review questionnaire that steps have been taken (other than under the MLI) to implement the minimum standard in its agreements with Albania, Argentina, Armenia, Bangladesh*, Belgium, Bolivia*, Bosnia-Herzegovina, Canada, China (People's Republic of), Costa Rica, Côte d'Ivoire, Ecuador*, Egypt, Iceland, India, Indonesia, Iran*, Israel, Jamaica, Kazakhstan, Kenya, Korea, Kosovo*, Kuwait, Liberia, Malaysia, Mongolia, Montenegro, Morocco, Namibia, New Zealand, Norway, Pakistan, Poland, Portugal, the Russian Federation, Serbia, Slovenia, South Africa, Sri Lanka, Switzerland, Thailand, Trinidad and Tobago, Tunisia, Ukraine, Uruguay and Viet Nam.

Germany has signed a bilateral complying instrument with respect to its agreements with Bulgaria, Latvia, Lithuania, Mexico[61] and Sweden.

Germany indicated in its response to the Peer Review questionnaire that the agreement with Zambia does not give rise to material treaty-shopping concerns for Germany, noting the application of German domestic anti-abuse provisions such as Section 42 of the German Fiscal Code (GAAR) or in Section 50d para. 3 of the German Income Tax Act (anti-conduit rule), which permits the proportionate denial of tax treaty benefits to companies with non-eligible shareholders. Germany further indicated that the agreements with Azerbaijan, Belarus, Georgia, and North Macedonia do not give rise to material treaty-shopping concerns for Germany, because they contain a general reservation for the application of domestic anti-abuse provisions such as the two sections mentioned above and the CFC-legislation.

[60] The reservation was made under Article 35(7)(a) of the MLI.

[61] The bilateral complying instrument with respect to the agreement with Mexico entered into force on 6 August 2023.

Germany is implementing the minimum standard through the inclusion of the preamble statement and the PPT.[62]

B. Conclusion

Albania, Armenia, Bosnia-Herzegovina, China (People's Republic of), Côte d'Ivoire, Egypt, India, Jamaica, Kazakhstan, Malaysia, Morocco, Mongolia, Namibia, New Zealand, North Macedonia, Pakistan, Portugal, Serbia, Thailand, Tunisia, Ukraine, Uruguay and Viet Nam have listed their agreement with Germany under the MLI, which amount to requests to implement the minimum standard.

Recommendations

It is recommended that Germany completes the steps to have the MLI take effect with respect to its agreements listed under the MLI as those agreements will only be modified by the MLI (and come into compliance with the minimum standard) once the provisions of the MLI take effect.

Summary of the jurisdiction response – Germany

	1.Treaty partners	2. Compliance with the standard	3. Signature of a complying instrument	4. Minimum standard provision used
1	Albania	No	No	
2	Argentina	No	No	
3	Armenia	No	No	
4	Australia	Yes other		PPT
5	Austria	No	Yes MLI	PPT
6	Bangladesh*	No	No	
7	Belgium	No	No	
8	Bolivia*	No	No	
9	Bosnia-Herzegovina	No	No	
10	Bulgaria	No	Yes other	
11	Canada	No	No	
12	China (People's Republic of)	No	No	
13	Costa Rica	No	No	
14	Côte d'Ivoire	No	No	
15	Croatia	No	Yes MLI	PPT
16	Cyprus*	Yes other		PPT
17	Czechia	No	Yes MLI	PPT
18	Denmark	Yes other		PPT
19	Ecuador*	No	No	
20	Egypt	No	No	

[62] For its agreements listed under the MLI, Germany is implementing the preamble statement (Article 6 of the MLI) and the PPT (Article 7 of the MLI). Germany has made a reservation pursuant to Article 6(4) of the MLI not to apply Article 6(1) of the MLI with respect to agreements that already contain the relevant preamble language (covering one agreement). Germany has also made a reservation pursuant to 7(15)(b) of the MLI not to apply Article 7(1) of the MLI with respect to agreements which already contain a PPT (covering one agreement).

21	Estonia	Yes other		PPT
22	Finland	Yes other		PPT
23	France	No	Yes MLI	PPT
24	Greece	No	Yes MLI	PPT
25	Hungary	No	Yes MLI	PPT
26	Iceland	No	No	
27	India	No	No	
28	Indonesia	No	No	
29	Iran*	No	No	
30	Ireland	Yes other		PPT
31	Israel	No	No	
32	Italy	No	Yes MLI	PPT
33	Jamaica	No	No	
34	Japan	Yes other		PPT+LOB
35	Kazakhstan	No	No	
36	Kenya	No	No	
37	Korea	No	No	
38	Kosovo*	No	No	
39	Kuwait	No	No	
40	Latvia	No	Yes other	
41	Liberia	No	No	
42	Liechtenstein	Yes other		PPT
43	Lithuania	No	Yes other	
44	Luxembourg	No	Yes MLI	PPT
45	Malaysia	No	No	
46	Malta	No	Yes MLI	PPT
47	Mauritius	Yes other		PPT
48	Mexico	No	Yes other	PPT
49	Mongolia	No	No	
50	Montenegro	No	No	
51	Morocco	No	No	
52	Namibia	No	No	
53	Netherlands	Yes other		PPT
54	New Zealand	No	No	
55	Norway	No	No	
56	Pakistan	No	No	
57	Poland	No	No	
58	Portugal	No	No	
59	Romania	No	No	PPT
60	Russian Federation	No	No	
61	Serbia	No	No	
62	Singapore	Yes other		PPT
63	Slovak Republic	No	Yes MLI	PPT
64	Slovenia	No	No	
65	South Africa	No	No	
66	Spain	No	Yes MLI	PPT
67	Sri Lanka	No	No	
68	Sweden	No	Yes other	PPT
69	Switzerland	No	No	PPT
70	Thailand	No	No	
71	Trinidad and Tobago	No	No	
72	Tunisia	No	No	
73	Türkiye	No	Yes MLI	PPT

74	Ukraine	No	No	
75	United Kingdom	Yes other		PPT
76	United States	No	No	D-LOB
77	Uruguay	No	No	
78	Viet Nam	No	No	

Other agreements

	1.Treaty partners	2. Inclusive Framework member
1	Algeria*	No
2	Azerbaijan	Yes
3	Belarus	Yes
4	Georgia	Yes
5	Ghana*	No
6	Kyrgyzstan*	No
7	Moldova*	No
8	North Macedonia	Yes
9	Philippines	Yes
10	Syrian Arab Republic*	No
11	Tajikistan*	No
12	Turkmenistan*	No
13	Uzbekistan	Yes
14	Venezuela*	No
15	Zambia	Yes
16	Zimbabwe*	No

Gibraltar

A. Progress in the implementation of the minimum standard

Gibraltar has one tax agreement in force, the agreement with the United Kingdom, as reported in its response to the Peer Review questionnaire. This agreement complies with the minimum standard.

Gibraltar is implementing the minimum standard through the inclusion of the preamble statement and the PPT.

B. Conclusion

No jurisdiction has raised any concerns about Gibraltar.

Summary of the jurisdiction response – Gibraltar

	1.Treaty partners	2. Compliance with the standard	3. Signature of a complying instrument	4. Minimum standard provision used
1	United Kingdom	Yes other		PPT

Greece

A. Progress in the implementation of the minimum standard

Greece has 57 tax agreements in force as reported in its response to the Peer Review questionnaire. Forty-two of those agreements comply with the minimum standard.

Greece signed the MLI in 2017 and deposited its instrument of ratification on 30 March 2021, listing its non-compliant agreements. The MLI entered into force for Greece on 1 July 2021. The agreements modified by the MLI come into compliance with the minimum standard once the provisions of the MLI take effect.

Greece is implementing the minimum standard through the inclusion of the preamble statement and the PPT.[63]

B. Conclusion

No jurisdiction has raised any concerns about their agreements with Greece.

Summary of the jurisdiction response – Greece

	1.Treaty partners	2. Compliance with the standard	3. Signature of a complying instrument	4. Minimum standard provision used
1	Albania	Yes MLI		PPT
2	Armenia	No	Yes MLI	PPT
3	Austria	Yes MLI		PPT
4	Azerbaijan	No	No	PPT
5	Belgium	Yes MLI		PPT
6	Bosnia-Herzegovina	Yes MLI		PPT
7	Bulgaria	Yes MLI		PPT
8	Canada	Yes MLI		PPT
9	China (People's Republic of)	Yes MLI		PPT
10	Croatia	Yes MLI		PPT
11	Cyprus*	Yes MLI		PPT
12	Czechia	Yes MLI		PPT
13	Denmark	Yes MLI		PPT
14	Egypt	Yes MLI		PPT
15	Estonia	No	Yes MLI	PPT
16	Finland	Yes MLI		PPT
17	France	Yes MLI		PPT
18	Georgia	Yes MLI		PPT
19	Germany	No	Yes MLI	PPT
20	Hungary	Yes MLI		PPT
21	Iceland	Yes MLI		PPT
22	India	Yes MLI		PPT

[63] For its agreements listed under the MLI, Greece is implementing the preamble statement (Article 6 of the MLI) and the PPT (Article 7 of the MLI). Greece has also adopted the asymmetrical application of the simplified LOB under Article 7(7)(b) of the MLI.

23	Ireland	Yes MLI		PPT
24	Israel	Yes MLI		PPT
25	Italy	No	Yes MLI	PPT
26	Korea	Yes MLI		PPT
27	Kuwait	No	Yes MLI	PPT
28	Latvia	Yes MLI		PPT
29	Lithuania	Yes MLI		PPT
30	Luxembourg	Yes MLI		PPT
31	Malta	Yes MLI		PPT
32	Mexico	No	Yes MLI	PPT
33	Moldova*	No	No	PPT
34	Morocco	No	Yes MLI	PPT
35	Netherlands	Yes MLI		PPT
36	Norway	Yes MLI		PPT
37	Poland	Yes MLI		PPT
38	Portugal	Yes MLI		PPT
39	Qatar	Yes MLI		PPT
40	Romania	No	Yes MLI	PPT
41	Russian Federation	Yes MLI		PPT
42	San Marino	Yes MLI		PPT
43	Saudi Arabia	Yes MLI		PPT
44	Serbia	Yes MLI		PPT
45	Singapore	Yes other		PPT
46	Slovak Republic	Yes MLI		PPT
47	Slovenia	Yes MLI		PPT
48	South Africa	Yes MLI		PPT
49	Spain	Yes MLI		PPT
50	Switzerland	No	No	PPT
51	Tunisia	No	Yes MLI	PPT
52	Türkiye	No	Yes MLI	PPT
53	Ukraine	Yes MLI		PPT
54	United Arab Emirates	Yes MLI		PPT
55	United Kingdom	Yes MLI		PPT
56	United States	No	No	
57	Uzbekistan	No	No	PPT

Greenland

A. Progress in the implementation of the minimum standard

Greenland has four tax agreements in force as reported in its response to the Peer Review questionnaire. One of those agreements, the agreement with the Faroe Islands, complies with the minimum standard.

Greenland has not signed the MLI.

Greenland indicated in its response to the Peer Review questionnaire that steps have been taken (other than under the MLI) to implement the minimum standard in its agreements with Denmark, Iceland and Norway.

Greenland is implementing the minimum standard through the inclusion of the preamble statement and the PPT.

B. Conclusion

No jurisdiction has raised any concerns about their agreements with Greenland.

Summary of the jurisdiction response – Greenland

	1.Treaty partners	2. Compliance with the standard	3. Signature of a complying instrument	4. Minimum standard provision used
1	Denmark	No	No	
2	Faroe Islands	Yes other		PPT
3	Iceland	No	No	
4	Norway	No	No	

Grenada

A. Progress in the implementation of the minimum standard

Grenada has four tax agreements in force as reported in its response to the Peer Review questionnaire, including the multilateral agreement among the members of the CARICOM concluded with ten treaty partners (the CARICOM Agreement). [64] None of those agreements comply with the minimum standard.

Grenada has not signed the MLI.

Grenada indicated in its response to the Peer Review questionnaire that steps have been taken (other than under the MLI) to implement the minimum standard in the CARICOM Agreement.

In its response to the Peer Review questionnaire, Switzerland indicated that its agreement with Grenada did not give rise to material treaty shopping concerns for Switzerland.

B. Conclusion

Recommendation

It is recommended that Grenada formulates a plan for the implementation of the minimum standard in its agreements for which no steps have yet been taken and that were concluded with members of the BEPS Inclusive Framework (South Africa and the United Kingdom).

Summary of the jurisdiction response – Grenada

	1.Treaty partners	2. Compliance with the standard	3. Signature of a complying instrument	4. Minimum standard provision used
1	CARICOM Agreement treaty partners (Antigua and Barbuda, Barbados, Belize, Dominica, Guyana*, Jamaica, Saint Kitts and Nevis, Saint Lucia, Saint Vincent and the Grenadines, Trinidad and Tobago)	No	No	PPT

[64] Agreement Among the Governments of the Member States of the Caribbean Community for the Avoidance of Double Taxation and the Prevention of Fiscal Evasion with Respect to Taxes on Income, Profits or Gains and Capital Gains and for the Encouragement of Regional Trade and Investment, St. Michael Barbados, 6 July 1994; between: Antigua and Barbuda (18 February 1998), Barbados (7 July 1995), Belize (30 November 1994), Dominica (19 June 1996), Grenada (1 March 1996), Guyana* (26 November 1997), Jamaica (16 February 1995), St. Kitts/Nevis (8 May 1997), St. Lucia (22 May 1995) St. Vincent (12 February 1998) and Trinidad & Tobago (29 November 1994).

Other agreements

	1.Treaty partners	2. Inclusive Framework member
1	South Africa	Yes
2	Switzerland	Yes
3	United Kingdom	Yes

Guernsey

A. Progress in the implementation of the minimum standard

Guernsey has 14 tax agreements in force as reported in its response to the Peer Review questionnaire. Thirteen of those agreements comply with the minimum standard.

Guernsey signed the MLI in 2017 and deposited its instrument of ratification on 12 February 2019. The MLI entered into force for Guernsey on 1 June 2019. The agreements modified by the MLI come into compliance with the minimum standard once the provisions of the MLI take effect.

Guernsey has not listed its agreements with Jersey under the MLI but indicated in its response to the Peer Review questionnaire that steps have been taken (other than under the MLI) to implement the minimum standard in that agreement.

Guernsey is implementing the minimum standard through the inclusion of the preamble statement and the PPT.[65]

B. Conclusion

No jurisdiction has raised any concerns about their agreements with Guernsey.

Summary of the jurisdiction response – Guernsey

	1.Treaty partners	2. Compliance with the standard	3. Signature of a complying instrument	4. Minimum standard provision used
1	Cyprus*	Yes MLI		PPT
2	Estonia	Yes other		PPT
3	Hong Kong (China)	Yes MLI		PPT
4	Isle of Man	Yes other		PPT
5	Jersey	No	No	PPT
6	Liechtenstein	Yes MLI		PPT
7	Luxembourg	Yes MLI		PPT
8	Malta	Yes MLI		PPT
9	Mauritius	Yes MLI		PPT
10	Monaco	Yes MLI		PPT
11	Qatar	Yes other		PPT
12	Seychelles	Yes MLI		PPT
13	Singapore	Yes MLI		PPT
14	United Kingdom	Yes other		PPT

[65] For its agreements listed under the MLI, Guernsey is implementing the preamble statement (Article 6 of the MLI) and the PPT (Article 7 of the MLI).

Haiti

A. Progress in the implementation of the minimum standard

Haiti has no tax agreements in force, as reported in its response to the Peer Review questionnaire.

B. Conclusion

No jurisdiction has raised any concerns about Haiti.

Honduras

A. Progress in the implementation of the minimum standard

Honduras has no tax agreements in force, as reported in its response to the Peer Review questionnaire.

B. Conclusion

No jurisdiction has raised any concerns about Honduras.

Hong Kong (China)

A. Progress in the implementation of the minimum standard

Hong Kong (China) has 43 tax agreements in force as reported in its response to the Peer Review questionnaire. Thirty-four of those agreements comply with the minimum standard.

Hong Kong (China) joined the MLI in 2017 and China (People's Republic of) deposited an instrument of approval that covered Hong Kong (China)'s agreements on 25 May 2022, listing its non-compliant agreements. The MLI entered into force on 1 September 2022.The agreements modified by the MLI come into compliance with the minimum standard once the provisions of the MLI take effect.

A reservation to delay the entry into effect of the provisions of the MLI until internal procedures are completed for this purpose with respect to each listed agreement was made under the MLI.[66] Notifications on the completion of internal procedures for the entry into effect of the MLI were made on 21 February 2023 with respect to the agreements with Austria, Belgium, Canada, Czechia, France, Guernsey, Hungary, India, Indonesia, Ireland, Japan, Jersey, Korea, Latvia, Liechtenstein, Luxembourg, Malaysia, Malta, Netherlands, New Zealand, Pakistan, Portugal, Qatar, Romania, Russian Federation, Saudi Arabia, South Africa, Spain, Thailand, United Arab Emirates, United Kingdom.

Hong Kong (China) is implementing the minimum standard through the inclusion of the preamble statement and the PPT.[67]

B. Conclusion

It is encouraged that the internal procedures for the entry into effect of the MLI be completed (and that such completion be notified) with respect to Hong Kong (China)'s listed agreements that are covered tax agreements under the MLI and for which no such notification has yet been made, as those agreements will only be modified by the MLI (and come into compliance with the minimum standard) following the notification of the completion of such procedures.

Summary of the jurisdiction response – Hong Kong (China)

	1.Treaty partners	2. Compliance with the standard	3. Signature of a complying instrument	4. Minimum standard provision used
1	Austria	Yes MLI		PPT
2	Belarus	Yes other		PPT
3	Belgium	Yes MLI		PPT
4	Brunei Darussalam	No	No	PPT
5	Cambodia*	No	No	PPT
6	Canada	Yes MLI		PPT

66 The reservation was made under Article 35(7)(a) of the MLI.

67 For its agreements listed under the MLI, Hong Kong (China) is implementing the preamble statement (Article 6 of the MLI) and the PPT (Article 7 of the MLI). Hong Kong (China) has made a reservation pursuant to Article 6(4) of the MLI not to apply Article 6(1) of the MLI with respect to agreements that already contain the relevant preamble language (covering one agreement). Hong Kong (China) has also made a reservation pursuant to Article 7(15)(b) of the MLI not to apply Article 7(1) of the MLI with respect to agreements that already contain a PPT (covering two agreements).

7	Czechia	Yes MLI		PPT
8	Estonia	Yes other		PPT
9	Finland	Yes other		PPT
10	France	Yes MLI		PPT
11	Georgia	Yes other		PPT
12	Guernsey	Yes MLI		PPT
13	Hungary	Yes MLI		PPT
14	India	Yes MLI		PPT
15	Indonesia	Yes MLI		PPT
16	Ireland	Yes MLI		PPT
17	Italy	No	Yes MLI	PPT
18	Japan	Yes MLI		PPT
19	Jersey	Yes MLI		PPT
20	Korea	Yes MLI		PPT
21	Kuwait	No	Yes MLI	PPT
22	Latvia	Yes MLI		PPT
23	Liechtenstein	Yes MLI		PPT
24	Luxembourg	Yes MLI		PPT
25	Malaysia	Yes MLI		PPT
26	Malta	Yes MLI		PPT
27	Mexico	No	Yes MLI	PPT
28	Netherlands	Yes MLI		PPT
29	New Zealand	Yes MLI		PPT
30	Pakistan	Yes MLI		PPT
31	Portugal	Yes MLI		PPT
32	Qatar	Yes MLI		PPT
33	Romania	No	Yes MLI	PPT
34	Russian Federation	No	Yes MLI	PPT
35	Saudi Arabia	Yes MLI		PPT
36	Serbia	Yes other		PPT
37	South Africa	Yes MLI		PPT
38	Spain	Yes MLI		PPT
39	Switzerland	No	No	PPT
40	Thailand	Yes MLI		PPT
41	United Arab Emirates	Yes MLI		PPT
42	United Kingdom	Yes MLI		PPT
43	Viet Nam	No	Yes MLI	PPT

Hungary

A. Progress in the implementation of the minimum standard

Hungary has 83 tax agreements in force as reported in its response to the Peer Review questionnaire. Fifty-five of those agreements comply with the minimum standard.

Hungary signed the MLI in 2017 and deposited its instrument of ratification on 25 March 2021. The MLI entered into force for Hungary on 1 July 2021. The agreements modified by the MLI come into compliance with the minimum standard once the provisions of the MLI take effect.

Hungary has not listed its agreements with Mongolia, Montenegro and Switzerland under the MLI and indicated in its response to the Peer Review questionnaire that steps have been taken (other than under the MLI) to implement the minimum standard in its agreement with Switzerland. Hungary also indicated in its response to the Peer Review questionnaire that the agreements with Mongolia and Montenegro do not give rise to material treaty-shopping concerns for Hungary and that those agreements may be amended bilaterally in the future to comply with the minimum standard. Mongolia has listed its agreement with Hungary under the MLI.

Hungary is implementing the minimum standard through the inclusion of the preamble statement and the PPT.[68]

B. Conclusion

Mongolia has listed its agreement with Hungary under the MLI, which amounts to requests to implement the minimum standard.

Hungary has developed a plan for the implementation of the minimum standard in its agreement with Mongolia. Hungary indicated in its response to the Peer Review questionnaire that it intends to expand its list of agreements to be covered under the MLI to include that agreement.

Summary of the jurisdiction response – Hungary

	1.Treaty partners	2. Compliance with the standard	3. Signature of a complying instrument	4. Minimum standard provision used
1	Albania	Yes MLI		PPT
2	Andorra	Yes other		PPT
3	Armenia	No	Yes MLI	PPT
4	Australia	Yes MLI		PPT
5	Austria	Yes MLI		PPT
6	Azerbaijan	No	No	PPT
7	Bahrain	Yes MLI		PPT
8	Belarus	No	No	PPT
9	Belgium	Yes MLI		PPT
10	Bosnia-Herzegovina	Yes MLI		PPT
11	Brazil	No	No	PPT

[68] For its agreements listed under the MLI, Hungary is implementing the preamble statement (Article 6 of the MLI) and the PPT (Article 7 of the MLI).

12	Bulgaria	Yes MLI		PPT
13	Canada	Yes MLI		PPT
14	China (People's Republic of)	Yes MLI		PPT
15	Croatia	Yes MLI		PPT
16	Cyprus*	Yes MLI		PPT
17	Czechia	Yes MLI		PPT
18	Denmark	Yes MLI		PPT
19	Egypt	Yes MLI		PPT
20	Estonia	No	Yes MLI	PPT
21	Finland	Yes MLI		PPT
22	France	Yes MLI		PPT
23	Georgia	Yes MLI		PPT
24	Germany	No	Yes MLI	PPT
25	Greece	Yes MLI		PPT
26	Hong Kong (China)	Yes MLI		PPT
27	Iceland	Yes MLI		PPT
28	India	Yes MLI		PPT
29	Indonesia	Yes MLI		PPT
30	Ireland	Yes MLI		PPT
31	Israel	Yes MLI		PPT
32	Italy	No	Yes MLI	PPT
33	Japan	Yes MLI		PPT
34	Kazakhstan	Yes MLI		PPT
35	Korea	Yes MLI		PPT
36	Kuwait	No	No	PPT
37	Kyrgyzstan*	Yes other		PPT
38	Latvia	Yes MLI		PPT
39	Liechtenstein	Yes MLI		PPT
40	Lithuania	Yes MLI		PPT
41	Luxembourg	Yes MLI		PPT
42	Malaysia	Yes MLI		PPT
43	Malta	Yes MLI		PPT
44	Mexico	No	Yes MLI	PPT
45	Morocco	No	Yes MLI	PPT
46	Netherlands	Yes MLI		PPT
47	North Macedonia	No	Yes MLI	PPT
48	Norway	No	No	PPT
49	Oman	Yes MLI		PPT
50	Pakistan	Yes MLI		PPT
51	Philippines	No	No	PPT
52	Poland	Yes MLI		PPT
53	Portugal	Yes MLI		PPT
54	Qatar	Yes MLI		PPT
55	Romania	No	Yes MLI	PPT
56	Russian Federation	Yes MLI		PPT
57	San Marino	Yes MLI		PPT
58	Saudi Arabia	Yes MLI		PPT
59	Serbia	Yes MLI		PPT
60	Singapore	Yes MLI		PPT
61	Slovak Republic	Yes MLI		PPT
62	Slovenia	Yes MLI		PPT
63	South Africa	Yes MLI		PPT
64	Spain	Yes MLI		PPT

65	Sweden	No	Yes MLI	PPT
66	Switzerland	No	No	PPT
67	Thailand	Yes MLI		PPT
68	Tunisia	No	Yes MLI	PPT
69	Türkiye	No	Yes MLI	PPT
70	Ukraine	Yes MLI		PPT
71	United Arab Emirates	Yes MLI		PPT
72	United Kingdom	Yes MLI		PPT
73	Uruguay	Yes MLI		PPT
74	Viet Nam	No	Yes MLI	PPT

Other agreements

	1.Treaty partners	2. Inclusive Framework member
1	Chinese Taipei*	No
2	Iran*	No
3	Iraq*	No
4	Kosovo*	No
5	Moldova*	No
6	Mongolia	Yes
7	Montenegro	Yes
8	Turkmenistan*	No
9	Uzbekistan	Yes

Iceland

A. Progress in the implementation of the minimum standard

Iceland has 41 tax agreements in force as reported in its response to the Peer Review questionnaire, including the multilateral Nordic Convention concluded with Denmark, the Faroe Islands, Finland, Norway and Sweden (the Nordic Convention).[69] Thirty-one of those agreements, including the Nordic Convention, comply with the minimum standard.

Iceland signed the MLI in 2017 and deposited its instrument of ratification on 26 September 2019. The MLI entered into force for Iceland on 1 January 2020. On 14 December 2021, Iceland made an additional notification to expand its list of agreements to be covered under the MLI. The agreements modified by the MLI come into compliance with the minimum standard once the provisions of the MLI take effect.

Iceland has not listed its agreements with Germany and Greenland under the MLI but indicated in its response to the Peer Review questionnaire that steps have been taken (other than under the MLI) to implement the minimum standard in those agreements.

Iceland is implementing the minimum standard through the inclusion of the preamble statement and PPT.[70]

B. Conclusion

No jurisdiction has raised any concerns about their agreements with Iceland.

Summary of the jurisdiction response – Iceland

	1.Treaty partners	2. Compliance with the standard	3. Signature of a complying instrument	4. Minimum standard provision used
1	Albania	Yes MLI		PPT
2	Austria	No	No	
3	Barbados	Yes MLI		PPT
4	Belgium	Yes MLI		PPT
5	Canada	Yes MLI		PPT
6	China (People's Republic of)	Yes MLI		PPT
7	Croatia	Yes MLI		PPT
8	Cyprus*	Yes MLI		PPT
9	Czechia	Yes MLI		PPT
10	Estonia	No	Yes MLI	PPT
11	France	Yes MLI		PPT
12	Georgia	Yes MLI		PPT
13	Germany	No	No	
14	Greece	Yes MLI		PPT
15	Greenland	No	No	

[69] See the Multilateral convention concluded by Denmark, Finland, the Faroe Islands, Iceland, Norway and Sweden: for the avoidance of double taxation with respect to taxes on income and on capital (1996, 1997, 2008 and 2018).

[70] For its agreements listed under the MLI, Iceland is implementing the preamble statement (Article 6 of the MLI) and the PPT (Article 7 of the MLI). Under Article 7(7)(a) of the MLI, Iceland is also implementing the simplified LOB (Article 7(8 to 13) of the MLI) in agreements concluded with treaty partners that have adopted the simplified LOB.

16	Hungary	Yes MLI		PPT
17	India	Yes MLI		PPT+LOB
18	Ireland	Yes MLI		PPT
19	Italy	No	Yes MLI	PPT
20	Japan	Yes other		PPT+LOB
21	Korea	Yes MLI		PPT
22	Latvia	Yes MLI		PPT
23	Liechtenstein	Yes other		PPT
24	Lithuania	Yes MLI		PPT
25	Luxembourg	Yes MLI		PPT
26	Malta	Yes MLI		PPT
27	Mexico	No	Yes MLI	PPT+LOB
28	Netherlands	Yes MLI		PPT
29	Nordic Convention treaty partners (Denmark, Faroe Islands, Finland, Norway, Sweden)	Yes other		PPT
30	Poland	Yes MLI		PPT
31	Portugal	Yes MLI		PPT
32	Romania	No	Yes MLI	PPT
33	Russian Federation	Yes MLI		PPT+LOB
34	Slovak Republic	Yes MLI		PPT+LOB
35	Slovenia	Yes MLI		PPT
36	Spain	Yes MLI		PPT
37	Switzerland	No	Yes MLI	PPT
38	Ukraine	Yes MLI		PPT
39	United Kingdom	Yes MLI		PPT
40	United States	No	No	D-LOB
41	Viet Nam	No	Yes MLI	PPT

India

A. Progress in the implementation of the minimum standard

India has 96 tax agreements in force as reported in its response to the Peer Review questionnaire. Fifty-four of those agreements comply with the minimum standard.

India signed the MLI in 2017 and deposited its instrument of ratification on 25 June 2019, listing its non-compliant agreements. The MLI entered into force for India on 1 October 2019. The agreements modified by the MLI come into compliance with the minimum standard once the provisions of the MLI take effect.

India has signed a bilateral compliant instrument with respect to its agreement with Brazil.

India is implementing the minimum standard through the inclusion of the preamble statement and the PPT combined with the LOB.[71]

B. Conclusion

No jurisdiction has raised any concerns about their agreements with India.

Summary of the jurisdiction response – India

	1.Treaty partners	2. Compliance with the standard	3. Signature of a complying instrument	4. Minimum standard provision used
1	Albania	Yes MLI		PPT
2	Armenia	No	Yes MLI	PPT+LOB
3	Australia	Yes MLI		PPT
4	Austria	Yes MLI		PPT
5	Bangladesh*	No	No	
6	Belarus	No	No	
7	Belgium	Yes MLI		PPT
8	Bhutan*	No	No	
9	Botswana	No	No	
10	Brazil	No	Yes Other	PPT + LOB
11	Bulgaria	Yes MLI		PPT
12	Canada	Yes MLI		PPT
13	Chile	Yes other		PPT + LOB
14	China (People's Republic of)	Yes other		PPT
15	Colombia	No	Yes MLI	PPT+LOB
16	Croatia	Yes MLI		PPT
17	Cyprus*	Yes MLI		PPT
18	Czechia	Yes MLI		PPT
19	Denmark	Yes MLI		PPT+LOB
20	Egypt	Yes MLI		PPT

[71] For its agreements listed under the MLI, India is implementing the preamble statement (Article 6 of the MLI), the PPT (Article 7 of the MLI) and the simplified LOB (Article 7(6) of the MLI). India expressed a statement, in accordance with Article 7(17)(a) of the MLI, that while it accepts the application of PPT alone as an interim measure, it intends where possible to adopt an LOB provision in addition to or in replacement of the PPT through bilateral negotiation.

21	Estonia	Yes MLI		PPT
22	Ethiopia*	No	No	
23	Fiji*	No	Yes MLI	PPT
24	Finland	Yes MLI		PPT
25	France	Yes MLI		PPT
26	Georgia	Yes MLI		PPT
27	Germany	No	No	
28	Greece	Yes MLI		PPT+LOB
29	Hong Kong (China)	Yes MLI		PPT
30	Hungary	Yes MLI		PPT
31	Iceland	Yes MLI		PPT+LOB
32	Indonesia	Yes MLI		PPT
33	Iran*	Yes other		PPT
34	Ireland	Yes MLI		PPT
35	Israel	Yes MLI		PPT
36	Italy	No	Yes MLI	PPT
37	Japan	Yes MLI		PPT
38	Jordan	Yes MLI		PPT
39	Kazakhstan	Yes MLI		PPT+LOB
40	Kenya	No	Yes MLI	PPT+LOB
41	Korea	Yes MLI		PPT
42	Kuwait	No	Yes MLI	PPT
43	Kyrgyzstan*	No	No	
44	Latvia	Yes MLI		PPT
45	Libya*	No	No	
46	Lithuania	Yes MLI		PPT
47	Luxembourg	Yes MLI		PPT
48	Malaysia	Yes MLI		PPT
49	Malta	Yes MLI		PPT
50	Mauritius	No	No	
51	Mexico	No	Yes MLI	PPT
52	Mongolia	No	Yes MLI	PPT + LOB
53	Montenegro	No	No	
54	Morocco	No	Yes MLI	PPT
55	Mozambique*	No	No	
56	Myanmar*	No	No	
57	Namibia	No	Yes MLI	PPT+LOB
58	Nepal*	No	No	
59	Netherlands	Yes MLI		PPT
60	New Zealand	Yes MLI		PPT
61	North Macedonia	No	Yes MLI	PPT
62	Norway	Yes MLI		PPT+LOB
63	Oman	No	No	
64	Philippines	No	No	
65	Poland	Yes MLI		PPT
66	Portugal	Yes MLI		PPT
67	Qatar	Yes MLI		PPT
68	Romania	Yes MLI		PPT
69	Russian Federation	Yes MLI		PPT+LOB
70	Saudi Arabia	Yes MLI		PPT
71	Serbia	Yes MLI		PPT
72	Singapore	Yes MLI		PPT
73	Slovak Republic	Yes MLI		PPT+LOB

74	Slovenia	Yes MLI		PPT
75	South Africa	Yes MLI		PPT
76	Spain	Yes MLI		PPT
77	Sri Lanka	No	No	
78	Sudan*	No	No	
79	Sweden	No	Yes MLI	PPT
80	Switzerland	No	No	
81	Syria*	No	No	
82	Tajikistan*	No	No	
83	Tanzania*	No	No	
84	Thailand	Yes MLI		PPT
85	Trinidad and Tobago	No	No	
86	Türkiye	No	Yes MLI	PPT
87	Turkmenistan*	No	No	
88	United Arab Emirates	Yes MLI		PPT
89	Uganda*	No	No	
90	Ukraine	Yes MLI		PPT
91	United Kingdom	Yes MLI		PPT
92	United States	No	No	
93	Uruguay	Yes MLI		PPT+LOB
94	Uzbekistan	No	No	
95	Viet Nam	No	Yes MLI	PPT
96	Zambia	No	No	

Indonesia

A. Progress in the implementation of the minimum standard

Indonesia has 70 tax agreements in force as reported in its response to the Peer Review questionnaire. Thirty-one of those agreements comply with the minimum standard.

Indonesia signed the MLI in 2017 and deposited its instrument of ratification on 28 April 2020. The MLI entered into force for Indonesia on 1 August 2020. On 27 November 2023, Indonesia made an additional notification to expand its list of agreements to be covered under the MLI The agreements modified by the MLI come into compliance with the minimum standard once the provisions of the MLI take effect.

Indonesia reserved the right to delay the entry into effect of the provisions of the MLI until Indonesia has completed its internal procedures for this purpose with respect to each of its listed agreements.[72] Indonesia notified that it completed its internal procedures for the entry into effect of the MLI with respect to its agreements with Australia, Belgium, Canada, Denmark, Finland, France, India, Japan, Korea, Luxembourg, Netherlands, New Zealand, Poland, Portugal, Qatar, the Russian Federation, Serbia, Singapore, the Slovak Republic, Sweden, the United Arab Emirates and the United Kingdom on 26 November 2020, with respect to its agreements with Croatia, Egypt, Hungary, Malaysia and Pakistan on 21 October 2021, with respect to its agreements with China (People's Republic of), Hong Kong (China), the Seychelles, Thailand, Romania and Spain on 10 November 2022, and with respect to its agreements with Bulgaria, Mexico, South Africa and Viet Nam on 27 November 2023.

Indonesia is implementing the minimum standard through the inclusion of the preamble statement and the PPT.[73]

B. Conclusion

Indonesia has given effect to its plan for the implementation of the minimum standard in its agreements with Belarus, Jordan, Mongolia, Morocco, Papua New Guinea, Sri Lanka, Tunisia and Ukraine. Indonesia made an additional notification in November 2023 to expand its list of agreements to be covered under the MLI to include those agreements.

Summary of the jurisdiction response – Indonesia

	1.Treaty partners	2. Compliance with the standard	3. Signature of a complying instrument	4. Minimum standard provision used
1	Armenia	No	Yes MLI	PPT
2	Australia	Yes MLI		PPT
3	Austria	No	No	
4	Belarus	No	No	
5	Belgium	Yes MLI		PPT
6	Brunei Darussalam	No	No	PPT
7	Bulgaria	No	Yes MLI	PPT

72 The reservation was made under Article 35(7)(a) of the MLI.

73 For its agreements listed under the MLI, Indonesia is implementing the preamble statement (Article 6 of the MLI) and the PPT (Article 7 of the MLI).

8	Canada	Yes MLI		
9	China (People's Republic of)	Yes MLI		PPT
10	Croatia	Yes MLI		PPT
11	Czechia	No	No	PPT
12	Denmark	Yes MLI		PPT
13	Egypt	Yes MLI		PPT
14	Finland	Yes MLI		PPT
15	France	Yes MLI		PPT
16	Germany	No	No	
17	Hong Kong (China)	Yes MLI		PPT
18	Hungary	Yes MLI		PPT
19	India	Yes MLI		PPT
20	Italy	No	Yes MLI	PPT
21	Japan	Yes MLI		PPT
22	Jordan	No	Yes MLI	PPT
23	Korea	Yes MLI		PPT
24	Kuwait	No	No	
25	Lao People's Democratic Republic*	No	No	PPT
26	Luxembourg	Yes MLI		PPT
27	Malaysia	Yes MLI		PPT
28	Mexico	No	Yes MLI	PPT
29	Mongolia	No		PPT
30	Morocco	No		PPT
31	Netherlands	Yes MLI		PPT
32	New Zealand	Yes MLI		PPT
33	Norway	No	No	PPT
34	Pakistan	Yes MLI		PPT
35	Papua New Guinea	No	Yes MLI	PPT
36	Philippines	No	No	PPT
37	Poland	Yes MLI		PPT
38	Portugal	Yes MLI		PPT
39	Qatar	Yes MLI		PPT
40	Romania	No	Yes MLI	PPT
41	Russia	Yes MLI		PPT
42	Serbia	Yes MLI		PPT
43	Seychelles	Yes MLI		PPT
44	Singapore	Yes other		PPT
45	Slovak Republic	Yes MLI		PPT
46	South Africa	No	Yes MLI	PPT
47	Spain	Yes MLI		PPT
48	Sri Lanka	No	No	
49	Sweden	No	Yes MLI	PPT
50	Switzerland	No	No	PPT
51	Thailand	Yes MLI		PPT
52	Türkiye	No	Yes MLI	PPT
53	Tunisia	No	Yes MLI	PPT
54	Ukraine	No	Yes MLI	PPT
55	United Arab Emirates	Yes other		PPT
56	United Kingdom	Yes MLI		PPT
57	United States	No	No	
58	Viet Nam	No	Yes MLI	PPT

Other agreements

	1.Treaty partners	2. Inclusive Framework member
1	Algeria*	No
2	Bangladesh*	No
3	Cambodia*	No
4	Chinese Taipei*	No
5	Democratic People's Republic of Korea*	No
6	Iran*	No
7	Sudan*	No
8	Suriname*	No
9	Syrian Arab Republic*	No
10	Tajikistan*	No
11	Uzbekistan	Yes
12	Venezuela*	No

Ireland

A. Progress in the implementation of the minimum standard

Ireland has 74 tax agreements in force as reported in its response to the Peer Review questionnaire. Fifty-five of those agreements comply with the minimum standard.

Ireland signed the MLI in 2017 and deposited its instrument of ratification on 29 January 2019. The MLI entered into force for Ireland on 1 May 2019. The agreements modified by the MLI come into compliance with the minimum standard once the provisions of the MLI take effect.

Ireland is implementing the minimum standard through the inclusion of the preamble statement and the PPT.[74]

B. Conclusion

No jurisdiction has raised any concerns about their agreements with Ireland.

Summary of the jurisdiction response – Ireland

	1.Treaty partners	2. Compliance with the standard	3. Signature of a complying instrument	4. Minimum standard provision used
1	Albania	Yes MLI		PPT
2	Armenia	No	Yes MLI	PPT
3	Australia	Yes MLI		PPT
4	Austria	Yes MLI		PPT
5	Bahrain	Yes MLI		PPT
6	Belarus	No	No	PPT
7	Belgium	Yes MLI		PPT
8	Bosnia-Herzegovina	Yes MLI		PPT
9	Botswana	No	No	PPT
10	Bulgaria	Yes MLI		PPT
11	Canada	Yes MLI		PPT
12	Chile	Yes MLI		PPT
13	China (People's Republic of)	Yes MLI		PPT
14	Croatia	Yes MLI		PPT
15	Cyprus*	Yes MLI		PPT
16	Czechia	Yes MLI		PPT
17	Denmark	Yes MLI		PPT
18	Egypt	Yes MLI		PPT
19	Estonia	No	Yes MLI	PPT
20	Ethiopia*	No	No	PPT
21	Finland	Yes MLI		PPT
22	France	Yes MLI		PPT
23	Georgia	Yes MLI		PPT
24	Germany	Yes other		PPT

[74] For its agreements listed under the MLI, Ireland is implementing the preamble statement (Article 6 of the MLI) and the PPT (Article 7 of the MLI).

25	Greece	Yes MLI		PPT
26	Hong Kong (China)	Yes MLI		PPT
27	Hungary	Yes MLI		PPT
28	Iceland	Yes MLI		PPT
29	India	Yes MLI		PPT
30	Israel	Yes MLI		PPT
31	Italy	No	Yes MLI	PPT
32	Japan	Yes MLI		PPT
33	Kazakhstan	Yes MLI		PPT
34	Korea	Yes MLI		PPT
35	Kosovo*	Yes other		PPT
36	Kuwait	No	Yes MLI	PPT
37	Latvia	Yes MLI		PPT
38	Lithuania	Yes MLI		PPT
39	Luxembourg	Yes MLI		PPT
40	Malaysia	Yes MLI		PPT
41	Malta	Yes MLI		PPT
42	Mexico	No	Yes MLI	PPT
43	Moldova*	No	No	PPT
44	Montenegro	No	No	PPT
45	Morocco	No	Yes MLI	PPT
46	Netherlands	Yes other		PPT
47	New Zealand	Yes MLI		PPT
48	North Macedonia	No	Yes MLI	PPT
49	Norway	Yes MLI		PPT
50	Pakistan	Yes MLI		PPT
51	Panama	Yes MLI		PPT
52	Poland	Yes MLI		PPT
53	Portugal	Yes MLI		PPT
54	Qatar	Yes MLI		PPT
55	Romania	No	Yes MLI	PPT
56	Russian Federation	Yes MLI		PPT
57	Saudi Arabia	Yes MLI		PPT
58	Serbia	Yes MLI		PPT
59	Singapore	Yes MLI		PPT
60	Slovak Republic	Yes MLI		PPT
61	Slovenia	Yes MLI		PPT
62	South Africa	Yes MLI		PPT
63	Spain	Yes MLI		PPT
64	Sweden	No	Yes MLI	PPT
65	Switzerland	Yes other		PPT
66	Thailand	Yes MLI		PPT
67	Türkiye	No	Yes MLI	PPT
68	Ukraine	Yes MLI		PPT
69	United Arab Emirates	Yes MLI		PPT
70	United Kingdom	Yes MLI		PPT
71	United States	No	No	LOB
72	Uzbekistan	No	No	PPT
73	Viet Nam	No	Yes MLI	PPT
74	Zambia	No	No	PPT

Isle of Man

A. Progress in the implementation of the minimum standard

The Isle of Man has ten tax agreements in force as reported in its response to the Peer Review questionnaire. Nine of those agreements comply with the minimum standard.

The Isle of Man signed the MLI in 2017 and deposited its instrument of ratification on 25 October 2017. The MLI entered into force for the Isle of Man on 1 July 2018. The agreements modified by the MLI come into compliance with the minimum standard once the provisions of the MLI take effect.

The Isle of Man has not listed its agreement with Jersey under the MLI but indicated in its response to the Peer Review questionnaire that steps have been taken (other than under the MLI) to implement the minimum standard in that agreement.

The Isle of Man is implementing the minimum standard through the inclusion of the preamble statement and the PPT.[75]

B. Conclusion

No jurisdiction has raised any concerns about their agreements with the Isle of Man.

Summary of the jurisdiction response – Isle of Man

	1.Treaty partners	2. Compliance with the standard	3. Signature of a complying instrument	4. Minimum standard provision used
1	Bahrain	Yes MLI		PPT
2	Estonia	Yes MLI		PPT
3	Guernsey	Yes other		PPT
4	Jersey	No	No	PPT
5	Luxembourg	Yes MLI		PPT
6	Malta	Yes MLI		PPT
7	Qatar	Yes MLI		PPT
8	Seychelles	Yes MLI		PPT
9	Singapore	Yes MLI		PPT
10	United Kingdom	Yes other		PPT

[75] For its agreements listed under the MLI, the Isle of Man is implementing the preamble statement (Article 6 of the MLI) and the PPT (Article 7 of the MLI).

Israel

A. Progress in the implementation of the minimum standard

Israel has 60 tax agreements in force as reported in its response to the Peer Review questionnaire. Thirty-nine of those agreements comply with the minimum standard.

Israel signed the MLI in 2017 and deposited its instrument of ratification on 13 September 2018. The MLI entered into force for Israel on 1 January 2019. The agreements modified by the MLI come into compliance with the minimum standard once the provisions of the MLI take effect.

Israel has not listed its agreements with Germany and Switzerland under the MLI but indicated in its response to the Peer Review questionnaire that steps have been taken (other than under the MLI) to implement the minimum standard in those agreements.

Israel is implementing the minimum standard through the inclusion of the preamble statement and the PPT.[76]

B. Conclusion

No jurisdiction has raised any concerns about their agreements with Israel.

Summary of the jurisdiction response – Israel

	1.Treaty partners	2. Compliance with the standard	3. Signature of a complying instrument	4. Minimum standard provision used
1	Albania	Yes other		PPT
2	Armenia	No	No	PPT
3	Australia	Yes other		PPT
4	Austria	Yes MLI		PPT
5	Azerbaijan	No	No	PPT
6	Belarus	No	No	PPT
7	Belgium	Yes MLI		PPT
8	Brazil	No	No	PPT
9	Bulgaria	Yes MLI		PPT
10	Canada	Yes MLI		PPT
11	China (People's Republic of)	Yes MLI		PPT
12	Chinese Taipei*	No	No	PPT
13	Croatia	Yes MLI		PPT
14	Czechia	Yes MLI		PPT
15	Denmark	Yes MLI		PPT
16	Estonia	No	Yes MLI	PPT
17	Ethiopia*	No	No	PPT
18	Finland	Yes MLI		PPT
19	France	Yes MLI		PPT
20	Georgia	Yes MLI		PPT

[76] For its agreements listed under the MLI, Israel is implementing the preamble statement (Article 6 of the MLI) and the PPT (Article 7 of the MLI).

21	Germany	No	No	PPT
22	Greece	Yes MLI		PPT
23	Hungary	Yes MLI		PPT
24	India	Yes MLI		PPT
25	Ireland	Yes MLI		PPT
26	Italy	No	Yes MLI	PPT
27	Jamaica	No	Yes MLI	PPT
28	Japan	Yes MLI		PPT
29	Korea	Yes MLI		PPT
30	Latvia	Yes MLI		PPT
31	Lithuania	Yes MLI		PPT
32	Luxembourg	Yes MLI		PPT
33	Malta	Yes MLI		PPT
34	Mexico	No	Yes MLI	PPT
35	Moldova*	No	No	PPT
36	Netherlands	Yes MLI		PPT
37	North Macedonia	No	Yes MLI	PPT
38	Norway	No	No	PPT
39	Panama	Yes MLI		PPT
40	Philippines	No	No	PPT
41	Poland	Yes MLI		PPT
42	Portugal	Yes MLI		PPT
43	Romania	Yes MLI		PPT
44	Russian Federation	Yes MLI		PPT
45	Serbia	Yes other		PPT
46	Singapore	Yes MLI		PPT
47	Slovak Republic	Yes MLI		PPT
48	Slovenia	Yes MLI		PPT
49	South Africa	Yes MLI		PPT
50	Spain	Yes MLI		PPT
51	Sweden	No	Yes MLI	PPT
52	Switzerland	No	No	PPT
53	Thailand	Yes MLI		PPT
54	Türkiye	No	Yes MLI	PPT
55	Ukraine	Yes MLI		PPT
56	United Arab Emirates	Yes other		PPT
57	United Kingdom	Yes other		PPT
58	United States	No	No	
59	Uzbekistan	No	No	PPT
60	Viet Nam	No	Yes MLI	PPT

Italy

A. Progress in the implementation of the minimum standard

Italy has 103 tax agreements in force as reported in its response to the Peer Review questionnaire. Four of those agreements comply with the minimum standard.

Italy signed the MLI in 2017. The agreements modified by the MLI come into compliance with the minimum standard once the provisions of the MLI take effect.

Italy has not listed its agreements with Albania, Belarus, Congo, Montenegro, North Macedonia, Oman, and Panama. These agreements will therefore not, at this stage, be modified by the MLI. Albania, North Macedonia, Oman and Panama have listed their agreements with Italy under the MLI.

Italy indicated in its response to the Peer Review questionnaire that steps have been taken (other than under the MLI) to implement the minimum standard in its agreements with Brazil, Norway and Uzbekistan.

Italy indicated in its response to the Peer Review questionnaire that the agreements with Belarus, Congo, Ecuador*, Ethiopia*, Ghana*, Kyrgyzstan*, Montenegro, Mozambique*, Syria*, Tajikistan*, Trinidad and Tobago and Venezuela* do not give rise to material treaty-shopping concerns for Italy as they contain specific features and as Italy's domestic anti-abuse legislation applies.

Italy is implementing the minimum standard through the inclusion of the preamble statement and the PPT.[77]

B. Conclusion

Albania, North Macedonia, Oman and Panama have listed their agreements with Italy under the MLI, which amount to requests to implement the minimum standard.

Italy has developed a plan for the implementation of the minimum standard in its agreements with Albania, North Macedonia, Oman and Panama. Italy indicated in its response to the Peer Review questionnaire that it intends to expand its list of agreements to be covered under the MLI to include those agreements.

Recommendation

It is recommended that Italy completes the steps to have the MLI take effect with respect to its agreements listed under the MLI as those agreements will only be modified by the MLI (and come into compliance with the minimum standard) once the provisions of the MLI take effect.

Summary of the jurisdiction response – Italy

	1.Treaty partners	2. Compliance with the standard	3. Signature of a complying instrument	4. Minimum standard provision used
1	Argentina	No	Yes MLI	PPT

[77] For its agreements listed under the MLI, Italy is implementing the preamble statement (Article 6 of the MLI) and the PPT (Article 7 of the MLI). Italy has made a reservation pursuant to Article 7(15)(b) of the MLI not to apply Article 7(1) of the MLI with respect to agreements that already contain a PPT (covering thirteen agreements).

2	Armenia	No	Yes MLI	PPT
3	Australia	No	Yes MLI	PPT
4	Austria	No	Yes MLI	PPT
5	Azerbaijan	No	No	PPT
6	Bangladesh*	No	No	PPT
7	Barbados	No	Yes MLI	PPT
8	Belgium	No	Yes MLI	PPT
9	Bosnia-Herzegovina	No	Yes MLI	PPT
10	Brazil	No	No	PPT
11	Bulgaria	No	Yes MLI	PPT
12	Canada	No	Yes MLI	PPT
13	Chile	Yes other		PPT
14	China (People's Republic of)	No	Yes MLI	PPT
15	Colombia	Yes other		PPT
16	Côte d'Ivoire	No	Yes MLI	PPT
17	Croatia	No	Yes MLI	PPT
18	Cyprus*	No	Yes MLI	PPT
19	Czechia	No	Yes MLI	PPT
20	Denmark	No	Yes MLI	PPT
21	Egypt	No	Yes MLI	PPT
22	Estonia	No	Yes MLI	PPT
23	Finland	No	Yes MLI	PPT
24	France	No	Yes MLI	PPT
25	Georgia	No	Yes MLI	PPT
26	Germany	No	Yes MLI	PPT
27	Greece	No	Yes MLI	PPT
28	Hong Kong (China)	No	Yes MLI	PPT
29	Hungary	No	Yes MLI	PPT
30	Iceland	No	Yes MLI	PPT
31	India	No	Yes MLI	PPT
32	Indonesia	No	Yes MLI	PPT
33	Ireland	No	Yes MLI	PPT
34	Israel	No	Yes MLI	PPT
35	Jamaica	Yes other		PPT
36	Japan	No	Yes MLI	PPT
37	Jordan	No	Yes MLI	PPT
38	Kazakhstan	No	Yes MLI	PPT
39	Korea	No	Yes MLI	PPT
40	Kuwait	No	No	PPT
41	Latvia	No	Yes MLI	PPT
42	Lebanon*	No	No	PPT
43	Lithuania	No	Yes MLI	PPT
44	Luxembourg	No	Yes MLI	PPT
45	Malaysia	No	Yes MLI	PPT
46	Malta	No	Yes MLI	PPT
47	Mauritius	No	Yes MLI	PPT
48	Mexico	No	Yes MLI	PPT
49	Moldova*	No	No	PPT
50	Mongolia	No	Yes MLI	PPT
51	Morocco	No	Yes MLI	PPT
52	Netherlands	No	Yes MLI	PPT
53	New Zealand	No	Yes MLI	PPT
54	Norway	No	No	PPT

55	Pakistan	No	Yes MLI	PPT
56	Philippines	No	No	PPT
57	Poland	No	Yes MLI	PPT
58	Portugal	No	Yes MLI	PPT
59	Qatar	No	Yes MLI	PPT
60	Romania	No	Yes MLI	PPT
61	Russian Federation	No	Yes MLI	PPT
62	San Marino	No	Yes MLI	PPT
63	Saudi Arabia	No	Yes MLI	PPT
64	Senegal	No	Yes MLI	PPT
65	Serbia	No	Yes MLI	PPT
66	Singapore	No	Yes MLI	PPT
67	Slovak Republic	No	Yes MLI	PPT
68	Slovenia	No	Yes MLI	PPT
69	South Africa	No	Yes MLI	PPT
70	Spain	No	Yes MLI	PPT
71	Sri Lanka	No	No	PPT
72	Sweden	No	Yes MLI	PPT
73	Switzerland	No	Yes MLI	PPT
74	Tanzania*	No	No	PPT
75	Thailand	No	Yes MLI	PPT
76	Tunisia	No	Yes MLI	PPT
77	Türkiye	No	Yes MLI	PPT
78	Uganda*	No	No	PPT
79	Ukraine	No	Yes MLI	PPT
80	United Arab Emirates	No	Yes MLI	PPT
81	United Kingdom	No	Yes MLI	PPT
82	United States	No	No	LOB
83	Uruguay	Yes other		PPT
84	Uzbekistan	No	No	PPT
85	Viet Nam	No	Yes MLI	PPT
86	Zambia	No	No	PPT

Other agreements

	1.Treaty partners	2. Inclusive Framework member
1	Albania	Yes
2	Algeria*	No
3	Belarus	Yes
4	Congo	Yes
5	Ecuador*	No
6	Ethiopia*	No
7	Ghana*	No
8	Kyrgyzstan*	No
9	Montenegro	Yes
10	Mozambique*	No
11	North Macedonia	Yes
12	Oman	Yes
13	Panama	Yes
14	Syrian Arab Republic*	No
15	Tajikistan*	No
16	Trinidad and Tobago	Yes
17	Venezuela*	No

Jamaica

A. Progress in the implementation of the minimum standard

Jamaica has 16 tax agreements in force, as reported in its response to the Peer Review questionnaire, including the multilateral agreement among the members of the CARICOM concluded with ten treaty partners (the CARICOM Agreement).[78] Two of those agreements comply with the minimum standard.

Jamaica signed the MLI in 2018 and listed its non-compliant bilateral agreements. The agreements modified by the MLI come into compliance with the minimum standard once the provisions of the MLI take effect.

Jamaica is implementing the minimum standard through the inclusion of the preamble statement and PPT combined with the LOB.[79]

B. Conclusion

Recommendation

It is recommended that Jamaica completes the steps to have the MLI take effect with respect to its agreements listed under the MLI as those agreements will only be modified by the MLI (and come into compliance with the minimum standard) once the provisions of the MLI take effect.

Summary of the jurisdiction response – Jamaica

	1.Treaty partners	2. Compliance with the standard	3. Signature of a complying instrument	4. Minimum standard provision used
1	Canada	No	Yes MLI	PPT
2	CARICOM Agreement treaty partners (Antigua and Barbuda, Barbados, Belize, Dominica, Grenada, Guyana*, Saint Kitts and Nevis, Saint Lucia, Saint Vincent and the Grenadines, Trinidad and Tobago)	No	No	PPT
3	China (People's Republic of)	No	Yes MLI	PPT

[78] Agreement Among the Governments of the Member States of the Caribbean Community for the Avoidance of Double Taxation and the Prevention of Fiscal Evasion with Respect to Taxes on Income, Profits or Gains and Capital Gains and for the Encouragement of Regional Trade and Investment, St. Michael Barbados, 6 July 1994; between: Antigua and Barbuda (18 February 1998), Barbados (7 July 1995), Belize (30 November 1994), Dominica (19 June 1996), Grenada (1 March 1996), Guyana* (26 November 1997), Jamaica (16 February 1995), St. Kitts/Nevis (8 May 1997), St. Lucia (22 May 1995) St. Vincent (12 February 1998) and Trinidad & Tobago (29 November 1994).

[79] For its agreements listed under the MLI, Jamaica is implementing the preamble statement (Article 6 of the MLI) and the PPT (Article 7 of the MLI). Under Article 7(7)(a) of the MLI, Jamaica is also implementing the simplified LOB (Article 7(8 to 13) of the MLI) in agreements concluded with treaty partners that adopted the simplified LOB.

4	Denmark	No	Yes MLI	PPT
5	France	No	Yes MLI	PPT
6	Germany	No	No	PPT+LOB
7	Israel	No	Yes MLI	PPT
8	Italy	Yes other		PPT
9	Japan	Yes other		PPT
10	Mexico	No	Yes MLI	PPT+LOB
11	Norway	No	No	PPT+LOB
12	Spain	No	Yes MLI	PPT
13	Sweden	No	Yes MLI	PPT
14	Switzerland	No	No	PPT+LOB
15	United Kingdom	No	Yes MLI	PPT
16	United States	No	No	

Japan

A. Progress in the implementation of the minimum standard

Japan has 79 tax agreements in force as reported in its response to the Peer Review questionnaire. Fifty-seven of those agreements comply with the minimum standard.

Japan signed the MLI in 2017 and deposited its instrument of acceptance on 26 September 2018. The MLI entered into force for Japan on 1 January 2019. Subsequently, Japan made additional notifications to expand its list of agreements to be covered under the MLI.[80] The agreements modified by the MLI come into compliance with the minimum standard once the provisions of the MLI take effect.

Japan has not listed its agreements with Armenia, Belarus, Brazil, Brunei Darussalam, Sri Lanka, the United States and Zambia, which have not joined the MLI or have joined the MLI but not listed the agreements with Japan in their definitive list of reservations and notifications under the MLI. These agreements will therefore not, at this stage, be modified by the MLI. Japan indicated that it would list such agreements once the treaty partners join the MLI and list the agreements with Japan in their definitive list of reservations and notifications under the MLI except for the cases where the agreement will be updated through bilateral negotiations to be compliant with the minimum standard.

Japan has signed a bilateral complying instrument with respect to its agreement with Azerbaijan.

Japan indicated in its response to the Peer Review questionnaire that the agreements with Armenia, Belarus, Brazil, Brunei Darussalam, Sri Lanka and Zambia do not give rise to material treaty-shopping concerns for Japan.

Japan is implementing the minimum standard through the inclusion of the preamble statement and the PPT for its compliant agreements with Bulgaria, Canada, Chile, China (People's Republic of), Czechia, Ecuador*, Egypt, Finland, Hong Kong (China), Hungary, India, Indonesia, Ireland, Israel, Jamaica, Kazakhstan, Korea, Luxembourg, Malaysia, Morocco, Norway, Oman, Pakistan, Peru, Poland, Portugal, Qatar, Saudi Arabia, Serbia, Singapore, the Slovak Republic, Slovenia, South Africa, Thailand, Ukraine, the United Arab Emirates and Uruguay. Japan is implementing the minimum standard through the inclusion of the preamble statement and the PPT combined with the LOB for its compliant agreements with Australia, Austria, Belgium, Croatia, Colombia, Denmark, Estonia, France, Georgia, Germany, Iceland, Latvia, Lithuania, Netherlands, New Zealand, Russian Federation, Spain, Switzerland, the United Kingdom and Uzbekistan.[81]

B. Conclusion

No jurisdiction has raised any concerns about their agreements with Japan.

---

[80] Japan made additional notifications to expand its list of agreements to be covered under the MLI on 14 February 2020 (Qatar), on 22 July 2020 (Oman), on 21 April 2022 (Thailand) and on 20 June 2023 (Viet Nam).

[81] For its agreements listed under the MLI, Japan is implementing the preamble statement (Article 6 of the MLI) and the PPT (Article 7 of the MLI). Japan has made a reservation pursuant to Article 6(4) of the MLI not to apply Article 6(1) of the MLI with respect to agreements that already contain the relevant preamble language (covering one agreement).

Summary of the jurisdiction response – Japan

	1.Treaty partners	2. Compliance with the standard	3. Signature of a complying instrument	4. Minimum standard provision used
1	Australia	Yes MLI		PPT+LOB
2	Austria	Yes other		PPT+LOB
3	Azerbaijan	No	Yes other	PPT
4	Belgium	Yes other		PPT+LOB
5	Bulgaria	Yes MLI		PPT
6	Canada	Yes MLI		PPT
7	Chile	Yes other		PPT
8	China (People's Republic of)	Yes MLI		PPT
9	Colombia	Yes other		PPT+LOB
10	Croatia	Yes other		PPT+LOB
11	Czechia	Yes MLI		PPT
12	Denmark	Yes other		PPT+LOB
13	Ecuador*	Yes other		PPT
14	Egypt	Yes MLI		PPT
15	Estonia	Yes other		PPT+LOB
16	Fiji*	No	Yes MLI	PPT
17	Finland	Yes MLI		PPT
18	France	Yes MLI		PPT+LOB
19	Georgia	Yes other		PPT+LOB
20	Germany	Yes other		PPT+LOB
21	Hong Kong (China)	Yes MLI		PPT
22	Hungary	Yes MLI		PPT
23	Iceland	Yes other		PPT+LOB
24	India	Yes MLI		PPT
25	Indonesia	Yes MLI		PPT
26	Ireland	Yes MLI		PPT
27	Israel	Yes MLI		PPT
28	Italy	No	Yes MLI	PPT
29	Jamaica	Yes other		PPT
30	Kazakhstan	Yes MLI		PPT
31	Korea	Yes MLI		PPT
32	Kuwait	No	Yes MLI	PPT
33	Latvia	Yes other		PPT+LOB
34	Lithuania	Yes other		PPT+LOB
35	Luxembourg	Yes MLI		PPT
36	Malaysia	Yes MLI		PPT
37	Mexico	No	Yes MLI	PPT
38	Morocco	Yes other		PPT
39	Netherlands	Yes MLI		PPT+LOB
40	New Zealand	Yes MLI		PPT+LOB
41	Norway	Yes MLI		PPT
42	Oman	Yes MLI		PPT
43	Pakistan	Yes MLI		PPT
44	Peru	Yes other		PPT
45	Poland	Yes MLI		PPT
46	Portugal	Yes MLI		PPT
47	Qatar	Yes MLI		PPT
48	Romania	No	Yes MLI	PPT
49	Russian Federation	Yes other		PPT+LOB

50	Saudi Arabia	Yes MLI		PPT
51	Serbia	Yes other		PPT
52	Singapore	Yes MLI		PPT
53	Slovak Republic	Yes MLI		PPT
54	Slovenia	Yes other		PPT
55	South Africa	Yes MLI		PPT
56	Spain	Yes other		PPT+LOB
57	Sweden	No	Yes MLI	PPT+LOB
58	Switzerland	Yes other		PPT+LOB
59	Thailand	Yes MLI		PPT
60	Türkiye	No	Yes MLI	PPT
61	Ukraine	Yes MLI		PPT
62	United Arab Emirates	Yes MLI		PPT
63	United Kingdom	Yes MLI		PPT+LOB
64	United States	No	No	D-LOB
65	Uruguay	Yes other		PPT
66	Uzbekistan	Yes other		PPT+LOB
67	Viet Nam	No	Yes MLI	PPT

Other agreements

	1.Treaty partners	2. Inclusive Framework member
1	Armenia	Yes
2	Bangladesh*	No
3	Belarus	Yes
4	Brazil	Yes
5	Brunei Darussalam	Yes
6	Kyrgyzstan*	No
7	Moldova*	No
8	Philippines	Yes
9	Sri Lanka	Yes
10	Tajikistan*	No
11	Turkmenistan*	No
12	Zambia	Yes

Jersey

A. Progress in the implementation of the minimum standard

Jersey has 15 tax agreements in force as reported in its response to the Peer Review questionnaire. Ten of those agreements comply with the minimum standard.

Jersey signed the MLI in 2017 and deposited its instrument of ratification on 15 December 2017. The MLI entered into force for Jersey on 1 July 2018. The agreements modified by the MLI come into compliance with the minimum standard once the provisions of the MLI take effect.

Jersey has not listed its agreement with Mauritius, but indicated in its response to the Peer Review questionnaire that steps have been taken (other than under the MLI) to implement the minimum standard in its agreements with Guernsey, the Isle of Man and Mauritius.

Jersey is implementing the minimum standard through the inclusion of the preamble statement and the PPT.[82]

B. Conclusion

No jurisdiction has raised any concerns about their agreements with Jersey.

Mauritius has listed its agreement with Jersey under the MLI, which amounts to a request to implement the minimum standard.

Summary of the jurisdiction response – Jersey

	1.Treaty partners	2. Compliance with the standard	3. Signature of a complying instrument	4. Minimum standard provision used
1	Cyprus*	Yes MLI		PPT
2	Estonia	No	Yes MLI	PPT
3	Guernsey	No	No	PPT
4	Hong Kong (China)	Yes MLI		PPT
5	Isle of Man	No	No	PPT
6	Liechtenstein	Yes other		PPT
7	Luxembourg	Yes MLI		PPT
8	Malta	Yes MLI		PPT
9	Mauritius	No	No	
10	Qatar	Yes MLI		PPT
11	Rwanda*	No	No	
12	Seychelles	Yes MLI		PPT
13	Singapore	Yes MLI		PPT
14	United Arab Emirates	Yes MLI		PPT
15	United Kingdom	Yes other		PPT

82 For its agreements listed under the MLI, Jersey is implementing the preamble statement (Article 6 of the MLI) and the PPT (Article 7 of the MLI).

Jordan

A. Progress in the implementation of the minimum standard

Jordan has 39 tax agreements in force as reported in its response to the Peer Review questionnaire. Twenty-one of those agreements comply with the minimum standard.

Jordan signed the MLI in 2019 and deposited its instrument of ratification on 29 September 2020, listing its non-compliant agreements. The MLI entered into force for Jordan on 1 January 2021. The agreements modified by the MLI come into compliance with the minimum standard once the provisions of the MLI take effect.

Jordan is implementing the minimum standard through the inclusion of the preamble statement and the PPT.[83]

B. Conclusion

No jurisdiction has raised any concerns about their agreements with Jordan.

Summary of the jurisdiction response - Jordan

	1.Treaty partners	2. Compliance with the standard	3. Signature of a complying instrument	4. Minimum standard provision used
1	Algeria*	No	No	
2	Azerbaijan	No	No	
3	Bahrain	Yes MLI		PPT
4	Bosnia-Herzegovina	Yes MLI		PPT
5	Bulgaria	Yes MLI		PPT
6	Canada	Yes MLI		PPT
7	Croatia	Yes MLI		PPT
8	Cyprus*	Yes other		PPT
9	Czechia	No	No	
10	Egypt	Yes MLI		PPT
11	France	Yes MLI		PPT
12	India	Yes MLI		PPT
13	Indonesia	No	No	
14	Iran*	No	No	
15	Italy	No	Yes MLI	PPT
16	Korea	Yes MLI		PPT
17	Kuwait	No	No	
18	Lebanon*	No	No	
19	Malaysia	Yes MLI		PPT
20	Malta	Yes MLI		PPT
21	Morocco	No	Yes MLI	PPT
22	Netherlands	Yes MLI		PPT
23	Pakistan	Yes MLI		PPT

83 For its agreements listed under the MLI, Jordan is implementing the preamble statement (Article 6 of the MLI) and the PPT (Article 7 of the MLI).

24	Palestine*	No	No	
25	Poland	Yes MLI		PPT
26	Qatar	Yes MLI		PPT
27	Romania	No	Yes MLI	PPT
28	Saudi Arabia	Yes MLI		PPT
29	Singapore	Yes other		PPT
30	Sudan*	No	No	
31	Syria*	No	No	
32	Tajikistan*	No	No	
33	Tunisia	No	Yes MLI	PPT
34	Türkiye	No	Yes MLI	PPT
35	Ukraine	Yes MLI		PPT
36	United Arab Emirates	Yes MLI		PPT
37	United Kingdom	Yes MLI		PPT
38	Uzbekistan	No	No	
39	Yemen*	No	No	

Kazakhstan

A. Progress in the implementation of the minimum standard

Kazakhstan has 55 tax agreements in force as reported in its response to the Peer Review questionnaire. Thirty of those agreements comply with the minimum standard.

Kazakhstan signed the MLI in 2018 and deposited its instrument of ratification on 24 June 2020, listing its non-compliant agreements. The MLI entered into force for Kazakhstan on 1 October 2020. The agreements modified by the MLI come into compliance with the minimum standard once the provisions of the MLI take effect.

Kazakhstan indicated in its response to the Peer Review questionnaire that steps have been taken (other than under the MLI) to implement the minimum standard in its agreement with Cyprus*.

Kazakhstan is implementing the minimum standard through the inclusion of the preamble statement and the PPT combined with the LOB.[84]

B. Conclusion

No jurisdiction has raised any concerns about their agreements with Kazakhstan.

Summary of the jurisdiction response - Kazakhstan

	1.Treaty partners	2. Compliance with the standard	3. Signature of a complying instrument	4. Minimum standard provision used
1	Armenia	No	Yes MLI	PPT+LOB
2	Austria	No	No	
3	Azerbaijan	No	No	
4	Belarus	No	No	
5	Belgium	Yes MLI		PPT
6	Bulgaria	Yes MLI		PPT
7	Canada	Yes MLI		PPT
8	China (People's Republic of)	Yes MLI		PPT
9	Croatia	Yes MLI		PPT
10	Cyprus*	No	No	
11	Czechia	No	No	
12	Estonia	No	Yes MLI	PPT
13	Finland	Yes MLI		PPT
14	France	Yes MLI		PPT
15	Georgia	No	No	
16	Germany	No	No	
17	Hungary	Yes MLI		PPT
18	India	Yes MLI		PPT+LOB
19	Iran*	No	No	
20	Ireland	Yes MLI		PPT

[84] For its agreements listed under the MLI, Kazakhstan is implementing the preamble statement (Article 6 of the MLI) and the PPT (Article 7 of the MLI). Kazakhstan has also adopted the simplified LOB pursuant to Article 7(6) of the MLI.

21	Italy	No	Yes MLI	PPT
22	Japan	Yes MLI		PPT
23	Korea	Yes MLI		PPT
24	Kyrgyzstan*	No	No	
25	Latvia	Yes MLI		PPT
26	Lithuania	Yes MLI		PPT
27	Luxembourg	Yes MLI		PPT
28	Malaysia	Yes MLI		PPT
29	Moldova*	No	No	
30	Mongolia	No	Yes MLI	
31	Netherlands	Yes MLI		PPT
32	North Macedonia	No	Yes MLI	
33	Norway	No	No	
34	Pakistan	Yes MLI		PPT+LOB
35	Poland	Yes MLI		PPT
36	Qatar	Yes MLI		PPT+LOB
37	Romania	No	Yes MLI	PPT
38	Russian Federation	Yes MLI		PPT+LOB
39	Saudi Arabia	Yes MLI		PPT
40	Serbia	Yes MLI		PPT
41	Singapore	Yes MLI		PPT
42	Slovak Republic	Yes MLI		PPT+LOB
43	Slovenia	Yes MLI		PPT
44	Spain	Yes MLI		PPT
45	Sweden	No	Yes MLI	PPT
46	Switzerland	No	No	
47	Tajikistan*	No	No	
48	Türkiye	No	Yes MLI	PPT
49	Turkmenistan*	No	No	
50	Ukraine	Yes MLI		PPT
51	United Arab Emirates	Yes MLI		PPT
52	United Kingdom	Yes MLI		PPT
53	United States	No	No	
54	Uzbekistan	No	No	
55	Viet Nam	No	Yes MLI	

Kenya

A. Progress in the implementation of the minimum standard

Kenya has 15 tax agreements in force as reported in its response to the Peer Review questionnaire. None of those agreements comply with the minimum standard.

Kenya signed the MLI in 2019. The agreements modified by the MLI come into compliance with the minimum standard once the provisions of the MLI take effect.

Kenya indicated has not listed its agreements with Germany, Korea and Zambia under the MLI, but indicated in its response to the Peer Review questionnaire that steps have been taken (other than under the MLI) to implement the minimum standard in its agreement with Germany and Korea. Korea has listed its agreement with Kenya under the MLI.

Kenya is implementing the minimum standard through the inclusion of the preamble statement and the PPT combined with the LOB.[85]

B. Conclusion

Korea has listed its agreement with Kenya under the MLI, which amounts to a request to implement the minimum standard.

Kenya has developed a plan for the implementation of the minimum standard in its agreement with Zambia. Kenya indicated in its response to the Peer Review questionnaire that it intends to expand its list of agreements to be covered under the MLI to include that agreement.

Recommendation

It is recommended that Kenya completes the steps to have the MLI take effect with respect to its agreements listed under the MLI as those agreements will only be modified by the MLI (and come into compliance with the minimum standard) once the provisions of the MLI take effect.

Summary of the jurisdiction response - Kenya

	1.Treaty partners	2. Compliance with the standard	3. Signature of a complying instrument	4. Minimum standard provision used
1	Canada	No	Yes MLI	PPT
2	Denmark	No	Yes MLI	PPT+LOB
3	France	No	Yes MLI	
4	Germany	No	No	
5	India	No	Yes MLI	PPT+LOB
6	Korea	No	No	
7	Norway	No	No	

85 For its agreements listed under the MLI, Kenya is implementing the preamble statement (Article 6 of the MLI) and the PPT combined with the LOB (Article 7 of the MLI).

8	Qatar	No	Yes MLI	PPT
9	Seychelles	No	Yes MLI	PPT
10	South Africa	No	Yes MLI	PPT
11	Sweden	No	Yes MLI	PPT
12	United Arab Emirates	No	Yes MLI	PPT
13	United Kingdom	No	Yes MLI	PPT

Other agreements

	1.Treaty partners	2. Inclusive Framework member
1	Iran*	No
2	Zambia	Yes

Korea

A. Progress in the implementation of the minimum standard

Korea has 94 tax agreements in force as reported in its response to the Peer Review questionnaire. Fifty-seven of those agreements comply with the minimum standard.

Korea signed the MLI in 2017 and deposited its instrument of ratification on 13 May 2020. The MLI entered into force for Korea on 1 September 2020. The agreements modified by the MLI come into compliance with the minimum standard once the provisions of the MLI take effect.

Korea has not listed its agreements with Albania, Belarus, Brazil and Germany, but indicated in its response to the Peer Review questionnaire that steps have been taken (other than under the MLI) to implement the minimum standard in the agreements with Albania, Belarus, Brazil, Ecuador*, Ethiopia*, Germany, Iran*, Kyrgyzstan*, Lao People's Democratic Republic*, Myanmar*, Nepal*, and Venezuela*. Albania and Türkiye have listed their agreements with Korea under the MLI.

Korea has signed a bilateral complying instrument with respect to its agreement with Türkiye.

Korea is implementing the minimum standard through the inclusion of the preamble statement and the PPT.[86]

B. Conclusion

No jurisdiction has raised any concerns about their agreements with Korea.

Albania has listed their agreements with Korea under the MLI, which amount to requests to implement the minimum standard.

Summary of the jurisdiction response - Korea

	1.Treaty partners	2. Compliance with the standard	3. Signature of a complying instrument	4. Minimum standard provision used
1	Albania	No	No	PPT
2	Algeria*	No	No	PPT
3	Australia	Yes MLI		PPT
4	Austria	Yes other		PPT
5	Azerbaijan	No	No	PPT
6	Bahrain	Yes MLI		PPT
7	Bangladesh*	No	No	PPT
8	Belarus	No	No	PPT
9	Belgium	Yes MLI		PPT
10	Brazil	No	No	PPT
11	Brunei Darussalam	No	No	PPT
12	Bulgaria	Yes MLI		PPT
13	Cambodia*	Yes other		PPT
14	Canada	Yes MLI		PPT

[86] For its agreements listed under the MLI, Korea is implementing the preamble statement (Article 6 of the MLI) and the PPT (Article 7 of the MLI).

15	Chile	Yes MLI		PPT
16	China (People's Republic of)	Yes MLI		PPT
17	Colombia	No	Yes MLI	PPT
18	Croatia	Yes MLI		PPT
19	Czechia	Yes other		PPT
20	Denmark	Yes MLI		PPT
21	Ecuador*	No	No	PPT
22	Egypt	Yes MLI		PPT
23	Estonia	No	Yes MLI	PPT
24	Ethiopia*	No	No	PPT
25	Fiji*	No	Yes MLI	PPT
26	Finland	Yes MLI		PPT
27	France	Yes MLI		PPT
28	Gabon	No	No	PPT
29	Georgia	Yes MLI		PPT
30	Germany	No	No	PPT
31	Greece	Yes MLI		PPT
32	Hong Kong (China)	Yes MLI		PPT
33	Hungary	Yes MLI		PPT
34	Iceland	Yes MLI		PPT
35	India	Yes MLI		PPT
36	Indonesia	Yes MLI		PPT
37	Iran*	No	No	PPT
38	Ireland	Yes MLI		PPT
39	Israel	Yes MLI		PPT
40	Italy	No	Yes MLI	PPT
41	Japan	Yes MLI		PPT
42	Jordan	Yes MLI		PPT
43	Kazakhstan	Yes MLI		PPT
44	Kenya	No	No	PPT
45	Kuwait	No	Yes MLI	PPT
46	Kyrgyzstan*	No	No	PPT
47	Lao People's Democratic Republic*	No	No	PPT
48	Latvia	Yes MLI		PPT
49	Lithuania	Yes MLI		PPT
50	Luxembourg	Yes MLI		PPT
51	Malaysia	Yes MLI		PPT
52	Malta	Yes MLI		PPT
53	Mexico	No	Yes MLI	PPT
54	Mongolia	No	Yes MLI	PPT
55	Morocco	No	Yes MLI	PPT
56	Myanmar*	No	No	PPT
57	Nepal*	No	No	PPT
58	Netherlands	Yes MLI		PPT
59	New Zealand	Yes MLI		PPT
60	Norway	No	No	PPT
61	Oman	Yes MLI		PPT
62	Pakistan	Yes MLI		PPT
63	Panama	Yes MLI		PPT
64	Papua New Guinea	No	Yes MLI	PPT
65	Peru	No	Yes MLI	PPT
66	Philippines	No	No	PPT
67	Poland	Yes MLI		PPT

68	Portugal	Yes MLI		PPT
69	Qatar	Yes MLI		PPT
70	Romania	No	Yes MLI	PPT
71	Russian Federation	Yes MLI		PPT
72	Saudi Arabia	Yes MLI		PPT
73	Serbia	Yes MLI		PPT
74	Singapore	Yes other		PPT
75	Slovak Republic	Yes MLI		PPT
76	Slovenia	Yes MLI		PPT
77	South Africa	Yes MLI		PPT
78	Spain	Yes MLI		PPT
79	Sri Lanka	No	No	PPT
80	Sweden	No	Yes MLI	PPT
81	Switzerland	Yes other		PPT
82	Tajikistan*	Yes other		PPT
83	Thailand	Yes MLI		PPT
84	Tunisia	No	Yes MLI	PPT
85	Türkiye	No	Yes other	PPT
86	Turkmenistan*	Yes other		PPT
87	Ukraine	Yes MLI		PPT
88	United Arab Emirates	Yes MLI		PPT
89	United Kingdom	Yes MLI		PPT
90	United States	No	No	
91	Uruguay	Yes MLI		PPT
92	Uzbekistan	Yes other		PPT
93	Venezuela*	No	No	PPT
94	Viet Nam	No	Yes MLI	PPT

Latvia

A. Progress in the implementation of the minimum standard

Latvia has 64 tax agreements in force as reported in its response to the Peer Review questionnaire. Forty-four of those agreements comply with the minimum standard.

Latvia signed the MLI in 2017 and deposited its instrument of ratification on 29 October 2019. The MLI entered into force for Latvia on 1 February 2020. On 20 April 2020, Latvia made an additional notification to expand its list of agreements to be covered under the MLI. The agreements modified by the MLI come into compliance with the minimum standard once the provisions of the MLI take effect.

Latvia has not listed its agreement with Germany under the MLI but indicated in its response to the Peer Review questionnaire that steps have been taken (other than under the MLI) to implement the minimum standard in this agreement.

Latvia is implementing the minimum standard through the inclusion of the preamble statement and the PPT.[87]

B. Conclusion

No jurisdiction has raised any concerns about their agreements with Latvia.

Summary of the jurisdiction response - Latvia

	1.Treaty partners	2. Compliance with the standard	3. Signature of a complying instrument	4. Minimum standard provision used
1	Albania	Yes MLI		PPT
2	Armenia	No	Yes MLI	PPT
3	Austria	Yes MLI		PPT
4	Azerbaijan	No	No	PPT
5	Belarus	No	No	PPT
6	Belgium	Yes MLI		PPT
7	Bulgaria	Yes MLI		PPT
8	Canada	Yes MLI		PPT
9	China (People's Republic of)	Yes MLI		PPT
10	Croatia	Yes MLI		PPT
11	Cyprus*	Yes MLI		PPT
12	Czechia	Yes MLI		PPT
13	Denmark	Yes MLI		PPT
14	Estonia	Yes MLI		PPT
15	Finland	Yes MLI		PPT
16	France	Yes MLI		PPT
17	Georgia	Yes MLI		PPT
18	Germany	No	No	PPT
19	Greece	Yes MLI		PPT

[87] For its agreements listed under the MLI, Latvia is implementing the preamble statement (Article 6 of the MLI) and the PPT (Article 7 of the MLI).

20	Hong Kong (China)	Yes MLI		PPT
21	Hungary	Yes MLI		PPT
22	Iceland	Yes MLI		PPT
23	India	Yes MLI		PPT
24	Ireland	Yes MLI		PPT
25	Israel	Yes MLI		PPT
26	Italy	No	Yes MLI	PPT
27	Japan	Yes other		PPT+LOB
28	Kazakhstan	Yes MLI		PPT
29	Korea	Yes MLI		PPT
30	Kosovo*	Yes other		PPT
31	Kuwait	No	No	PPT
32	Kyrgyzstan*	No	No	PPT
33	Lithuania	Yes MLI		PPT
34	Luxembourg	Yes MLI		PPT
35	Malta	Yes MLI		PPT
36	Mexico	No	Yes MLI	PPT
37	Moldova*	No	No	PPT
38	Montenegro	No	No	PPT
39	Morocco	No	Yes MLI	PPT
40	Netherlands	Yes MLI		PPT
41	North Macedonia	No	Yes MLI	PPT
42	Norway	Yes MLI		PPT
43	Poland	Yes MLI		PPT
44	Portugal	Yes MLI		PPT
45	Qatar	Yes MLI		PPT
46	Romania	No	Yes MLI	PPT
47	Russian Federation	Yes MLI		PPT
48	Saudi Arabia	Yes other		PPT
49	Serbia	Yes MLI		PPT
50	Singapore	Yes MLI		PPT
51	Slovak Republic	Yes MLI		PPT
52	Slovenia	Yes MLI		PPT
53	Spain	Yes MLI		PPT
54	Sweden	No	Yes MLI	PPT
55	Switzerland	Yes other		PPT
56	Tajikistan*	No	No	PPT
57	Türkiye	No	Yes MLI	PPT
58	Turkmenistan*	No	No	PPT
59	Ukraine	Yes MLI		PPT
60	United Arab Emirates	Yes MLI		PPT
61	United Kingdom	Yes MLI		PPT
62	United States	No	No	
63	Uzbekistan	No	No	PPT
64	Viet Nam	No	Yes MLI	PPT

Liberia

A. Progress in the implementation of the minimum standard

Liberia has three tax agreements in force, as reported in its response to the Peer Review questionnaire, including the multilateral Supplementary Act A/SA, 5/12/18 adopting community rules for the elimination of double taxation with respect to taxes on income, capital and inheritance and the prevention of tax evasion and avoidance within the ECOWAS Member States (the ECOWAS Supplementary Act) concluded with fourteen treaty partners. Two of those agreements, including the ECOWAS Supplementary Act, comply with the minimum standard. Liberia has not signed the MLI.

Liberia indicated in its response to the Peer Review questionnaire that steps have been taken (other than under the MLI) to implement the minimum standard in its agreement with Germany.

Liberia is implementing the minimum standard through the inclusion of the preamble statement and the PPT.

B. Conclusion

No jurisdiction has raised any concerns about their agreements with Liberia.

Summary of the jurisdiction response - Liberia

	1.Treaty partners	2. Compliance with the standard	3. Signature of a complying instrument	4. Minimum standard provision used
1	Morocco	Yes other		PPT
2	Germany	No	No	
3	ECOWAS Supplementary Act treaty partners (Benin, Burkina Faso, Cabo Verde, Côte d'Ivoire, The Gambia*, Ghana*, Guinea-Bissau*, Guinea Conakry*, Mali*, Niger*, Nigeria, Senegal, Sierra Leone, Togo)	Yes other		PPT

Liechtenstein

A. Progress in the implementation of the minimum standard

Liechtenstein has 21 tax agreements in force as reported in its response to the Peer Review questionnaire. Each of its agreements complies with the minimum standard.

Liechtenstein signed the MLI in 2017 and deposited its instrument of ratification on 19 December 2019. The MLI entered into force for Liechtenstein on 1 April 2020. The agreements modified by the MLI come into compliance with the minimum standard once the provisions of the MLI take effect.

Liechtenstein is implementing the minimum standard through the inclusion of the preamble statement and the PPT.[88]

B. Conclusion

No jurisdiction has raised any concerns about their agreements with Liechtenstein.

Summary of the jurisdiction response – Liechtenstein

	1.Treaty partners	2. Compliance with the standard	3. Signature of a complying instrument	4. Minimum standard provision used
1	Andorra	Yes MLI		PPT
2	Austria	Yes other		PPT
3	Czechia	Yes MLI		PPT
4	Georgia	Yes MLI		PPT
5	Germany	Yes other		PPT
6	Guernsey	Yes MLI		PPT
7	Hong Kong (China)	Yes MLI		PPT
8	Hungary	Yes MLI		PPT
9	Iceland	Yes other		PPT
10	Jersey	Yes other		PPT
11	Lithuania	Yes other		PPT
12	Luxembourg	Yes MLI		PPT
13	Malta	Yes MLI		PPT
14	Monaco	Yes other		PPT
15	Netherlands	Yes other		PPT
16	San Marino	Yes MLI		PPT
17	Singapore	Yes MLI		PPT
18	Switzerland	Yes other		PPT
19	United Arab Emirates	Yes MLI		PPT
20	United Kingdom	Yes MLI		PPT
21	Uruguay	Yes MLI		PPT

88 For its agreements listed under the MLI, Liechtenstein is implementing the preamble statement (Article 6 of the MLI) and the PPT (Article 7 of the MLI).

Lithuania

A. Progress in the implementation of the minimum standard

Lithuania has 58 tax agreements in force as reported in its response to the Peer Review questionnaire. Forty-one of those agreements comply with the minimum standard.

Lithuania signed the MLI in 2017 and deposited its instrument of ratification on 11 September 2018. The MLI entered into force for the Lithuania on 1 January 2019. The agreements modified by the MLI come into compliance with the minimum standard once the provisions of the MLI take effect.

Lithuania has signed a bilateral complying instrument with respect to its agreement with Germany[89].

Lithuania is implementing the minimum standard through the inclusion of the preamble statement and the PPT.[90]

B. Conclusion

No jurisdiction has raised any concerns about their agreements with Lithuania.

Summary of the jurisdiction response - Lithuania

	1.Treaty partners	2. Compliance with the standard	3. Signature of a complying instrument	4. Minimum standard provision used
1	Armenia	No	Yes MLI	PPT
2	Austria	Yes MLI		PPT
3	Azerbaijan-	No	No	PPT
4	Belarus	No	No	PPT
5	Belgium	Yes MLI		PPT
6	Bulgaria	Yes MLI		PPT
7	Canada	Yes MLI		PPT
8	China (People's Republic of)	Yes MLI		PPT
9	Croatia	Yes MLI		PPT
10	Cyprus*	Yes MLI		PPT
11	Czechia	Yes MLI		PPT
12	Denmark	Yes MLI		PPT
13	Estonia	Yes MLI		PPT
14	Finland	Yes MLI		PPT
15	France	Yes MLI		PPT
16	Georgia	Yes MLI		PPT
17	Germany	No	Yes other	PPT
18	Greece	Yes MLI		PPT
19	Hungary	Yes MLI		PPT
20	Iceland	Yes MLI		PPT
21	India	Yes MLI		PPT

[89] Lithuania ratified the complying instrument with respect to the agreement with Germany on 23 May 2023.

[90] For its agreements listed under the MLI, Lithuania is implementing the preamble statement (Article 6 of the MLI) and the PPT (Article 7 of the MLI).

22	Ireland	Yes MLI		PPT
23	Israel	Yes MLI		PPT
24	Italy	No	Yes MLI	PPT
25	Japan	Yes other		PPT+LOB
26	Kazakhstan	Yes MLI		PPT
27	Korea	Yes MLI		PPT
28	Kosovo*	Yes other		PPT
29	Kuwait	No	Yes MLI	PPT
30	Kyrgyzstan*	No	No	PPT
31	Latvia	Yes MLI		PPT
32	Liechtenstein	Yes other		PPT
33	Luxembourg	Yes MLI		PPT
34	Malta	Yes MLI		PPT
35	Mexico	No	Yes MLI	PPT
36	Moldova*	No	No	PPT
37	Morocco	No	Yes MLI	PPT
38	Netherlands	Yes MLI		PPT
39	North Macedonia	No	Yes MLI	PPT
40	Norway	Yes MLI		PPT
41	Poland	Yes MLI		PPT
42	Portugal	Yes MLI		PPT
43	Romania	No	Yes MLI	PPT
44	Russian Federation	Yes MLI		PPT
45	Serbia	Yes MLI		PPT
46	Singapore	Yes MLI		PPT
47	Slovak Republic	Yes MLI		PPT
48	Slovenia	Yes MLI		PPT
49	Spain	Yes MLI		PPT
50	Sweden	No	Yes MLI	PPT
51	Switzerland	Yes MLI		PPT
52	Türkiye	No	Yes MLI	PPT
53	Turkmenistan*	No	No	PPT
54	Ukraine	Yes MLI		PPT
55	United Arab Emirates	Yes MLI		PPT
56	United Kingdom	Yes MLI		PPT
57	United States	No	No	
58	Uzbekistan	No	No	PPT

Luxembourg

A. Progress in the implementation of the minimum standard

Luxembourg has 84 tax agreements in force as reported in its response to the Peer Review questionnaire. Sixty-two of those agreements comply with the minimum standard.

Luxembourg signed the MLI in 2017 and deposited its instrument of ratification on 9 April 2019, listing its non-compliant agreements. The MLI entered into force for Luxembourg on 1 August 2019. The agreements modified by the MLI come into compliance with the minimum standard once the provisions of the MLI take effect.

Luxembourg is implementing the minimum standard through the inclusion of the preamble statement and the PPT.[91]

B. Conclusion

No jurisdiction has raised any concerns about their agreements with Luxembourg.

Summary of the jurisdiction response - Luxembourg

	1.Treaty partners	2. Compliance with the standard	3. Signature of a complying instrument	4. Minimum standard provision used
1	Andorra	Yes MLI		PPT
2	Armenia	No	Yes MLI	PPT
3	Austria	Yes MLI		PPT
4	Azerbaijan	No	No	PPT
5	Bahrain	Yes MLI		PPT
6	Barbados	Yes MLI		PPT
7	Belgium	Yes MLI		PPT
8	Botswana	Yes other		PPT
9	Brazil	No	No	PPT
10	Brunei Darussalam	No	No	PPT
11	Bulgaria	Yes MLI		PPT
12	Canada	Yes MLI		PPT
13	China (People's Republic of)	Yes MLI		PPT
14	Chinese Taipei*	No	No	PPT
15	Croatia	Yes MLI		PPT
16	Cyprus*	Yes other		PPT
17	Czechia	Yes MLI		PPT
18	Denmark	Yes MLI		PPT
19	Estonia	No	Yes MLI	PPT
20	Finland	Yes MLI		PPT

[91] For its agreements listed under the MLI, Luxembourg is implementing the preamble statement (Article 6 of the MLI) and the PPT (Article 7 of the MLI). Luxembourg has made a reservation pursuant to Article 6(4) MLI not to apply Article 6(1) of the MLI with respect to agreements that already contain the relevant preamble language (covering one agreement). Luxembourg has also made a reservation pursuant to Article 7(15)(b) MLI not to apply Article 7(1) of the MLI with respect to agreements that already contain a PPT (covering one agreement).

21	France	Yes other		PPT
22	Georgia	Yes MLI		PPT
23	Germany	No	Yes MLI	PPT
24	Greece	Yes MLI		PPT
25	Guernsey	Yes MLI		PPT
26	Hong Kong (China)	Yes MLI		PPT
27	Hungary	Yes MLI		PPT
28	Iceland	Yes MLI		PPT
29	India	Yes MLI		PPT
30	Indonesia	Yes MLI		PPT
31	Ireland	Yes MLI		PPT
32	Isle of Man	Yes MLI		PPT
33	Israel	Yes MLI		PPT
34	Italy	No	Yes MLI	PPT
35	Japan	Yes MLI		PPT
36	Jersey	Yes MLI		PPT
37	Kazakhstan	Yes MLI		PPT
38	Korea	Yes MLI		PPT
39	Kosovo*	Yes other		PPT
40	Lao People's Democratic Republic*	No	No	PPT
41	Latvia	Yes MLI		PPT
42	Liechtenstein	Yes MLI		PPT
43	Lithuania	Yes MLI		PPT
44	Malaysia	Yes MLI		PPT
45	Malta	Yes MLI		PPT
46	Mauritius	Yes MLI		PPT
47	Mexico	No	Yes MLI	PPT
48	Moldova*	No	No	PPT
49	Monaco	Yes MLI		PPT
50	Morocco	No	Yes MLI	PPT
51	Netherlands	Yes MLI		PPT
52	North Macedonia	No	Yes MLI	PPT
53	Norway	Yes MLI		PPT
54	Panama	Yes MLI		PPT
55	Poland	Yes MLI		PPT
56	Portugal	Yes MLI		PPT
57	Qatar	Yes MLI		PPT
58	Romania	No	Yes MLI	PPT
59	Russian Federation	Yes MLI		PPT
60	San Marino	Yes MLI		PPT
61	Saudi Arabia	Yes MLI		PPT
62	Senegal	Yes other		PPT
63	Serbia	Yes MLI		PPT
64	Seychelles	Yes MLI		PPT
65	Singapore	Yes MLI		PPT
66	Slovak Republic	Yes MLI		PPT
67	Slovenia	Yes MLI		PPT
68	South Africa	Yes MLI		PPT
69	Spain	Yes MLI		PPT
70	Sri Lanka	No	No	PPT
71	Sweden	No	Yes MLI	PPT
72	Switzerland	Yes MLI		PPT
73	Tajikistan*	No	No	PPT

74	Thailand	Yes MLI		PPT
75	Trinidad and Tobago	No	No	PPT
76	Tunisia	No	Yes MLI	PPT
77	Türkiye	No	Yes MLI	PPT
78	Ukraine	Yes MLI		PPT
79	United Arab Emirates	Yes MLI		PPT
80	United Kingdom	Yes MLI		PPT
81	United States	No	No	D-LOB
82	Uruguay	Yes MLI		PPT
83	Uzbekistan	Yes other		PPT
84	Viet Nam	No	Yes MLI	PPT

Macau (China)

A. Progress in the implementation of the minimum standard

Macau (China) has four tax agreements in force, as reported in its response to the Peer Review questionnaire. None of those agreements comply with the minimum standard.

Macau (China) has not joined the MLI.

Macau (China) indicated in its response to the Peer Review questionnaire that steps have been taken (other than under the MLI) to implement the minimum standard in its agreements with Cabo Verde, Mozambique*, Portugal and Viet Nam.

B. Conclusion

No jurisdiction has raised any concerns about their agreements with Macau (China).

Summary of the jurisdiction response – Macau (China)

	1.Treaty partners	2. Compliance with the standard	3. Signature of a complying instrument	4. Minimum standard provision used
1	Cabo Verde	No	No	PPT
2	Mozambique*	No	No	PPT
3	Portugal	No	No	
4	Viet Nam	No	No	

Malaysia

A. Progress in the implementation of the minimum standard

Malaysia has 74 tax agreements in force as reported in its response to the Peer Review questionnaire. Forty-four of those comply with the minimum standard.

Malaysia signed the MLI in 2018 and deposited its instrument of ratification on 18 February 2021, listing its non-compliant agreements in force at the time. On 10 November 2022, Malaysia made an additional notification to expand its list of agreements to be covered under the MLI. The MLI entered into force for Malaysia on 1 June 2021. The agreements modified by the MLI come into compliance with the minimum standard once the provisions of the MLI take effect.

Malaysia is implementing the minimum standard through the inclusion of the preamble statement and the PPT.[92]

B. Conclusion

No jurisdiction has raised any concerns about their agreements with Malaysia.

Summary of the jurisdiction response - Malaysia

	1.Treaty partners	2. Compliance with the standard	3. Signature of a complying instrument	4. Minimum standard provision used
1	Albania	Yes MLI		PPT
2	Australia	Yes MLI		PPT
3	Austria	No	No	PPT
4	Bahrain	Yes MLI		PPT
5	Bangladesh*	No	No	PPT
6	Belgium	Yes MLI		PPT
7	Bosnia-Herzegovina	Yes MLI		PPT
8	Brunei Darussalam	No	No	PPT
9	Cambodia*	Yes other		PPT
10	Canada	Yes MLI		PPT
11	Chile	Yes MLI		PPT
12	China (People's Republic of)	Yes MLI		PPT
13	Croatia	Yes MLI		PPT
14	Czechia	No	No	PPT
15	Denmark	Yes MLI		PPT
16	Egypt	Yes MLI		PPT
17	Fiji*	No	Yes MLI	PPT
18	Finland	Yes MLI		PPT
19	France	Yes MLI		PPT
20	Germany	No	No	PPT
21	Hong Kong (China)	Yes MLI		PPT
22	Hungary	Yes MLI		PPT

92 For its agreements listed under the MLI, Malaysia is implementing the preamble statement (Article 6 of the MLI) and the PPT (Article 7 of the MLI).

23	India	Yes MLI		PPT
24	Indonesia	Yes MLI		PPT
25	Iran*	No	No	PPT
26	Ireland	Yes MLI		PPT
27	Italy	No	Yes MLI	PPT
28	Japan	Yes MLI		PPT
29	Jordan	Yes MLI		PPT
30	Kazakhstan	Yes MLI		PPT
31	Korea	Yes MLI		PPT
32	Kuwait	No	Yes MLI	PPT
33	Kyrgyzstan*	No	No	PPT
34	Lao People's Democratic Republic*	No	No	PPT
35	Lebanon*	No	No	PPT
36	Luxembourg	Yes MLI		PPT
37	Malta	Yes MLI		PPT
38	Mauritius	Yes MLI		PPT
39	Mongolia	No	Yes MLI	PPT
40	Morocco	No	Yes MLI	PPT
41	Myanmar*	No	No	PPT
42	Namibia	No	Yes MLI	PPT
43	Netherlands	Yes MLI		PPT
44	New Zealand	Yes MLI		PPT
45	Norway	No	No	PPT
46	Pakistan	Yes MLI		PPT
47	Papua New Guinea	No	Yes MLI	PPT
48	Philippines	No	No	PPT
49	Poland	Yes MLI		PPT
50	Qatar	Yes MLI		PPT
51	Romania	Yes MLI		PPT
52	Russian Federation	Yes MLI		PPT
53	San Marino	Yes MLI		PPT
54	Saudi Arabia	Yes MLI		PPT
55	Seychelles	Yes MLI		PPT
56	Singapore	Yes MLI		PPT
57	Slovak Republic	Yes MLI		PPT
58	South Africa	Yes MLI		PPT
59	Spain	Yes MLI		PPT
60	Sri Lanka	No	No	PPT
61	Sudan*	No	No	PPT
62	Sweden	No	Yes MLI	PPT
63	Switzerland	No	No	PPT
64	Syrian Arab Republic*	No	No	PPT
65	Thailand	Yes MLI		PPT
66	Türkiye	No	Yes MLI	PPT
67	Turkmenistan*	No	No	PPT
68	Ukraine	Yes MLI		PPT
69	United Arab Emirates	Yes MLI		PPT
70	United Kingdom	Yes MLI		PPT
71	Uzbekistan	No	No	PPT
72	Venezuela*	No	No	PPT
73	Viet Nam	No	Yes MLI	PPT
74	Zimbabwe*	No	No	PPT

Maldives

A. Progress in the implementation of the minimum standard

The Maldives has one tax agreement in force[93], the agreement with the United Arab Emirates, as reported in its response to the Peer Review questionnaire. This agreement does not comply with the minimum standard.

The Maldives has not signed the MLI.

The Maldives indicated in its response to the Peer Review questionnaire that steps have been taken (other than under the MLI) to implement the minimum standard in its agreement with the United Arab Emirates.

B. Conclusion

No jurisdiction has raised any concerns about their agreements with the Maldives.

Summary of the jurisdiction response – Maldives

	1.Treaty partners	2. Compliance with the standard	3. Signature of a complying instrument	4. Minimum standard provision used
1	United Arab Emirates	No	No	

[93] The Maldives has also concluded an agreement with Bangladesh*, which was ratified on 23 December 2021.

Malta

A. Progress in the implementation of the minimum standard

Malta has 78 tax agreements in force, as reported in its response to the Peer Review questionnaire. Fifty-six of those agreements comply with the minimum standard.

Malta signed the MLI in 2017 and deposited its instrument of ratification on 18 December 2018. The MLI entered into force for Malta on 1 April 2019. The agreements modified by the MLI come into compliance with the minimum standard once the provisions of the MLI take effect.[94]

Malta has not listed its agreements with Botswana, Bulgaria and Monaco under the MLI, but indicated in its response to the Peer Review questionnaire that steps have been taken (other than under the MLI) to implement the minimum standard in the agreements with Botswana, Bulgaria, Georgia, Moldova*, Monaco, Montenegro and the United States.

Malta is implementing the minimum standard through the inclusion of the preamble statement and the PPT.[95]

B. Conclusion

No jurisdiction has raised any concerns about their agreements with Malta.

Summary of the jurisdiction response – Malta

	1.Treaty partners	2. Compliance with the standard	3. Signature of a complying instrument	4. Minimum standard provision used
1	Albania	Yes MLI		PPT
2	Andorra	Yes MLI		PPT
3	Armenia	Yes other		PPT
4	Australia	Yes MLI		PPT
5	Austria	Yes MLI		PPT
6	Azerbaijan	No	No	
7	Bahrain	Yes MLI		PPT
8	Barbados	Yes MLI		PPT
9	Belgium	Yes MLI		PPT
10	Botswana	No	No	
11	Bulgaria	No	No	
12	Canada	Yes MLI		PPT
13	China (People's Republic of)	Yes MLI		PPT
14	Croatia	Yes MLI		PPT
15	Cyprus*	Yes MLI		PPT

[94] Malta chose to replace, under Article 35(3) of the MLI, the reference to "taxable periods beginning on or after the expiration of a period" with a reference to "taxable periods beginning on or after 1 January of the next calendar year beginning on or after the expiration of a period" for the purposes of its own application of Article 35(1)(b) and (5)(b) (Entry into effect) of the MLI.

[95] For its agreements listed under the MLI, Malta is implementing the preamble statement (Article 6 of the MLI) and the PPT (Article 7 of the MLI).

16	Czechia	Yes MLI		
17	Denmark	Yes MLI		PPT
18	Egypt	Yes MLI		PPT
19	Estonia	No	Yes MLI	PPT
20	Finland	Yes MLI		PPT
21	France	Yes MLI		PPT
22	Georgia	No	No	PPT
23	Germany	No	Yes MLI	PPT
24	Greece	Yes MLI		PPT
25	Guernsey	Yes MLI		PPT
26	Hong Kong (China)	Yes MLI		PPT
27	Hungary	Yes MLI		PPT
28	Iceland	Yes MLI		PPT
29	India	Yes MLI		PPT
30	Ireland	Yes MLI		PPT
31	Isle of Man	Yes MLI		PPT
32	Israel	Yes MLI		PPT
33	Italy	No	Yes MLI	PPT
34	Jersey	Yes MLI		PPT
35	Jordan	Yes MLI		PPT
36	Korea	Yes MLI		PPT
37	Kosovo*	Yes other		PPT
38	Kuwait	No	Yes MLI	PPT
39	Latvia	Yes MLI		PPT
40	Lebanon*	No	No	
41	Libya*	No	No	
42	Liechtenstein	Yes MLI		PPT
43	Lithuania	Yes MLI		PPT
44	Luxembourg	Yes MLI		PPT
45	Malaysia	Yes MLI		PPT
46	Mauritius	Yes MLI		PPT
47	Mexico	No	Yes MLI	PPT
48	Moldova*	No	No	
49	Monaco	No	No	
50	Montenegro	No	No	
51	Morocco	No	Yes MLI	PPT
52	Netherlands	Yes MLI		PPT
53	Norway	Yes MLI		PPT
54	Pakistan	Yes MLI		PPT
55	Poland	Yes MLI		PPT
56	Portugal	Yes MLI		PPT
57	Qatar	Yes MLI		PPT
58	Romania	No	Yes MLI	PPT
59	Russian Federation	Yes MLI		PPT
60	San Marino	Yes MLI		PPT
61	Saudi Arabia	Yes MLI		PPT
62	Serbia	Yes MLI		PPT
63	Singapore	Yes MLI		PPT
64	Slovak Republic	Yes MLI		PPT
65	Slovenia	Yes MLI		PPT
66	South Africa	Yes MLI		PPT
67	Spain	Yes MLI		PPT
68	Sweden	No	Yes MLI	PPT

69	Switzerland	Yes other		PPT
70	Syria*	No	No	
71	Tunisia	No	Yes MLI	PPT
72	Türkiye	No	Yes MLI	PPT
73	Ukraine	Yes MLI		PPT
74	United Arab Emirates	Yes MLI		PPT
75	United Kingdom	Yes MLI		PPT
76	United States	No	No	
77	Uruguay	Yes MLI		PPT
78	Viet Nam	No	Yes MLI	PPT

Mauritania

A. Progress in the implementation of the minimum standard

Mauritania has six tax agreements in force, as reported in its response to the Peer Review questionnaire, including the Arab Maghreb Union Income Agreement concluded with four treaty partners (the UMA Agreement).

None of those agreements comply with the minimum standard.

Mauritania has not signed the MLI.

B. Conclusion

Mauritania has developed a plan for the implementation of the minimum standard in its agreements with France, Senegal, Tunisia and the United Arab Emirates. Mauritania indicated in its response to the Peer Review questionnaire that it intends to sign the MLI and list those agreements to be covered.

Other agreements

This Table shows the agreements that are not compliant, not subject to a complying instrument, not covered by a general statement on the implementation of the detailed LOB and for which no steps have been taken to implement the minimum standard.

	1.Treaty partners	2. Inclusive Framework member
1	Algeria*	No
2	France	Yes
3	UMA Agreement treaty partners (Algeria*, Libya*, Morocco, Tunisia)	Yes (Morocco, Tunisia) No (Algeria*, Libya*)
4	Morocco	Yes
5	Senegal	Yes
6	Tunisia	Yes

Mauritius

A. Progress in the implementation of the minimum standard

Mauritius has 44 tax agreements in force, as reported in its response to the Peer Review questionnaire. Twenty-three of those agreements comply with the minimum standard.

Mauritius signed the MLI in 2017 and deposited its instrument of ratification on 18 October 2019. The MLI entered into force for Mauritius on 1 February 2020. The agreements modified by the MLI come into compliance with the minimum standard once the provisions of the MLI take effect.

Mauritius has not listed its agreement with India under the MLI but indicated in its response to the Peer Review questionnaire that steps have been taken (other than under the MLI) to implement the minimum standard in its agreements with Bangladesh*, Botswana, Cabo Verde, India, Jersey, Madagascar*, Mozambique*, Rwanda*, Tunisia and Uganda*. India has listed its agreement with Mauritius under the MLI.

Mauritius is implementing the minimum standard in its tax agreements through the inclusion of the preamble statement and the PPT.[96]

B. Conclusion

No jurisdiction has raised any concerns about their agreements with Mauritius.

India has listed its agreement with Mauritius under the MLI, which amounts to a request to implement the minimum standard.

Summary of the jurisdiction response - Mauritius

	1.Treaty partners	2. Compliance with the standard	3. Signature of a complying instrument	4. Minimum standard provision used
1	Bangladesh*	No	No	PPT
2	Barbados	Yes MLI		PPT
3	Belgium	Yes MLI		PPT
4	Botswana	No	No	PPT
5	Cabo Verde	No	No	PPT
6	China (People's Republic of)	Yes MLI		PPT
7	Congo	No	No	PPT
8	Croatia	Yes MLI		PPT
9	Cyprus*	Yes MLI		PPT
10	Egypt	Yes MLI		PPT
11	Estonia	Yes other		PPT
12	Eswatini	No	No	PPT
13	France	Yes MLI		PPT
14	Germany	Yes other		PPT
15	Ghana*	No	No	PPT

[96] For its agreements listed under the MLI, Mauritius is implementing the preamble statement (Article 6 of the MLI) and the PPT (Article 7 of the MLI). Mauritius has stated that while it accepts the application of the PPT under the MLI, it intends where possible to adopt an LOB provision through bilateral negotiation.

16	Guernsey	Yes MLI		PPT
17	India	No	No	PPT
18	Italy	No	Yes MLI	PPT
19	Jersey	No	No	PPT
20	Kuwait	No	Yes MLI	PPT
21	Lesotho*	Yes other		PPT
22	Luxembourg	Yes MLI		PPT
23	Madagascar*	No	No	PPT
24	Malaysia	Yes MLI		PPT
25	Malta	Yes MLI		PPT
26	Monaco	Yes MLI		PPT
27	Mozambique*	No	No	PPT
28	Namibia	No	Yes MLI	PPT
29	Nepal*	No	No	PPT
30	Oman	Yes MLI		PPT
31	Pakistan	Yes MLI		PPT
32	Qatar	Yes MLI		PPT
33	Rwanda*	No	No	PPT
34	Seychelles	Yes MLI		PPT
35	Singapore	Yes MLI		PPT
36	South Africa	No	Yes MLI	PPT
37	Sri Lanka	No	No	PPT
38	Sweden	No	Yes MLI	PPT
39	Thailand	Yes MLI		PPT
40	Tunisia	No	No	PPT
41	Uganda*	No	No	PPT
42	United Arab Emirates	Yes MLI		PPT
43	United Kingdom	Yes MLI		PPT
44	Zimbabwe*	No	No	PPT

Mexico

A. Progress in the implementation of the minimum standard

Mexico has 60 tax agreements in force, as reported in its response to the Peer Review questionnaire. Three of those agreements comply with the minimum standard.

Mexico signed the MLI in 2017 and deposited its instrument of ratification on 15 March 2023, listing its non-compliant agreements. The MLI entered into force for Mexico on 1 July 2023. The agreements modified by the MLI come into compliance with the minimum standard once the provisions of the MLI take effect.

Mexico has signed a bilateral complying instrument with respect to its agreement with Germany.

Mexico is implementing the minimum standard through the inclusion of the preamble statement and the PPT combined with the LOB.[97]

B. Conclusion

No jurisdiction has raised any concerns about their agreements with Mexico.

Summary of the jurisdiction response - Mexico

	1.Treaty partners	2. Compliance with the standard	3. Signature of a complying instrument	4. Minimum standard provision used
1	Argentina	Yes other		PPT+LOB
2	Australia	No	Yes MLI	PPT
3	Austria	No	Yes MLI	PPT
4	Bahrain	No	Yes MLI	PPT
5	Barbados	No	Yes MLI	PPT
6	Belgium	No	Yes MLI	PPT
7	Brazil	No	No	
8	Canada	No	Yes MLI	PPT
9	Chile	No	Yes MLI	PPT+LOB
10	China (People's Republic of)	No	Yes MLI	PPT
11	Colombia	No	Yes MLI	PPT+LOB
12	Costa Rica	No	Yes MLI	PPT
13	Czechia	No	Yes MLI	PPT
14	Denmark	No	Yes MLI	PPT+LOB
15	Ecuador*	No	No	PPT
16	Estonia	No	Yes MLI	PPT

[97] For its agreements listed under the MLI, Mexico is implementing the preamble statement (Article 6 of the MLI) and the PPT (Article 7 of the MLI). Mexico has also adopted the simplified LOB under Article 7(6) of the MLI. Mexico has made a reservation pursuant to Article 6(4) of the MLI not to apply Article 6(1) of the MLI with respect to agreements which already contain the relevant preamble language (covering four agreements). Mexico has also made a reservation pursuant to Article 7(15)(b) of the MLI not to apply Article 7(1) of the MLI with respect to agreements which already contain a PPT (covering three agreements).

17	Finland	No	Yes MLI	PPT
18	France	No	Yes MLI	PPT
19	Germany	No	Yes other	PPT
20	Greece	No	Yes MLI	PPT+LOB
21	Hong Kong (China)	No	Yes MLI	PPT
22	Hungary	No	Yes MLI	PPT
23	Iceland	No	Yes MLI	PPT+LOB
24	India	No	Yes MLI	PPT
25	Indonesia	No	Yes MLI	PPT
26	Ireland	No	Yes MLI	PPT
27	Israel	No	Yes MLI	PPT
28	Italy	No	Yes MLI	PPT
29	Jamaica	No	Yes MLI	PPT+LOB
30	Japan	No	Yes MLI	PPT
31	Korea	No	Yes MLI	PPT
32	Kuwait	No	Yes MLI	PPT
33	Latvia	No	Yes MLI	PPT
34	Lithuania	No	Yes MLI	PPT
35	Luxembourg	No	Yes MLI	PPT
36	Malta	No	Yes MLI	PPT
37	Netherlands	No	Yes MLI	PPT
38	New Zealand	No	Yes MLI	PPT
39	Norway	No	Yes MLI	PPT+LOB
40	Panama	No	Yes MLI	PPT
41	Peru	No	Yes MLI	PPT
42	Philippines	Yes other		PPT
43	Poland	No	Yes MLI	PPT
44	Portugal	No	Yes MLI	PPT
45	Qatar	No	Yes MLI	PPT
46	Romania	No	Yes MLI	PPT
47	Russian Federation	No	Yes MLI	PPT+LOB
48	Saudi Arabia	No	Yes MLI	PPT
49	Singapore	No	Yes MLI	PPT
50	Slovak Republic	No	Yes MLI	PPT+LOB
51	South Africa	No	Yes MLI	PPT
52	Spain	Yes other		PPT
53	Sweden	No	Yes MLI	PPT
54	Switzerland	No	Yes MLI	PPT
55	Türkiye	No	Yes MLI	PPT
56	Ukraine	No	Yes MLI	PPT
57	United Arab Emirates	No	Yes MLI	PPT
58	United Kingdom	No	Yes MLI	PPT
59	United States	No	No	
60	Uruguay	No	Yes MLI	PPT+LOB

Monaco

A. Progress in the implementation of the minimum standard

Monaco has eleven tax agreements in force, as reported in its response to the Peer Review questionnaire. Eight of those agreements comply with the minimum standard.

Monaco signed the MLI in 2017 and deposited its instrument of ratification on 10 January 2019. The MLI entered into force for Monaco on 1 May 2019. The agreements modified by the MLI come into compliance with the minimum standard once the provisions of the MLI take effect.

Monaco has not listed its agreement with Malta under the MLI but indicated in its response to the Peer Review questionnaire that steps have been taken (other than under the MLI) to implement the minimum standard in its agreements with Malta and Mali*.

Monaco is implementing the minimum standard through the inclusion of the preamble statement and the PPT.[98]

B. Conclusion

No jurisdiction has raised any concerns about their agreements with Monaco.

Summary of the jurisdiction response - Monaco

	1.Treaty partners	2. Compliance with the standard	3. Signature of a complying instrument	4. Minimum standard provision used
1	France	Yes MLI		PPT
2	Guernsey	Yes MLI		PPT
3	Liechtenstein	Yes other		PPT
4	Luxembourg	Yes MLI		PPT
5	Mali*	No	No	
6	Malta	No	No	
7	Mauritius	Yes MLI		PPT
8	Montenegro	Yes other		PPT
9	Qatar	Yes MLI		PPT
10	Saint Kitts and Nevis	No	No	
11	Seychelles	Yes MLI		PPT

98 For its agreements listed under the MLI, Monaco is implementing the preamble statement (Article 6 of the MLI) and the PPT (Article 7 of the MLI).

Mongolia

A. Progress in the implementation of the minimum standard

Mongolia has 26 tax agreements in force, as reported in its response to the Peer Review questionnaire. None of those agreements comply with the minimum standard.

Mongolia signed the MLI in October 2022, listing its non-compliant agreements. The agreements modified by the MLI will come into compliance with the minimum standard once the provisions of the MLI take effect.

Mongolia is implementing the minimum standard through the inclusion of the preamble statement and the PPT.[99]

B. Conclusion

Recommendation

It is recommended that Mongolia completes the steps to have the MLI take effect with respect to its agreements listed under the MLI as those agreements will only be modified by the MLI (and come into compliance with the minimum standard) once the provisions of the MLI take effect.

Summary of the jurisdiction response - Mongolia

	1.Treaty partners	2. Compliance with the standard	3. Signature of a complying instrument	4. Minimum standard provision used
1	Austria	No	No	
2	Belarus	No	No	
3	Belgium	No	Yes MLI	PPT
4	Bulgaria	No	Yes MLI	PPT
5	Canada	No	Yes MLI	PPT
6	China (People's Republic of)	No	Yes MLI	PPT
7	Czechia	No	No	
8	Democratic People's Republic of Korea*	No	No	
9	France	No	Yes MLI	PPT
10	Germany	No	No	
11	Hungary	No	No	
12	India	No	Yes MLI	PPT+LOB
13	Indonesia	No	No	
14	Italy	No	Yes MLI	PPT
15	Kazakhstan	No	Yes MLI	PPT+LOB
16	Korea	No	Yes MLI	PPT
17	Kyrgyzstan*	No	No	

99 For its agreements listed under the MLI, Mongolia is implementing the preamble statement (Article 6 of the MLI) and the PPT (Article 7 of the MLI).

18	Malaysia	No	Yes MLI	PPT
19	Poland	No	Yes MLI	PPT
20	Russian Federation	No	Yes MLI	PPT+LOB
21	Singapore	No	Yes MLI	PPT
22	Switzerland	No	No	
23	Türkiye	No	Yes MLI	PPT
24	Ukraine	No	Yes MLI	PPT
25	United Kingdom	No	Yes MLI	PPT
26	Viet Nam	No	Yes MLI	PPT

Montenegro

A. Progress in the implementation of the minimum standard

Montenegro has 43 tax agreements in force, as reported in its response to the Peer Review questionnaire. None of those agreements comply with the minimum standard.

Montenegro has not signed the MLI.

Montenegro indicated in its response to the Peer Review questionnaire that steps have been taken (other than under the MLI) to implement the minimum standard in its agreements with Czechia, Poland, the Slovak Republic and Slovenia.

Montenegro indicated in its response to the Peer Review questionnaire that it intends to join the MLI.

In their responses to the Peer Review questionnaire, Hungary, Italy and Sweden indicated that their agreements with Montenegro did not give rise to material shopping concerns for their respective jurisdictions.

B. Conclusion

Montenegro has developed a plan for the implementation of the minimum standard in its agreements with Albania, Austria, Azerbaijan, Belarus, Belgium, Bosnia-Herzegovina, Bulgaria, China (People's Republic of), Croatia, Denmark, Egypt, Finland, France, Germany, Hungary, Ireland, Italy, Latvia, Malaysia, Malta, Netherlands, North Macedonia, Norway, Portugal, Romania, the Russian Federation, Serbia, Sri Lanka, Sweden, Switzerland, Türkiye, Ukraine, the United Emirates and the United Kingdom. Montenegro indicated in its response to the Peer Review questionnaire that it intends to sign the MLI and list those agreements to be covered.

Summary of the jurisdiction response - Montenegro

	1.Treaty partners	2. Compliance with the standard	3. Signature of a complying instrument	4. Minimum standard provision used
1	Czechia	No	No	
3	Poland	No	No	
4	Slovak Republic	No	No	
5	Slovenia	No	No	

Other agreements

	1.Treaty partners	2. Inclusive Framework member
1	Albania	Yes
2	Austria	Yes
3	Azerbaijan	Yes
4	Belarus	Yes
5	Belgium	Yes
6	Bosnia-Herzegovina	Yes
7	Bulgaria	Yes
8	China (People's Republic of)	Yes

9	Croatia	Yes
10	Cyprus*	No
11	Democratic People's Republic of Korea*	No
12	Denmark	Yes
13	Egypt	Yes
14	Finland	Yes
15	France	Yes
16	Germany	Yes
17	Hungary	Yes
18	Iran*	No
19	Ireland	Yes
20	Italy	Yes
21	Kuwait	Yes
22	Latvia	Yes
23	Malaysia	Yes
24	Malta	Yes
25	Moldova*	No
26	Netherlands	Yes
27	North Macedonia	Yes
28	Norway	Yes
29	Portugal	Yes
30	Romania	Yes
31	Russian Federation	Yes
32	Serbia	Yes
33	Sri Lanka	Yes
34	Sweden	Yes
35	Switzerland	Yes
36	Türkiye	Yes
37	Ukraine	Yes
38	United Emirates	Yes
39	United Kingdom	Yes

Montserrat

A. Progress in the implementation of the minimum standard

Montserrat has two tax agreements in force, as reported in its response to the Peer Review questionnaire. Neither of those agreements comply with the minimum standard.

Montserrat has not joined the MLI.

Montserrat indicated in its response to the Peer Review questionnaire that steps have been taken (other than under the MLI) to implement the minimum standard in its arrangement with the United Kingdom.

In its response to the Peer Review questionnaire, Switzerland indicated that its agreement with Montserrat did not give rise to material treaty shopping concerns for Switzerland.

B. Conclusion

No jurisdiction has raised any concerns about their agreements with Montserrat.

Summary of the jurisdiction response - Montserrat

	1.Treaty partners	2. Compliance with the standard	3. Signature of a complying instrument	4. Minimum standard provision used
1	United Kingdom	No	No	PPT

Other agreements

	1.Treaty partners	2. Inclusive Framework member
1	Switzerland	Yes

Morocco

A. Progress in the implementation of the minimum standard

Morocco has 65 tax agreements in force, as reported in its response to the Peer Review questionnaire, including the Arab Maghreb Union Income Agreement concluded with four treaty partners (the UMA Agreement). Two of those agreements, the agreements with Japan and Benin, comply with the minimum standard.

Morocco signed the MLI in 2019 and listed its non-compliant tax agreements. The agreements that will be modified by the MLI will come into compliance with the minimum standard once the provisions of the MLI take effect.

Morocco is implementing the minimum standard through the inclusion of the preamble statement and the PPT.[100]

B. Conclusion

Recommendation

It is recommended that Morocco completes the steps to have the MLI take effect with respect to its agreements listed under the MLI as those agreements will only be modified by the MLI (and come into compliance with the minimum standard) once the provisions of the MLI take effect.

Summary of the jurisdiction response - Morocco

	1.Treaty partners	2. Compliance with the standard	3. Signature of a complying instrument	4. Minimum standard provision used
1	Austria	No	No	PPT
2	Bahrain	No	Yes MLI	PPT
3	Belgium	No	Yes MLI	PPT
4	Benin	Yes other		PPT
5	Bulgaria	No	Yes MLI	PPT
6	Cameroon	No	Yes MLI	PPT
7	Canada	No	Yes MLI	PPT
8	China (People's Republic of)	No	Yes MLI	PPT
9	Côte d'Ivoire	No	Yes MLI	PPT
10	Croatia	No	Yes MLI	PPT
11	Czechia	No	No	PPT
12	Denmark	No	Yes MLI	PPT
13	Egypt	No	Yes MLI	PPT
14	Ethiopia*	No	No	PPT
15	Finland	No	Yes MLI	PPT

[100] For its agreements listed under the MLI, Morocco is implementing the preamble statement (Article 6 of the MLI) and the PPT (Article 7 of the MLI).

16	France	No	Yes MLI	PPT
17	Gabon	No	Yes MLI	PPT
18	Germany	No	No	PPT
19	Ghana	No	No	PPT
20	Greece	No	Yes MLI	PPT
21	Guinea*	No	No	PPT
22	Hungary	No	Yes MLI	PPT
23	India	No	Yes MLI	PPT
24	Indonesia	No	No	PPT
25	Ireland	No	Yes MLI	PPT
26	Italy	No	Yes MLI	PPT
27	Japan	Yes other		PPT
28	Jordan	No	Yes MLI	PPT
29	Korea	No	Yes MLI	PPT
30	Kuwait	No	Yes MLI	PPT
31	Latvia	No	Yes MLI	PPT
32	Lebanon*	No	No	PPT
33	Lithuania	No	Yes MLI	PPT
34	Luxembourg	No	Yes MLI	PPT
35	Madagascar	No	No	PPT
36	Malaysia	No	Yes MLI	PPT
37	Mali*	No	No	PPT
38	Malta	No	Yes MLI	PPT
39	Netherlands	No	Yes MLI	PPT
40	North Macedonia	No	Yes MLI	PPT
41	Norway	No	No	PPT
42	Oman	No	Yes MLI	PPT
43	Pakistan	No	Yes MLI	PPT
44	Partenaires conventionnels de l'UMA (Algérie*, Libye*, Mauritanie, Tunisie)	No	No	PPT
45	Poland	No	Yes MLI	PPT
46	Portugal	No	Yes MLI	PPT
47	Qatar	No	Yes MLI	PPT
48	Romania	No	Yes MLI	PPT
49	Russian Federation	No	Yes MLI	PPT
50	Rwanda*	No	No	PPT
51	Saudi Arabia	No	Yes MLI	PPT
52	Senegal	No	Yes MLI	PPT
53	Serbia	No	Yes MLI	PPT
54	Singapore	No	Yes MLI	PPT
55	Slovenia	No	Yes MLI	PPT
56	Spain	No	Yes MLI	PPT
57	Switzerland	No	No	PPT
58	Syria*	No	No	PPT
59	Türkiye	No	Yes MLI	PPT
60	Ukraine	No	Yes MLI	PPT
61	United Arab Emirates	No	Yes MLI	PPT
62	United Kingdom	No	Yes MLI	PPT
63	United States	No	No	PPT
64	Viet Nam	No	Yes MLI	PPT
65	Zambia	No	No	PPT

Namibia

A. Progress in the implementation of the minimum standard

Namibia has eleven tax agreements in force, as reported in its response to the Peer Review questionnaire. None of those agreements comply with the minimum standard.

Namibia signed the MLI in September 2021 and listed its non-compliant agreements. The agreements that will be modified by the MLI will come into compliance with the minimum standard once the provisions of the MLI take effect.

Namibia is implementing the minimum standard through the inclusion of the preamble statement and the PPT combined with the LOB.[101]

B. Conclusion

Recommendation

It is recommended that Namibia completes the steps to have the MLI take effect with respect to its agreements listed under the MLI as those agreements will only be modified by the MLI (and come into compliance with the minimum standard) once the provisions of the MLI take effect.

Summary of the jurisdiction response - Namibia

	1.Treaty partners	2. Compliance with the standard	3. Signature of a complying instrument	4. Minimum standard provision used
1	Botswana	No	No	PPT+LOB
2	France	No	Yes MLI	PPT+LOB
3	Germany	No	No	PPT+LOB
4	India	No	Yes MLI	PPT+LOB
5	Malaysia	No	Yes MLI	PPT+LOB
6	Mauritius	No	Yes MLI	PPT+LOB
7	Romania	No	Yes MLI	PPT+LOB
8	Russian Federation	No	No	PPT+LOB
9	South Africa	No	Yes MLI	PPT+LOB
10	Sweden	No	Yes MLI	PPT+LOB
11	United Kingdom	No	Yes MLI	PPT+LOB

101 For its agreements listed under the MLI, Namibia is implementing the preamble statement (Article 6 of the MLI) and the PPT (Article 7 of the MLI) and the simplified LOB (Article 7(6) of the MLI). Namibia expressed a statement, in accordance with Article 7(17)(a) of the MLI, that while it accepts the application of PPT alone as an interim measure, it intends where possible to adopt an LOB provision in addition to or in replacement of the PPT through bilateral negotiation.

Netherlands

A. Progress in the implementation of the minimum standard

The Netherlands has 94 tax agreements in force, as reported in its response to the Peer Review questionnaire. Fifty-nine of the Netherlands' agreements comply with the minimum standard.

The Netherlands signed the MLI in 2017 and deposited its instrument of acceptance on 29 March 2019. The MLI entered into force for the Netherlands on 1 July 2019. On 25 November 2021, the Netherlands made an additional notification to expand its list of agreements to be covered under the MLI. The agreements modified by the MLI come into compliance with the minimum standard once the provisions of the MLI take effect.

The Netherlands has not listed its agreements with Brazil and Spain under the MLI but indicated in its response to the Peer Review questionnaire that steps have been taken (other than under the MLI) to implement the minimum standard in those agreements, as well as in the agreements with Aruba, Bangladesh*, Curaçao, Moldova*, Suriname*, Thailand and Uganda*.

The Netherlands has signed a bilateral complying instrument with respect to its agreement with Germany.

The Netherlands' arrangements with Aruba, Curaçao and Sint Maarten* are arrangements governed by the domestic law of the Kingdom of the Netherlands.

The Netherlands is implementing the minimum standard through the inclusion of the preamble statement and the PPT.[102]

B. Conclusion

No jurisdiction has raised any concerns about their agreements with the Netherlands.

Summary of the jurisdiction response - Netherlands

	1.Treaty partners	2. Compliance with the standard	3. Signature of a complying instrument	4. Minimum standard provision used
1	Albania	Yes MLI		PPT
2	Algeria*	Yes other		PPT
3	Argentina	No	Yes MLI	PPT
4	Armenia	No	Yes MLI	PPT
5	Aruba	No	No	
6	Australia	Yes MLI		PPT
7	Austria	Yes MLI		PPT
8	Azerbaijan	No	No	PPT
9	Bahrain	Yes MLI		PPT
10	Bangladesh*	No	No	PPT
11	Barbados	Yes MLI		PPT
12	Belarus	No	No	PPT

[102] For its agreements listed under the MLI, Netherlands is implementing the preamble statement (Article 6 of the MLI) and the PPT (Article 7 of the MLI). Netherlands' agreements with Aruba, Curaçao and Sint Maarten* are not listed under the MLI as they are arrangements governed by the domestic law of the Kingdom of Netherlands.

13	Belgium	Yes MLI		PPT
14	Bosnia-Herzegovina	Yes MLI		PPT
15	Brazil	No	No	
16	Bulgaria	Yes other		PPT
17	Canada	Yes MLI		PPT
18	Chile	Yes other		PPT+LOB
19	China (People's Republic of)	Yes MLI		PPT
20	Croatia	Yes MLI		PPT
21	Curaçao	No	No	
22	Czechia	Yes MLI		PPT
23	Denmark	Yes other		PPT
24	Egypt	Yes MLI		PPT
25	Estonia	No	Yes MLI	PPT
26	Ethiopia*	No	No	PPT
27	Finland	Yes MLI		PPT
28	France	Yes MLI		PPT
29	Georgia	Yes MLI		PPT
30	Germany	Yes other		PPT
31	Ghana*	Yes other		PPT
32	Greece	Yes MLI		PPT
33	Hong Kong (China)	Yes MLI		PPT
34	Hungary	Yes MLI		PPT
35	Iceland	Yes MLI		PPT
36	India	Yes MLI		PPT
37	Indonesia	Yes MLI		PPT
38	Ireland	Yes other		PPT
39	Israel	Yes MLI		PPT
40	Italy	No	Yes MLI	PPT
41	Japan	Yes MLI		PPT+LOB
42	Jordan	Yes MLI		PPT
43	Kazakhstan	Yes MLI		PPT
44	Korea	Yes MLI		PPT
45	Kosovo*	Yes other		PPT
46	Kuwait	No	Yes MLI	PPT
47	Latvia	Yes MLI		PPT
48	Liechtenstein	Yes other		PPT
49	Lithuania	Yes MLI		PPT
50	Luxembourg	Yes MLI		PPT
51	Malaysia	Yes MLI		PPT
52	Malta	Yes MLI		PPT
53	Mexico	No	Yes MLI	PPT
54	Moldova*	No	No	PPT
55	Montenegro	No	No	PPT
56	Morocco	No	Yes MLI	PPT
57	New Zealand	Yes MLI		PPT
58	Nigeria	No	Yes MLI	PPT
59	North Macedonia	No	Yes MLI	PPT
60	Norway	Yes MLI		PPT
61	Oman	Yes MLI		PPT
62	Pakistan	Yes MLI		PPT
63	Panama	Yes MLI		PPT
64	Philippines	No	No	PPT
65	Poland	Yes other		PPT

66	Portugal	Yes MLI		PPT
67	Qatar	Yes MLI		PPT
68	Romania	No	Yes MLI	PPT
69	Saudi Arabia	Yes MLI		PPT
70	Serbia	Yes MLI		PPT
71	Singapore	Yes MLI		PPT
72	Slovak Republic	Yes MLI		PPT
73	Slovenia	Yes MLI		PPT
74	South Africa	Yes MLI		PPT
75	Spain	No	No	
76	Sri Lanka	No	No	PPT
77	Suriname*	No	No	PPT
78	Sweden	No	Yes MLI	PPT
79	Switzerland	Yes other		PPT
80	Thailand	No	No	PPT
81	Tunisia	No	Yes MLI	PPT
82	Türkiye	No	Yes MLI	PPT
83	Uganda*	No		PPT
84	Ukraine	Yes other		PPT
85	United Arab Emirates	Yes MLI		PPT
86	United Kingdom	Yes MLI		PPT
87	United States	No	No	
88	Uzbekistan	Yes other		PPT
89	Venezuela*	No	No	PPT
90	Viet Nam	No	Yes MLI	PPT
91	Zambia	No	No	PPT
92	Zimbabwe*	No	No	PPT

Other agreements

	1.Treaty partners	2. Inclusive Framework member
1	Chinese Taipei*	No
2	Sint Maarten	No

New Zealand

A. Progress in the implementation of the minimum standard

New Zealand has 40 tax agreements in force, as reported in its response to the Peer Review questionnaire. Twenty-seven of those agreements comply with the minimum standard.

New Zealand signed the MLI in 2017 and deposited its instrument of ratification on the 27 June 2018, listing its non-compliant agreements. The MLI entered into force for New Zealand on 1 October 2018. The agreements modified by the MLI come into compliance with the minimum standard once the provisions of the MLI take effect.

New Zealand indicated in its response to the Peer Review questionnaire that steps have been taken (other than under the MLI) to implement the minimum standard in its agreements with Austria, Germany and Norway.

New Zealand is implementing the minimum standard through the inclusion of the preamble statement and the PPT.[103]

B. Conclusion

No jurisdiction has raised any concerns about their agreements with New Zealand.

Summary of the jurisdiction response – New Zealand

	1.Treaty partners	2. Compliance with the standard	3. Signature of a complying instrument	4. Minimum standard provision used
1	Australia	Yes MLI		PPT
2	Austria	No	No	PPT
3	Belgium	Yes MLI		PPT
4	Canada	Yes MLI		PPT
5	Chile	Yes MLI		PPT
6	China (People's Republic of)	Yes other		PPT
7	Czechia	Yes MLI		PPT
8	Denmark	Yes MLI		PPT
9	Fiji*	No	Yes MLI	PPT
10	Finland	Yes MLI		PPT
11	France	Yes MLI		PPT
12	Germany	No	No	PPT
13	Hong Kong (China)	Yes MLI		PPT
14	India	Yes MLI		PPT
15	Indonesia	Yes MLI		PPT
16	Ireland	Yes MLI		PPT
17	Italy	No	Yes MLI	PPT
18	Japan	Yes MLI		PPT+LOB
19	Korea	Yes MLI		PPT

[103] For its agreements listed under the MLI, New Zealand is implementing the preamble statement (Article 6 of the MLI) and the PPT (Article 7 of the MLI).

	Malaysia	Yes MLI		PPT
21	Mexico	No	Yes MLI	PPT
22	Netherlands	Yes MLI		PPT
23	Norway	No	No	PPT
24	Papua New Guinea	No	Yes MLI	PPT
25	Philippines	No	No	PPT
26	Poland	Yes MLI		PPT
27	Russian Federation	Yes MLI		PPT
28	Samoa	Yes other		PPT
29	Singapore	Yes MLI		PPT
30	South Africa	Yes MLI		PPT
31	Spain	Yes MLI		PPT
32	Sweden	No	Yes MLI	PPT
33	Switzerland	Yes other		PPT
34	Thailand	Yes MLI		PPT
35	Türkiye	No	Yes MLI	PPT
36	United Arab Emirates	Yes MLI		PPT
37	United Kingdom	Yes MLI		PPT
38	United States	No	No	D-LOB
39	Viet Nam	No	Yes MLI	PPT

Other agreements

	1.Treaty partners	2. Inclusive Framework member
1	Chinese Taipei*	No

Nigeria

A. Progress in the implementation of the minimum standard

Nigeria has 16 tax agreements in force, as reported in its response to the Peer Review questionnaire, including the multilateral Supplementary Act A/SA, 5/12/18 adopting community rules for the elimination of double taxation with respect to taxes on income, capital and inheritance and the prevention of tax evasion and avoidance within the ECOWAS Member States (the ECOWAS Supplementary Act) concluded with fourteen treaty partners. One of those agreements, the ECOWAS Supplementary Act, complies with the minimum standard.

Nigeria signed the MLI in 2017 and listed its non-compliant agreements. The agreements that will be modified by the MLI will come into compliance with the minimum standard once the provisions of the MLI take effect.

Nigeria is implementing the minimum standard through the inclusion of the preamble statement and the PPT.[104]

B. Conclusion

Recommendation

It is recommended that Nigeria completes the steps to have the MLI take effect with respect to its agreements listed under the MLI as those agreements will only be modified by the MLI (and come into compliance with the minimum standard) once the provisions of the MLI take effect.

Summary of the jurisdiction response - Nigeria

	1.Treaty partners	2. Compliance with the standard	3. Signature of a complying instrument	4. Minimum standard provision used
1	Belgium	No	Yes MLI	PPT
2	Canada	No	Yes MLI	PPT
3	China (People's Republic of)	No	Yes MLI	PPT
4	Czechia	No	Yes MLI	PPT
5	ECOWAS Member States (Benin, Burkina Faso, Cabo Verde, Côte d'Ivoire, The Gambia*, Ghana*, Guinea-Bissau*, Guinea Conakry*, Liberia, Mali*, Niger*, Senegal, Sierra Leone, Togo)	Yes other		PPT
6	France	No	Yes MLI	PPT
7	Netherlands	No	Yes MLI	PPT
8	Pakistan	No	Yes MLI	PPT

104 For its agreements listed under the MLI, Nigeria is implementing the preamble statement (Article 6 of the MLI) and the PPT (Article 7 of the MLI).

9	Philippines	No	No	PPT
10	Romania	No	Yes MLI	PPT
11	Singapore	No	Yes MLI	PPT
12	Slovak Republic	No	Yes MLI	PPT
13	South Africa	No	Yes MLI	PPT
14	Spain	No	Yes MLI	PPT
15	Sweden	No	Yes MLI	PPT
16	United Kingdom	No	Yes MLI	PPT

North Macedonia

A. Progress in the implementation of the minimum standard

The Republic of North Macedonia has 48 tax agreements in force, as reported in its response to the Peer Review questionnaire. None of those agreements comply with the minimum standard.

The Republic of North Macedonia signed the MLI in 2020. The agreements that will be modified by the MLI will come into compliance with the minimum standard once the provisions of the MLI take effect.

The Republic of North Macedonia has signed a bilateral complying instrument with respect to its agreement with Switzerland.

The Republic of North Macedonia is implementing the minimum standard through the inclusion of the preamble statement and the PPT.[105]

B. Conclusion

Recommendation

It is recommended that the Republic of North Macedonia completes the steps to have the MLI take effect with respect to its agreements listed under the MLI as those agreements will only be modified by the MLI (and come into compliance with the minimum standard) once the provisions of the MLI take effect.

Summary of the jurisdiction response – North Macedonia

	1.Treaty partners	2. Compliance with the standard	3. Signature of a complying instrument	4. Minimum standard provision used
1	Albania	No	Yes MLI	PPT
2	Austria	No	No	PPT
3	Azerbaijan	No	No	PPT
4	Belarus	No	No	PPT
5	Belgium	No	Yes MLI	PPT
6	Bosnia-Herzegovina	No	Yes MLI	PPT
7	Bulgaria	No	Yes MLI	PPT
8	China (People's Republic of)	No	Yes MLI	PPT
9	Chinese Taipei*	No	No	PPT
10	Croatia	No	Yes MLI	PPT
11	Czechia	No	No	PPT
12	Denmark	No	Yes MLI	PPT
13	Estonia	No	Yes MLI	PPT
14	Finland	No	Yes MLI	PPT

105 For its agreements listed under the MLI, the Republic of North Macedonia is implementing the preamble statement (Article 6 of the MLI) and the PPT (Article 7 of the MLI).

15	France	No	Yes MLI	PPT
16	Germany	No	No	PPT
17	Hungary	No	Yes MLI	PPT
18	India	No	Yes MLI	PPT
19	Iran*	No	No	PPT
20	Ireland	No	Yes MLI	PPT
21	Israel	No	Yes MLI	PPT
22	Italy	No	No	PPT
23	Kazakhstan	No	Yes MLI	PPT
24	Kosovo*	No	No	PPT
25	Kuwait	No	No	PPT
26	Latvia	No	Yes MLI	PPT
27	Lithuania	No	Yes MLI	PPT
28	Luxembourg	No	Yes MLI	PPT
29	Moldova*	No	No	PPT
30	Montenegro	No	No	PPT
31	Morocco	No	Yes MLI	PPT
32	Netherlands	No	Yes MLI	PPT
33	Norway	No	No	PPT
34	Poland	No	Yes MLI	PPT
35	Qatar	No	Yes MLI	PPT
36	Romania	No	Yes MLI	PPT
37	Russian Federation	No	No	PPT
38	Saudi Arabia	No	Yes MLI	PPT
39	Serbia	No	Yes MLI	PPT
40	Slovak Republic	No	Yes MLI	PPT
41	Slovenia	No	Yes MLI	PPT
42	Spain	No	Yes MLI	PPT
43	Sweden	No	Yes MLI	PPT
44	Switzerland	No	Yes other	PPT
45	Türkiye	No	Yes MLI	PPT
46	Ukraine	No	Yes MLI	PPT
47	United Arab Emirates	No	Yes MLI	PPT
48	United Kingdom	No	Yes MLI	PPT

Norway

A. Progress in the implementation of the minimum standard

Norway has 84 tax agreements in force, as reported in its response to the Peer Review questionnaire, including the multilateral Nordic Convention concluded with Denmark, the Faroe Islands, Finland, Iceland and Sweden (the "Nordic Convention").[106] Twenty-six of those agreements, including the Nordic Convention, comply with the minimum standard.

Norway signed the MLI in 2017 and deposited its instrument of ratification on the 17 July 2019, listing 28 of its agreements in force at that time. The MLI entered into force for Norway on 1 November 2019. The agreements modified by the MLI come into compliance with the minimum standard once the provisions of the MLI take effect.

Norway has not listed its agreements with Albania, Austria, Azerbaijan, Barbados, Benin, Bosnia-Herzegovina, Canada, Côte d'Ivoire, Croatia, Curaçao, Egypt, France, Germany, Greenland, Hungary, Indonesia, Israel, Italy, Jamaica, Kazakhstan, Kenya, Korea, Malaysia, Montenegro, Morocco, New Zealand, North Macedonia, Pakistan, Qatar, Senegal, Sierra Leone, Singapore, the Slovak Republic, Spain, Sri Lanka, Switzerland, Thailand, Tunisia, Ukraine, Viet Nam and Zambia to be covered under the MLI. These agreements will therefore not, at this stage, be modified by the MLI. Albania, Barbados, Bosnia-Herzegovina, Canada, Côte d'Ivoire, Croatia, Curaçao, Egypt, France, Hungary, Indonesia, Israel, Italy, Jamaica, Kazakhstan, Kenya, Korea, Malaysia, Morocco, New Zealand, North Macedonia, Pakistan, Senegal, Singapore, the Slovak Republic, Tunisia, Ukraine and Viet Nam have listed their agreements with Norway under the MLI.

Norway indicated in its response to the Peer Review questionnaire that steps have been taken (other than under the MLI) to implement the minimum standard in its agreements with Austria, Canada, France, Germany, Greenland, Israel, Italy, Korea, Malaysia, New Zealand, Pakistan, Qatar, Singapore, Slovak Republic, Spain, Thailand and the United States.

Norway has signed a bilateral complying instrument with respect to its agreement with Belgium, Brazil and Ghana*.

Norway indicated in its response to the Peer Review questionnaire that the agreements with Azerbaijan, Bangladesh*, Gambia*, Malawi*, Nepal*, Uganda*, Venezuela*, and Zimbabwe* do not give rise to material treaty-shopping concerns for Norway.

Norway is implementing the minimum standard through the inclusion of the preamble statement and the PPT.[107]

---

[106] See the Multilateral convention concluded by Denmark, Finland, the Faroe Islands, Iceland, Norway and Sweden: for the avoidance of double taxation with respect to taxes on income and on capital (1996, 1997, 2008 and 2018).

[107] For its agreements listed under the MLI, Norway is implementing the preamble statement (Article 6 of the MLI) and the PPT (Article 7 of the MLI). Under Article 7(7)(a) of the MLI, Norway is also implementing the simplified LOB (Article 7(8 to 13) of the MLI) in agreements concluded with treaty partners that adopted the simplified LOB. Norway expressed a statement, in accordance with Article 7(17)(a) of the MLI, that while it accepts the application of PPT alone as an interim measure, it intends where possible to adopt an LOB provision in addition to or in replacement of the PPT through bilateral negotiation.

B. Conclusion

Albania, Barbados, Bosnia-Herzegovina, Canada, Côte d'Ivoire, Croatia, Curaçao, Egypt, France, Hungary, Indonesia, Israel, Italy, Jamaica, Kazakhstan, Kenya, Korea, Malaysia, Morocco, New Zealand, North Macedonia, Pakistan, Senegal, Singapore, the Slovak Republic, Tunisia, Ukraine and Viet Nam have listed their agreements with Norway under the MLI, which amount to requests to implement the minimum standard.

Norway has started to give effect to its plan for the implementation of the minimum standard in its agreements with Albania, Barbados, Benin, Bosnia-Herzegovina, Côte d'Ivoire, Croatia, Curaçao, Egypt, Hungary, Indonesia, Jamaica, Kazakhstan, Kenya, Montenegro, Morocco, North Macedonia, Senegal, Sierra Leone, Sri Lanka, Tunisia, Ukraine, Viet Nam and Zambia. Norway indicated in its response to the Peer Review questionnaire that bilateral discussions would be pursued with respect to those agreements.

Summary of the jurisdiction response - Norway

	1.Treaty partners	2. Compliance with the standard	3. Signature of a complying instrument	4. Minimum standard provision used
1	Argentina	No	Yes MLI	PPT+LOB
2	Australia	Yes MLI		PPT
3	Austria	No	No	
4	Belgium	No	Yes other	PPT
5	Brazil	No	Yes other	PPT+LOB
6	Bulgaria	Yes MLI		PPT
7	Canada	No	No	
8	Chile	Yes MLI		PPT+LOB
9	China (People's Republic of)	Yes MLI		
10	Cyprus*	Yes MLI		PPT
11	Czechia	Yes MLI		PPT
12	Estonia	Yes MLI		PPT
13	France	No	No	
14	Georgia	Yes MLI		PPT
15	Germany	No	No	
16	Ghana*	No	Yes other	PPT+LOB
17	Greece	Yes MLI		PPT
18	Greenland	No	No	
19	India	Yes MLI		PPT+LOB
20	Ireland	Yes MLI		PPT
21	Israel	No	No	
22	Italy	No	No	
23	Japan	Yes MLI		PPT
24	Korea	No	No	
25	Latvia	Yes MLI		PPT
26	Lithuania	Yes MLI		PPT
27	Luxembourg	Yes MLI		PPT
28	Malaysia	No	No	
29	Malta	Yes MLI		PPT
30	Mexico	No	Yes MLI	PPT+LOB
31	Netherlands	Yes MLI		PPT
32	New Zealand	No	No	
33	Nordic Convention treaty partners (Denmark, Faroe Islands, Finland, Iceland,	Yes other		PPT

	Sweden)			
34	Pakistan	No	No	
35	Poland	Yes MLI		PPT
36	Portugal	Yes MLI		PPT
37	Qatar	No	No	
38	Romania	No	Yes MLI	PPT
39	Russian Federation	Yes MLI		PPT
40	Serbia	Yes MLI		PPT
41	Singapore	No	No	
42	Slovak Republic	No	No	
43	Slovenia	Yes MLI		PPT
44	South Africa	Yes MLI		PPT
45	Spain	No	No	
46	Switzerland	Yes other		PPT
47	Thailand	No	No	
48	Türkiye	No	Yes MLI	PPT
49	United Kingdom	Yes MLI		PPT
50	United States	No	No	

Other agreements

	1.Treaty partners	2. Inclusive Framework member
1	Albania	Yes
2	Azerbaijan	Yes
3	Bangladesh*	No
4	Barbados	Yes
5	Benin	Yes
6	Bosnia-Herzegovina	Yes
7	Côte d'Ivoire	Yes
8	Croatia	Yes
9	Curaçao	Yes
10	Egypt	Yes
11	Gambia*	No
12	Hungary	Yes
13	Indonesia	Yes
14	Jamaica	Yes
15	Kazakhstan	Yes
16	Kenya	Yes
17	Malawi*	No
18	Montenegro	Yes
19	Morocco	Yes
20	Nepal*	No
21	North Macedonia	Yes
22	Philippines	Yes
23	Senegal	Yes
24	Sierra Leone	Yes
25	Sri Lanka	Yes
26	Tanzania*	No
27	Trinidad and Tobago	Yes
28	Tunisia	Yes
29	Uganda*	No
30	Ukraine	Yes

31	Venezuela*	No
32	Viet Nam	Yes
33	Zambia	Yes
34	Zimbabwe*	No

Oman

A. Progress in the implementation of the minimum standard

Oman has 37 tax agreements in force, as reported in its response to the Peer Review questionnaire. Seventeen of those agreements comply with the minimum standard.

Oman signed the MLI in 2019 and deposited its instrument of ratification on the 7 July 2020. The MLI entered into force for Oman on 1 November 2020. The agreements modified by the MLI come into compliance with the minimum standard once the provisions of the MLI take effect.

Oman has not listed its agreement with India under the MLI but indicated that steps have been taken (other than under the MLI) to implement the minimum standard in that agreement. India has listed its agreement with Oman under the MLI.

Oman is implementing the minimum standard through the inclusion of the preamble statement and the PPT.[108]

B. Conclusion

No jurisdiction has raised any concerns about their agreements with Oman.

India has listed its agreement with Oman under the MLI, which amounts to a request to implement the minimum standard.

Summary of the jurisdiction response - Oman

	1.Treaty partners	2. Compliance with the standard	3. Signature of a complying instrument	4. Minimum standard provision used
1	Algeria*	No	No	PPT
2	Belarus	No	No	PPT
3	Brunei Darussalam	No	No	PPT
4	Canada	Yes MLI		PPT
5	China (People's Republic of)	Yes MLI		PPT
6	Croatia	Yes MLI		PPT
7	France	Yes MLI		PPT
8	Hungary	Yes MLI		PPT
9	India	No	No	
10	Iran*	No	No	
11	Italy	No	No	
12	Japan	Yes MLI		PPT
13	Korea	Yes MLI		PPT
14	Lebanon*	No	No	PPT
15	Mauritius	Yes MLI		
16	Moldova*	No	No	PPT
17	Morocco	No	Yes MLI	PPT
18	Netherlands	Yes MLI		PPT

[108] For its agreements listed under the MLI, Oman is implementing the preamble statement (Article 6 of the MLI) and the PPT (Article 7 of the MLI).

19	Pakistan	Yes MLI		PPT
20	Portugal	Yes MLI		PPT
21	Qatar	Yes other		PPT
22	Seychelles	Yes MLI		PPT
23	Singapore	Yes MLI		PPT
24	Slovak Republic	No	No	
25	South Africa	No	Yes MLI	PPT
26	Spain	Yes MLI		PPT
27	Sri Lanka	No	No	PPT
28	Sudan*	No	No	
29	Switzerland	No	No	
30	Syrian Arab Republic*	No	No	
31	Thailand	Yes MLI		PPT
32	Tunisia	No	Yes MLI	PPT
33	Türkiye	No	Yes MLI	PPT
34	United Kingdom	Yes MLI		PPT
35	Uzbekistan	No	No	PPT
36	Viet Nam	No	Yes MLI	PPT
37	Yemen*	No	No	PPT

Pakistan

A. Progress in the implementation of the minimum standard

Pakistan has 66 tax agreements in force, as reported in its response to the Peer Review questionnaire. Thirty-eight of those agreements comply with the minimum standard.

Pakistan signed the MLI in 2017 and deposited its instrument of ratification on 18 December 2020, listing its non-compliant agreements. The MLI entered into force for Pakistan on 1 April 2021. The agreements modified by the MLI come into compliance with the minimum standard once the provisions of the MLI take effect.

Pakistan is implementing the minimum standard through the inclusion of the preamble statement and the PPT.[109]

B. Conclusion

No jurisdiction has raised any concerns about their agreements with Pakistan.

Summary of the jurisdiction response - Pakistan

	1.Treaty partners	2. Compliance with the standard	3. Signature of a complying instrument	4. Minimum standard provision used
1	Austria	Yes MLI		PPT
2	Azerbaijan	No	No	
3	Bahrain	Yes MLI		PPT
4	Bangladesh*	No	No	
5	Belarus	No	No	
6	Belgium	Yes MLI		PPT
7	Bosnia-Herzegovina	Yes MLI		PPT
8	Brunei Darussalam	No	No	
9	Bulgaria	Yes other		PPT
10	Canada	Yes MLI		PPT
11	China (People's Republic of)	Yes MLI		PPT
12	Czechia	Yes MLI		PPT
13	Denmark	Yes MLI		PPT+LOB
14	Egypt	Yes MLI		PPT
15	Finland	Yes MLI		PPT
16	France	Yes MLI		PPT
17	Germany	No	No	N/A
18	Hong Kong (China)	Yes MLI		PPT
19	Hungary	Yes MLI		PPT
20	Indonesia	Yes MLI		PPT
21	Iran*	No	No	
22	Ireland	Yes MLI		PPT
23	Italy	No	Yes MLI	PPT

[109] For its agreements listed under the MLI, Pakistan is implementing the preamble statement (Article 6 of the MLI) and the PPT (Article 7 of the MLI).

24	Japan	Yes MLI		PPT
25	Jordan	Yes MLI		PPT
26	Kazakhstan	Yes MLI		PPT+LOB
27	Korea	Yes MLI		PPT
28	Kuwait	No	Yes MLI	PPT
29	Kyrgyzstan*	No	No	
30	Lebanon*	No	No	
31	Libya*	No	No	
32	Malaysia	Yes MLI		PPT
33	Malta	Yes MLI		PPT
34	Mauritius	Yes MLI		PPT
35	Morocco	No	Yes MLI	PPT
36	Nepal*	No	No	
37	Netherlands	Yes MLI		PPT
38	Nigeria	No	Yes MLI	PPT
39	Norway	No	No	
40	Oman	Yes MLI		PPT
41	Philippines	No	No	
42	Poland	Yes MLI		PPT
43	Portugal	Yes MLI		PPT
44	Qatar	Yes MLI		PPT
45	Romania	Yes MLI		PPT
46	Saudi Arabia	Yes MLI		PPT
47	Serbia	Yes MLI		PPT
48	Singapore	Yes MLI		PPT
49	South Africa	Yes MLI		PPT
50	Spain	Yes MLI		PPT
51	Sri Lanka	No	No	
52	Sweden	No	Yes MLI	PPT
53	Switzerland	No	No	
54	Syria*	No	No	
55	Tajikistan*	No	No	
56	Thailand	Yes MLI		PPT
57	Tunisia	No	Yes MLI	PPT
58	Türkiye	No	Yes MLI	PPT
59	Turkmenistan*	No	No	
60	Ukraine	Yes MLI		PPT
61	United Arab Emirates	Yes MLI		PPT
62	United Kingdom	Yes MLI		PPT
63	United States	No	No	
64	Uzbekistan	No	No	
65	Viet Nam	No	Yes MLI	PPT
66	Yemen*	No	No	

Panama

A. Progress in the implementation of the minimum standard

Panama has 17 tax agreements in force, as reported in its response to the Peer Review questionnaire. Thirteen of those agreements comply with the minimum standard.

Panama signed the MLI in 2018 and deposited its instrument of ratification on 5 November 2020, listing its non-compliant agreements. The MLI entered into force for Panama on 1 March 2021. The agreements modified by the MLI come into compliance with the minimum standard once the provisions of the MLI take effect.

Panama is implementing the minimum standard through the inclusion of the preamble statement and the PPT.[110]

B. Conclusion

No jurisdiction has raised any concerns about their agreements with Panama.

Summary of the jurisdiction response - Panama

	1.Treaty partners	2. Compliance with the standard	3. Signature of a complying instrument	4. Minimum standard provision used
1	Barbados	Yes MLI		PPT
2	Czechia	No	No	PPT
3	France	Yes MLI		PPT
4	Ireland	Yes MLI		PPT
5	Israel	Yes MLI		PPT
6	Italy	No	No	PPT
7	Korea	Yes MLI		PPT
8	Luxembourg	Yes MLI		PPT
9	Mexico	No	Yes MLI	PPT
10	Netherlands	Yes MLI		PPT
11	Portugal	Yes MLI		PPT
12	Qatar	Yes MLI		PPT
13	Singapore	Yes MLI		PPT
14	Spain	Yes MLI		PPT
15	United Arab Emirates	Yes MLI		PPT
16	United Kingdom	Yes MLI		PPT
17	Viet Nam	No	Yes MLI	PPT

110 For its agreements listed under the MLI, Panama is implementing the preamble statement (Article 6 of the MLI) and the PPT (Article 7 of the MLI).

Papua New Guinea

A. Progress in the implementation of the minimum standard

Papua New Guinea has ten tax agreements in force, as reported in its response to the Peer Review questionnaire. None of those agreements comply with the minimum standard.

Papua New Guinea signed the MLI in 2019 and deposited its instrument of ratification on 31 August 2023, listing its non-compliant agreements. The MLI enters into force for Papua New Guinea on 1 December 2023. The agreements modified by the MLI come into compliance with the minimum standard once the provisions of the MLI take effect.

Papua New Guinea is implementing the minimum standard through the inclusion of the preamble statement and the PPT.[111]

B. Conclusion

No jurisdiction has raised any concerns about their agreements with Papua New Guinea.

Summary of the jurisdiction response - Papua New Guinea

	1.Treaty partners	2. Compliance with the standard	3. Signature of a complying instrument	4. Minimum standard provision used
1	Australia	No	Yes MLI	PPT
2	Canada	No	Yes MLI	PPT
3	China (People's Republic of)	No	Yes MLI	PPT
4	Fiji*	No	No	PPT
5	Indonesia	No	No	PPT
6	Korea	No	Yes MLI	PPT
7	Malaysia	No	Yes MLI	PPT
8	New Zealand	No	Yes MLI	PPT
9	Singapore	No	Yes MLI	PPT
10	United Kingdom	No	Yes MLI	PPT

[111] For its agreements listed under the MLI, Papua New Guinea is implementing the preamble statement (Article 6 of the MLI) and the PPT (Article 7 of the MLI).

Paraguay

A. Progress in the implementation of the minimum standard

Paraguay has five tax agreements in force, as reported in its response to the Peer Review questionnaire. One of those agreements, the agreement with Uruguay, complies with the minimum standard.

Paraguay has not signed the MLI.

Paraguay indicated in its response to the Peer Review questionnaire that steps have been taken (other than under the MLI) to implement the minimum standard in its agreement with Chile.

Paraguay is implementing the minimum standard through the inclusion of the preamble statement and the PPT combined with the LOB.

B. Conclusion

Paraguay is currently developing a plan, in consultation with the Secretariat, for the implementation of the minimum standard in its agreements with Qatar and the United Arab Emirates.

Summary of the jurisdiction response - Paraguay

	1.Treaty partners	2. Compliance with the standard	3. Signature of a complying instrument	4. Minimum standard provision used
1	Chile	No	No	PPT+LOB
2	Uruguay	Yes other		PPT+LOB

Other agreements

	1.Treaty partners	2. Inclusive Framework member
1	Chinese Taipei*	No
2	Qatar	Yes
3	United Arab Emirates	Yes

Peru

A. Progress in the implementation of the minimum standard

Peru has nine tax agreements in force, as reported in its response to the Peer Review questionnaire, including the Decision 578 of the Andean Community Commission (Decision 578) for the members of the Andean Community (the Andean Community Agreement).[112] One of those agreements, the agreement with Japan, complies with the minimum standard.

Peru signed the MLI in 2018 and listed its non-compliant bilateral agreements. The agreements modified by the MLI will come into compliance with the minimum standard once the provisions of the MLI take effect.

Peru indicated in its response to the Peer Review questionnaire that it is currently renegotiating the Andean Community Agreement to implement the minimum standard. Peru further indicated that steps have been taken (other than under the MLI) to implement the minimum standard in its agreements with Brazil and Switzerland.

Peru is implementing the minimum standard through the inclusion of the preamble statement and the PPT.[113]

B. Conclusion

Recommendation

It is recommended that Peru completes the steps to have the MLI take effect with respect to its agreements listed under the MLI as those agreements will only be modified by the MLI (and come into compliance with the minimum standard) once the provisions of the MLI take effect.

Summary of the jurisdiction response – Peru

	1.Treaty partners	2. Compliance with the standard	3. Signature of a complying instrument	4. Minimum standard provision used
1	Brazil	No	No	
2	Canada	No	Yes MLI	PPT
3	Chile	No	Yes MLI	PPT
4	Decision 578 treaty partners (Bolivia*, Colombia, Ecuador*)	No	No	PPT

[112] The Decision of the Commission of the Andean Community 578 on the regime for the avoidance of double taxation and the prevention of fiscal evasion, adopted on 4 May 2004. The current members of the Andean Community are Bolivia*, Colombia, Ecuador* and Peru.

[113] For its agreements listed under the MLI, Peru is implementing the preamble statement (Article 6 of the MLI) and the PPT (Article 7 of the MLI). Peru expressed a statement, in accordance with Article 7(17)(a) of the MLI, that while it accepts the application of the PPT under the MLI, it intends where possible to adopt an LOB provision through bilateral negotiation.

5	Japan	Yes other		PPT
6	Korea	No	Yes MLI	PPT
7	Mexico	No	Yes MLI	PPT
8	Portugal	No	Yes MLI	PPT
9	Switzerland	No	No	

Poland

A. Progress in the implementation of the minimum standard

Poland has 82 tax agreements in force, as reported in its response to the Peer Review questionnaire. Fifty-two of those agreements comply with the minimum standard.

Poland signed the MLI in 2017 and deposited its instrument of ratification of the MLI on 23 January 2018. The MLI entered into force for Poland on 1 July 2018. The agreements modified by the MLI come into compliance with the minimum standard once the provisions of the MLI take effect.

Poland has not listed its agreements with Germany, Montenegro, Switzerland and the United States under the MLI, but indicated in its response to the Peer Review questionnaire that steps have been taken (other than under the MLI) to implement the minimum standard in each of those agreements.

Poland is implementing the minimum standard through the inclusion of the preamble statement and the PPT.[114]

B. Conclusion

No jurisdiction has raised any concerns about their agreements with Poland.

Summary of the jurisdiction response - Poland

	1. Treaty partners	2. Compliance with the standard	3. Signature of a complying instrument	4. Minimum standard provision used
1	Albania	Yes MLI		PPT
2	Armenia	No	Yes MLI	PPT
3	Australia	Yes MLI		PPT
4	Austria	Yes MLI		PPT
5	Azerbaijan	No	No	PPT
6	Bangladesh*	No	No	PPT
7	Belarus	No	No	PPT
8	Belgium	Yes MLI		PPT
9	Bosnia-Herzegovina	Yes MLI		PPT
10	Bulgaria	Yes MLI		PPT
11	Canada	Yes MLI		PPT
12	Chile	Yes MLI		PPT
13	China (People's Republic of)	Yes MLI		PPT
14	Croatia	Yes MLI		PPT
15	Cyprus*	Yes MLI		PPT
16	Czechia	Yes MLI		PPT
17	Denmark	Yes MLI		PPT
18	Egypt	Yes MLI		PPT
19	Estonia	Yes MLI		PPT

114 For its agreements listed under the MLI, Poland is implementing the preamble statement (Article 6 of the MLI) and the PPT (Article 7 of the MLI). Poland expressed a statement that while it accepts the application of the PPT under the MLI, it intends where possible to adopt an LOB provision through bilateral negotiation.

20	Ethiopia*	No	No	PPT
21	Finland	Yes MLI		PPT
22	France	Yes MLI		PPT
23	Georgia	Yes other		PPT
24	Germany	No	No	
25	Greece	Yes MLI		PPT
26	Hungary	Yes MLI		PPT
27	Iceland	Yes MLI		PPT
28	India	Yes MLI		PPT
29	Indonesia	Yes MLI		PPT
30	Iran*	No	No	PPT
31	Ireland	Yes MLI		PPT
32	Israel	Yes MLI		PPT
33	Italy	No	Yes MLI	PPT
34	Japan	Yes MLI		PPT
35	Jordan	Yes MLI		PPT
36	Kazakhstan	Yes MLI		PPT
37	Korea	Yes MLI		PPT
38	Kuwait	No	No	PPT
39	Kyrgyzstan*	No	No	PPT
40	Latvia	Yes MLI		PPT
41	Lebanon*	No	No	PPT
42	Lithuania	Yes MLI		PPT
43	Luxembourg	Yes MLI		PPT
44	Malaysia	Yes MLI		PPT
45	Malta	Yes MLI		PPT
46	Mexico	No	Yes MLI	PPT
47	Moldova*	No	No	PPT
48	Mongolia	No	Yes MLI	PPT
49	Montenegro	No	No	
50	Morocco	No	Yes MLI	PPT
51	Netherlands	Yes other		PPT
52	New Zealand	Yes MLI		PPT
53	North Macedonia	No	Yes MLI	PPT
54	Norway	Yes MLI		PPT
55	Pakistan	Yes MLI		PPT
56	Philippines	No	No	PPT
57	Portugal	Yes MLI		PPT
58	Qatar	Yes MLI		PPT
59	Romania	No	Yes MLI	PPT
60	Russian Federation	Yes MLI		PPT
61	Saudi Arabia	Yes MLI		PPT
62	Serbia	Yes MLI		PPT
63	Singapore	Yes MLI		PPT
64	Slovak Republic	Yes MLI		PPT
65	Slovenia	Yes MLI		PPT
66	South Africa	Yes MLI		PPT
67	Spain	Yes MLI		PPT
68	Sri Lanka	No	No	PPT
69	Sweden	No	Yes MLI	PPT
70	Switzerland	No	No	
71	Syrian Arab Republic*	No	No	PPT
72	Tajikistan*	No	No	PPT

73	Thailand	Yes MLI		PPT
74	Tunisia	No	Yes MLI	PPT
75	Türkiye	No	Yes MLI	PPT
76	Ukraine	Yes MLI		PPT
77	United Arab Emirates	Yes MLI		PPT
78	United Kingdom	Yes MLI		PPT
79	United States	No	No	
80	Uzbekistan	No	No	PPT
81	Viet Nam	No	Yes MLI	PPT
82	Zimbabwe*	No	No	PPT

Portugal

A. Progress in the implementation of the minimum standard

Portugal has 78 tax agreements in force, as reported in its response to the Peer Review questionnaire. Fifty of those agreements comply with the minimum standard.

Portugal signed the MLI in 2017 and deposited its instrument of ratification on 28 February 2020, listing its non-compliant agreements. The MLI entered into force for Portugal on 1 June 2020. The agreements modified by the MLI come into compliance with the minimum standard once the provisions of the MLI take effect.

Portugal indicated in its response to the Peer Review questionnaire that steps have been taken (other than under the MLI) to implement the minimum standard in its agreements with Brazil, Cabo Verde, Germany, and Mozambique*.

Portugal is implementing the minimum standard through the inclusion of the preamble statement and the PPT.[115]

B. Conclusion

No jurisdiction has raised any concerns about their agreements with Portugal.

Summary of the jurisdiction response - Portugal

	1.Treaty partners	2. Compliance with the standard	3. Signature of a complying instrument	4. Minimum standard provision used
1	Algeria*	No	No	
2	Andorra	Yes MLI		PPT
3	Angola	Yes other		PPT
4	Austria	Yes MLI		PPT
5	Bahrain	Yes MLI		PPT
6	Barbados	Yes MLI		PPT
7	Belgium	Yes MLI		PPT
8	Brazil	No	No	
9	Bulgaria	Yes MLI		PPT
10	Cabo Verde	No	No	
11	Canada	Yes MLI		PPT
12	Chile	Yes MLI		PPT
13	China (People's Republic of)	Yes MLI		PPT
14	Colombia	No	Yes MLI	PPT
15	Côte d'Ivoire	No	Yes MLI	PPT
16	Croatia	Yes MLI		PPT
17	Cuba*	No	No	
18	Cyprus*	Yes MLI		PPT
19	Czechia	Yes MLI		PPT

115 For its agreements listed under the MLI, Portugal is implementing the preamble statement (Article 6 of the MLI) and the PPT (Article 7 of the MLI).

20	Denmark	Yes MLI		PPT
21	Estonia	No	Yes MLI	PPT
22	Ethiopia*	No	No	
23	France	Yes MLI		PPT
24	Georgia	Yes MLI		PPT
25	Germany	No	No	
26	Greece	Yes MLI		PPT
27	Guinea-Bissau*	No	No	
28	Hong Kong (China)	Yes MLI		PPT
29	Hungary	Yes MLI		PPT
30	Iceland	Yes MLI		PPT
31	India	Yes MLI		PPT
32	Indonesia	Yes MLI		PPT
33	Ireland	Yes MLI		PPT
34	Israel	Yes MLI		PPT
35	Italy	No	Yes MLI	PPT
36	Japan	Yes MLI		PPT
37	Korea	Yes MLI		PPT
38	Kuwait	No	Yes MLI	PPT
39	Latvia	Yes MLI		PPT
40	Lithuania	Yes MLI		PPT
41	Luxembourg	Yes MLI		PPT
42	Macau (China)	No	No	
43	Malta	Yes MLI		PPT
44	Mexico	No	Yes MLI	PPT
45	Moldova*	No	No	
46	Montenegro	No	No	
47	Morocco	No	Yes MLI	PPT
48	Mozambique*	No	No	
49	Netherlands	Yes MLI		PPT
50	Norway	Yes MLI		PPT
51	Oman	Yes MLI		PPT
52	Pakistan	Yes MLI		PPT
53	Panama	Yes MLI		PPT
54	Peru	No	Yes MLI	PPT
55	Poland	Yes MLI		PPT
56	Qatar	Yes MLI		PPT
57	Romania	No	Yes MLI	PPT
58	Russian Federation	Yes MLI		PPT
59	San Marino	Yes MLI		PPT
60	Sao Tome and Principe*	No	No	
61	Saudi Arabia	Yes MLI		PPT
62	Senegal	Yes MLI		PPT
63	Singapore	Yes MLI		PPT
64	Slovak Republic	Yes MLI		PPT
65	Slovenia	Yes MLI		PPT
66	South Africa	Yes MLI		PPT
67	Spain	Yes MLI		PPT
68	Switzerland	No	Yes MLI	PPT
69	Timor-Leste*	No	No	
70	Tunisia	No	Yes MLI	PPT
71	Türkiye	No	Yes MLI	PPT
72	Ukraine	Yes MLI		PPT

73	United Arab Emirates	Yes MLI		PPT
74	United Kingdom	Yes MLI		PPT
75	United States	No	No	
76	Uruguay	Yes MLI		PPT
77	Venezuela*	No	No	
78	Viet Nam	No	Yes MLI	

Qatar

A. Progress in the implementation of the minimum standard

Qatar has 80 tax agreements in force, as reported in its response to the Peer Review questionnaire. Forty-four of those agreements comply with the minimum standard.

Qatar signed the MLI in 2018 and deposited its instrument of ratification on 23 December 2019. The MLI entered into force for Qatar on 1 April 2020. On 25 November 2021, Qatar made an additional notification to expand its list of agreements to be covered under the MLI. The agreements modified by the MLI come into compliance with the minimum standard once the provisions of the MLI take effect.

Qatar has not listed its agreements with Argentina, Austria, Norway and Switzerland under the MLI but indicated in its response to the Peer Review questionnaire that steps have been taken (other than under the MLI) to implement the minimum standard in those agreements.

Qatar has concluded a bilateral complying instrument with respect to its agreement with Bermuda and Ukraine.

Qatar is implementing the minimum standard through the inclusion of the preamble statement and the PPT.[116]

B. Conclusion

No jurisdiction has raised any concerns about their agreements with Qatar.

Summary of the jurisdiction response – Qatar

	1.Treaty partners	2. Compliance with the standard	3. Signature of a complying instrument	4. Minimum standard provision used
1	Albania	Yes MLI		PPT
2	Algeria*	No	No	PPT
3	Argentina	No	No	PPT
4	Armenia	No	Yes MLI	PPT
5	Austria	No	No	PPT
6	Azerbaijan	No	No	PPT
7	Barbados	Yes MLI		PPT
8	Belarus	No	No	PPT
9	Bermuda	No	Yes other	PPT
10	Bosnia-Herzegovina	Yes MLI		PPT
11	Brunei Darussalam	No	No	PPT
12	Bulgaria	Yes MLI		PPT
13	Chad*	No	No	PPT
14	China (People's Republic of)	Yes MLI		PPT
15	Croatia	Yes MLI		PPT
16	Cuba*	No	No	PPT
17	Cyprus*	Yes MLI		PPT

[116] For its agreements listed under the MLI, Qatar is implementing the preamble statement (Article 6 of the MLI) and the PPT (Article 7 of the MLI).

18	Czechia	Yes other		PPT
19	Ecuador*	No	No	PPT
20	Fiji*	No	Yes MLI	PPT
21	France	Yes MLI		PPT
22	Georgia	No	No	PPT
23	Greece	Yes MLI		PPT
24	Guernsey	Yes other		PPT
25	Hong Kong (China)	Yes MLI		PPT
26	Hungary	Yes MLI		PPT
27	India	Yes MLI		PPT
28	Indonesia	Yes MLI		PPT
29	Iran*	No	No	PPT
30	Ireland	Yes MLI		PPT
31	Isle of Man	Yes MLI		PPT
32	Italy	No	Yes MLI	PPT
33	Japan	Yes MLI		PPT
34	Jersey	Yes MLI		PPT
35	Jordan	Yes MLI		PPT
36	Kazakhstan	Yes MLI		PPT
37	Kenya	No	Yes MLI	PPT
38	Korea	Yes MLI		PPT
39	Kyrgyzstan*	No	No	PPT
40	Latvia	Yes MLI		PPT
41	Lebanon*	No	No	PPT
42	Luxembourg	Yes MLI		PPT
43	Malaysia	Yes MLI		PPT
44	Malta	Yes MLI		PPT
45	Mauritius	Yes MLI		PPT
46	Mexico	No	Yes MLI	PPT
47	Monaco	Yes MLI		PPT
48	Morocco	No	Yes MLI	PPT
49	Nepal*	No	No	PPT
50	Netherlands	Yes MLI		PPT
51	Nigeria	No	Yes MLI	PPT
52	North Macedonia	No	Yes MLI	PPT
53	Norway	No	No	PPT
54	Oman	Yes other		PPT
55	Pakistan	Yes MLI		PPT
56	Panama	Yes MLI		PPT
57	Philippines	No	No	PPT
58	Poland	Yes MLI		PPT
59	Portugal	Yes MLI		PPT
60	Romania	No	Yes MLI	PPT
61	Russian Federation	Yes MLI		PPT
62	San Marino	Yes MLI		PPT
63	Senegal	Yes MLI		PPT
64	Serbia	Yes MLI		PPT
65	Seychelles	Yes MLI		PPT
66	Singapore	Yes MLI		PPT
67	Slovenia	Yes MLI		PPT
68	South Africa	Yes MLI		PPT
69	Spain	Yes MLI		PPT
70	Sri Lanka	No	No	PPT

71	Sudan*	No	No	PPT
72	Switzerland	No	No	PPT
73	Syrian Arab Republic*	No	No	PPT
74	Tunisia	No	No	PPT
75	Türkiye	No	Yes MLI	PPT
76	Ukraine	No	Yes other	PPT
77	United Kingdom	Yes MLI		PPT
78	Venezuela*	No	No	PPT
79	Viet Nam	No	Yes MLI	PPT
80	Yemen*	No	No	PPT

Romania

A. Progress in the implementation of the minimum standard

Romania has 88 tax agreements in force, as reported in its response to the Peer Review questionnaire. One of those agreements, the agreement with Spain, complies with the minimum standard.

Romania signed the MLI in 2017, and deposited its instrument of ratification on 28 February 2022, listing its non-compliant agreements. The MLI entered into force for Romania on 1 June 2022. The agreements modified by the MLI come into compliance with the minimum standard once the provisions of the MLI take effect.

Romania reserved the right to delay the entry into effect of the provisions of the MLI until Romania has completed its internal procedures for this purpose with respect to each of its listed agreements.[117] Romania notified that it completed its internal procedures for the entry into effect of the MLI with respect to its agreements with Australia, Austria, Belgium, Bosnia-Herzegovina, Bulgaria, Canada, China (People's Republic of), Croatia, Cyprus, Czechia, Denmark, Egypt, Estonia, Finland, France, Georgia, Greece, Hong Kong (China), Hungary, Iceland, India, Indonesia, Ireland, Israel, Japan, Jordan, Kazakhstan, Korea, Latvia, Lithuania, Luxembourg, Malaysia, Malta, Netherlands, Norway, Pakistan, Poland, Portugal, Qatar, Russian Federation, San Marino, Saudi Arabia, Serbia, Singapore, Slovak Republic, Slovenia, South Africa, Spain, Sweden, Thailand, Ukraine, United Arab Emirates, United Kingdom, United States and Uruguay on 6 March 2023, with respect to its agreement with Mexico on 3 July 2023, with respect to its agreement with Viet Nam on 5 September 2023, and with respect to its agreement with Tunisia on 10 November 2023.

Romania has not listed its agreement with Germany under the MLI but indicated in its response to the Peer Review questionnaire that steps have been taken (other than under the MLI) to implement the minimum standard in that agreement.

Romania is implementing the minimum standard through the inclusion of the preamble statement and the PPT.[118]

B. Conclusion

No jurisdiction has raised any concerns about their agreements with Romania.

Germany has listed its agreement with Romania under the MLI, which amounts to a request to implement the minimum standard.

Summary of the jurisdiction response - Romania

	1.Treaty partners	2. Compliance with the standard	3. Signature of a complying instrument	4. Minimum standard provision used

[117] The reservation was made under Article 35(7)(a) of the MLI.

[118] For its agreements listed under the MLI, Romania is implementing the preamble statement (Article 6 of the MLI) and the PPT (Article 7 of the MLI).

1	Albania	No	Yes MLI	PPT
2	Algeria*	No	No	PPT
3	Armenia	No	Yes MLI	PPT
4	Australia	No	Yes MLI	PPT
5	Austria	No	Yes MLI	PPT
6	Azerbaijan	No	No	PPT
7	Bangladesh*	No	No	PPT
8	Belarus	No	No	PPT
9	Belgium	No	Yes MLI	PPT
10	Bosnia-Herzegovina	No	Yes MLI	PPT
11	Bulgaria	No	Yes MLI	PPT
12	Canada	No	Yes MLI	PPT
13	China (People's Republic of)	No	Yes MLI	PPT
14	Croatia	No	Yes MLI	PPT
15	Cyprus*	No	Yes MLI	PPT
16	Czechia	No	Yes MLI	PPT
17	Democratic People's Republic of Korea*	No	No	PPT
18	Denmark	No	Yes MLI	PPT
19	Ecuador*	No	No	PPT
20	Egypt	No	Yes MLI	PPT
21	Estonia	No	Yes MLI	PPT
22	Ethiopia*	No	No	PPT
23	Finland	No	Yes MLI	PPT
24	France	No	Yes MLI	PPT
25	Georgia	No	Yes MLI	PPT
26	Germany	No	No	
27	Greece	No	Yes MLI	PPT
28	Hong Kong (China)	No	Yes MLI	PPT
29	Hungary	No	Yes MLI	PPT
30	Iceland	No	Yes MLI	PPT
31	India	No	Yes MLI	PPT
32	Indonesia	No	Yes MLI	PPT
33	Iran*	No	No	PPT
34	Ireland	No	Yes MLI	PPT
35	Israel	No	Yes MLI	PPT
36	Italy	No	Yes MLI	PPT
37	Japan	No	Yes MLI	PPT
38	Jordan	No	Yes MLI	PPT
39	Kazakhstan	No	Yes MLI	PPT
40	Korea	No	Yes MLI	PPT
41	Kuwait	No	Yes MLI	PPT
42	Latvia	No	Yes MLI	PPT
43	Lebanon*	No	No	PPT
44	Lithuania	No	Yes MLI	PPT
45	Luxembourg	No	Yes MLI	PPT
46	Malaysia	No	Yes MLI	PPT
47	Malta	No	Yes MLI	PPT
48	Mexico	No	Yes MLI	PPT
49	Moldova*	No	No	PPT
50	Montenegro	No	No	PPT
51	Morocco	No	Yes MLI	PPT
52	Namibia	No	Yes MLI	PPT
53	Netherlands	No	Yes MLI	PPT

54	Nigeria	No	Yes MLI	PPT
55	North Macedonia	No	Yes MLI	PPT
56	Norway	No	Yes MLI	PPT
57	Pakistan	No	Yes MLI	PPT
58	Philippines	No	No	PPT
59	Poland	No	Yes MLI	PPT
60	Portugal	No	Yes MLI	PPT
61	Qatar	No	Yes MLI	PPT
62	Russian Federation	No	Yes MLI	PPT
63	San Marino	No	Yes MLI	PPT
64	Saudi Arabia	No	Yes MLI	PPT
65	Serbia	No	Yes MLI	PPT
66	Singapore	No	Yes MLI	PPT
67	Slovak Republic	No	Yes MLI	PPT
68	Slovenia	No	Yes MLI	PPT
69	South Africa	No	Yes MLI	PPT
70	Spain	Yes other		PPT
71	Sri Lanka	No	No	PPT
72	Sudan*	No	No	PPT
73	Sweden	No	Yes MLI	PPT
74	Switzerland	No	No	
75	Syrian Arab Republic*	No	No	PPT
76	Tajikistan*	No	No	PPT
77	Thailand	No	Yes MLI	PPT
78	Tunisia	No	Yes MLI	PPT
79	Türkiye	No	Yes MLI	PPT
80	Turkmenistan*	No	No	PPT
81	Ukraine	No	Yes MLI	PPT
82	United Arab Emirates	No	Yes MLI	PPT
83	United Kingdom	No	Yes MLI	PPT
84	United States	No	No	
85	Uruguay	No	Yes MLI	PPT
86	Uzbekistan	No	No	PPT
87	Viet Nam	No	Yes MLI	PPT
88	Zambia	No	No	PPT

Saint Kitts and Nevis

A. Progress in the implementation of the minimum standard

Saint Kitts and Nevis has ten tax agreements in force, as reported in its response to the Peer Review questionnaire, including the multilateral agreement among the members of the CARICOM concluded with ten treaty partners (the CARICOM Agreement).[119] None of those agreements comply with the minimum standard.

Saint Kitts and Nevis has not signed the MLI.

Saint Kitts and Nevis indicated in its response to the Peer Review questionnaire that steps have been taken (other than under the MLI) to implement the minimum standard in the CARICOM Agreement.

Saint Kitts and Nevis indicated that the agreement with Switzerland does not give rise to material treaty-shopping concerns for Saint Kitts and Nevis. In its response to the Peer Review questionnaire, Switzerland also indicated that its agreement with Saint Kitts and Nevis did not give rise to material treaty shopping concerns for Switzerland.

B. Conclusion

Saint Kitts and Nevis is currently developing a plan, in consultation with the Secretariat, for the implementation of the minimum standard in its agreements with Denmark, Monaco, New Zealand, Norway, San Marino, Sweden and the United Kingdom.

Summary of the jurisdiction response – Saint Kitts and Nevis

	1.Treaty partners	2. Compliance with the standard	3. Signature of a complying instrument	4. Minimum standard provision used
1	CARICOM Agreement treaty partners (Antigua and Barbuda, Barbados, Belize, Dominica, Grenada, Guyana*, Jamaica, Saint Lucia, Saint Vincent and the Grenadines, Trinidad and Tobago)	No	No	

Other agreements

	1.Treaty partners	2. Inclusive Framework member
1	Canada	Yes
2	Denmark	Yes

119 Agreement Among the Governments of the Member States of the Caribbean Community for the Avoidance of Double Taxation and the Prevention of Fiscal Evasion with Respect to Taxes on Income, Profits or Gains and Capital Gains and for the Encouragement of Regional Trade and Investment, St. Michael Barbados, 6 July 1994; between: Antigua and Barbuda (18 February 1998), Barbados (7 July 1995), Belize (30 November 1994), Dominica (19 June 1996), Grenada (1 March 1996), Guyana* (26 November 1997), Jamaica (16 February 1995), St. Kitts/Nevis (8 May 1997), St. Lucia (22 May 1995) St. Vincent (12 February 1998) and Trinidad & Tobago (29 November 1994).

3	Monaco	Yes
4	New Zealand	Yes
5	Norway	Yes
6	San Marino	Yes
7	Sweden	Yes
8	Switzerland	Yes
9	United Kingdom	Yes

Saint Lucia

A. Progress in the implementation of the minimum standard

Saint Lucia has two tax agreements in force, as reported in its response to the Peer Review questionnaire, including the multilateral agreement among the members of the CARICOM concluded with ten treaty partners (the CARICOM Agreement).[120] Neither of those agreements comply with the minimum standard.

Saint Lucia has not signed the MLI.

Saint Lucia indicated in its response to the Peer Review questionnaire that steps have been taken (other than under the MLI) to implement the minimum standard in the CARICOM Agreement.

Saint Lucia indicated in its response to the Peer Review questionnaire that the agreement with Switzerland did not at this stage give rise to material treaty shopping concerns for Saint Lucia. In its response to the Peer Review questionnaire, Switzerland also indicated that its agreement with Saint Lucia did not give rise to material treaty shopping concerns for Switzerland.

B. Conclusion

No jurisdiction has raised any concerns about their agreements with Saint Lucia.

Summary of the jurisdiction response – Saint Lucia

	1.Treaty partners	2. Compliance with the standard	3. Signature of a complying instrument	4. Minimum standard provision used
1	CARICOM Agreement treaty partners (Antigua and Barbuda, Barbados, Belize, Dominica, Grenada, Guyana*, Jamaica, Saint Kitts and Nevis, Saint Vincent and the Grenadines, Trinidad and Tobago)	No	No	

Other agreements

	1.Treaty partners	2. Inclusive Framework member
1	Switzerland	Yes

[120] Agreement Among the Governments of the Member States of the Caribbean Community for the Avoidance of Double Taxation and the Prevention of Fiscal Evasion with Respect to Taxes on Income, Profits or Gains and Capital Gains and for the Encouragement of Regional Trade and Investment, St. Michael Barbados, 6 July 1994; between: Antigua and Barbuda (18 February 1998), Barbados (7 July 1995), Belize (30 November 1994), Dominica (19 June 1996), Grenada (1 March 1996), Guyana* (26 November 1997), Jamaica (16 February 1995), St. Kitts/Nevis (8 May 1997), St. Lucia (22 May 1995) St. Vincent (12 February 1998) and Trinidad & Tobago (29 November 1994).

Saint Vincent and the Grenadines

A. Progress in the implementation of the minimum standard

Saint Vincent and the Grenadines has three tax agreements in force, as reported in its response to the Peer Review questionnaire, including the multilateral agreement among the members of the CARICOM concluded with ten treaty partners (the CARICOM Agreement).[121] None of those agreements comply with the minimum standard.

Saint Vincent and the Grenadines has not signed the MLI.

Saint Vincent and the Grenadines has signed a bilateral complying instrument with respect to its agreement with the United Arab Emirates.

Saint Vincent and the Grenadines indicated in its response to the Peer Review questionnaire that steps have been taken (other than under the MLI) to implement the minimum standard in the CARICOM Agreement.

Saint Vincent and the Grenadines also indicated that the agreement with Switzerland does not give rise to material treaty-shopping concerns for Saint Vincent and the Grenadines. In its response to the Peer Review questionnaire, Switzerland also indicated that its agreement with Saint Vincent and the Grenadines did not give rise to material treaty shopping concerns for Switzerland.

B. Conclusion

No jurisdiction has raised any concerns about their agreements with Saint Vincent and the Grenadines.

Summary of the jurisdiction response – Saint Vincent and the Grenadines

	1.Treaty partners	2. Compliance with the standard	3. Signature of a complying instrument	4. Minimum standard provision used
1	CARICOM Agreement treaty partners (Antigua and Barbuda, Barbados, Belize, Dominica, Grenada, Guyana*, Jamaica, Saint Kitts and Nevis, Saint Lucia, Trinidad and Tobago)	No	No	
2	United Arab Emirates	No	Yes other	

[121] Agreement Among the Governments of the Member States of the Caribbean Community for the Avoidance of Double Taxation and the Prevention of Fiscal Evasion with Respect to Taxes on Income, Profits or Gains and Capital Gains and for the Encouragement of Regional Trade and Investment, St. Michael Barbados, 6 July 1994; between: Antigua and Barbuda (18 February 1998), Barbados (7 July 1995), Belize (30 November 1994), Dominica (19 June 1996), Grenada (1 March 1996), Guyana* (26 November 1997), Jamaica (16 February 1995), St. Kitts/Nevis (8 May 1997), St. Lucia (22 May 1995) St. Vincent (12 February 1998) and Trinidad & Tobago (29 November 1994).

Other agreements

	1.Treaty partners	2. Inclusive Framework member
1	Switzerland	Yes

Samoa

A. Progress in the implementation of the minimum standard

Samoa has one tax agreement in force, the agreement with New Zealand, as reported in its response to the Peer Review questionnaire. This agreement complies with the minimum standard.

B. Conclusion

No jurisdiction has raised any concerns about their agreements with Samoa.

Summary of the jurisdiction response – Samoa

	1.Treaty partners	2. Compliance with the standard	3. Signature of a complying instrument	4. Minimum standard provision used
1	New Zealand	Yes other		PPT

San Marino

A. Progress in the implementation of the minimum standard

San Marino has 25 tax agreements in force, as reported in its response to the Peer Review questionnaire. Eighteen of those agreements comply with the minimum standard.

San Marino signed the MLI in 2017 and deposited its instrument of ratification on 11 March 2020, listing its non-compliant agreements. The MLI entered into force for San Marino on 1 July 2020. The agreements modified by the MLI come into compliance with the minimum standard once the provisions of the MLI take effect.

San Marino is implementing the minimum standard through the inclusion of the preamble statement and the PPT.[122]

B. Conclusion

No jurisdiction has raised any concerns about their agreements with San Marino.

Summary of the jurisdiction response – San Marino

	1.Treaty partners	2. Compliance with the standard	3. Signature of a complying instrument	4. Minimum standard provision used
1	Andorra	Yes other		PPT
2	Austria	No	No	PPT
3	Azerbaijan	No	No	PPT
4	Barbados	Yes MLI		PPT
5	Belgium	Yes MLI		PPT
6	Croatia	Yes MLI		PPT
7	Cyprus*	Yes MLI		PPT
8	Czechia	Yes other		PPT
9	Georgia	Yes MLI		PPT
10	Greece	Yes MLI		PPT
11	Hungary	Yes MLI		PPT
12	Italy	No	Yes MLI	PPT
13	Liechtenstein	Yes MLI		PPT
14	Luxembourg	Yes MLI		PPT
15	Malaysia	Yes MLI		PPT
16	Malta	Yes MLI		PPT
17	Portugal	Yes MLI		PPT
18	Qatar	Yes MLI		PPT
19	Romania	No	Yes MLI	PPT
20	Saint Kitts and Nevis	No	No	PPT
21	Serbia	Yes other		PPT
22	Seychelles	Yes MLI		PPT

[122] For its agreements listed under the MLI, San Marino is implementing the preamble statement (Article 6 of the MLI) and the PPT (Article 7 of the MLI). San Marino made a reservation pursuant to Article 7(15)(b) of the MLI not to apply Article 7(1) of the MLI with respect to agreements that already contain a PPT (covering three agreements).

23	Singapore	Yes MLI		PPT
24	United Arab Emirates	No	No	PPT
25	Viet Nam	No	Yes MLI	PPT

Saudi Arabia

A. Progress in the implementation of the minimum standard

Saudi Arabia has 56 tax agreements in force, as reported in its response to the Peer Review questionnaire. Thirty of those agreements comply with the minimum standard.

Saudi Arabia signed the MLI in 2018 and deposited its instrument of ratification on 23 January 2020. The MLI entered into force for Saudi Arabia on 1 May 2020. The agreements modified by the MLI come into compliance with the minimum standard once the provisions of the MLI take effect.

Saudi Arabia is implementing the minimum standard through the inclusion of the preamble statement and the PPT.[123]

B. Conclusion

No jurisdiction has raised any concerns about their agreements with Saudi Arabia.

Summary of the jurisdiction response – Saudi Arabia

	1.Treaty partners	2. Compliance with the standard	3. Signature of a complying instrument	4. Minimum standard provision used
1	Albania	No	No	PPT
2	Algeria*	No	No	PPT
3	Austria	No	No	PPT
4	Azerbaijan	No	No	PPT
5	Bangladesh*	No	No	PPT
6	Belarus	No	No	PPT
7	Bulgaria	Yes other		PPT
8	China (People's Republic of)	Yes MLI		PPT
9	Cyprus*	Yes MLI		PPT
10	Czechia	No	No	PPT
11	Egypt	Yes MLI		PPT
12	Ethiopia*	No	No	PPT
13	France	Yes MLI		PPT
14	Gabon	No	No	PPT
15	Georgia	No	No	PPT
16	Greece	Yes MLI		PPT
17	Hong Kong (China)	Yes MLI		PPT
18	Hungary	Yes MLI		PPT
19	India	Yes MLI		PPT
20	Ireland	Yes MLI		PPT
21	Italy	No	Yes MLI	PPT
22	Japan	Yes MLI		PPT
23	Jordan	Yes MLI		PPT
24	Kazakhstan	Yes MLI		PPT

[123] For its agreements listed under the MLI, Saudi Arabia is implementing the preamble statement (Article 6 of the MLI) and the PPT (Article 7 of the MLI).

25	Korea	Yes MLI		PPT
26	Kyrgyzstan*	No	No	PPT
27	Latvia	Yes other		
28	Luxembourg	Yes MLI		PPT
29	Malaysia	Yes MLI		PPT
30	Malta	Yes MLI		PPT
31	Mexico	No	Yes MLI	PPT
32	Morocco	No	Yes MLI	PPT
33	Netherlands	Yes MLI		PPT
34	North Macedonia	No	Yes MLI	PPT
35	Pakistan	Yes MLI		PPT
36	Poland	Yes MLI		PPT
37	Portugal	Yes MLI		PPT
38	Romania	No	Yes MLI	PPT
39	Russian Federation	Yes MLI		PPT
40	Singapore	Yes MLI		PPT
41	South Africa	Yes MLI		PPT
42	Spain	Yes MLI		PPT
43	Sweden	No	Yes MLI	PPT
44	Switzerland	Yes other		PPT
45	Syria*	No	No	PPT
46	Tajikistan*	No	No	PPT
47	Tunisia	No	No	PPT
48	Türkiye	No	Yes MLI	PPT
49	Turkmenistan*	No	No	PPT
50	Ukraine	Yes MLI		PPT
51	United Arab Emirates	Yes other		PPT
52	United Kingdom	Yes MLI		PPT
53	Uzbekistan	No	No	PPT
54	Venezuela*	No	No	PPT
55	Viet Nam	No	Yes MLI	PPT

Other agreements

	1.Treaty partners	2. Inclusive Framework member
1	Kosovo*	No

Senegal

A. Progress in the implementation of the minimum standard

Senegal has 20 tax agreements in force, as reported in its response to the Peer Review questionnaire, including the multilateral Regulation 08/2008/COM adopting the rules for the avoidance of double taxation within the West African Economic and Monetary Union and the rule for assistance in tax matters (the UEMOA) concluded with seven treaty partners,[124] and the multilateral Supplementary Act A/SA, 5/12/18 adopting community rules for the elimination of double taxation with respect to taxes on income, capital and inheritance and the prevention of tax evasion and avoidance within the ECOWAS Member States (the ECOWAS Supplementary Act) concluded with fourteen treaty partners. Twelve of those agreements, including the ECOWAS Supplementary Act, comply with the minimum standard.

Senegal signed the MLI in 2017 and deposited its instrument of ratification on 10 May 2022, listing its non-compliant bilateral agreements concluded with other members of the Inclusive Framework. The MLI entered into force for Senegal on 1 September 2022. The agreements modified by the MLI come into compliance with the minimum standard once the provisions of the MLI take effect.

Senegal is implementing the minimum standard through the inclusion of the preamble statement and the PPT combined with the LOB.[125]

B. Conclusion

The UEMOA does not at this stage comply with the minimum standard and discussions to bring this agreement up to date should be contemplated.[126]

Summary of the jurisdiction response – Senegal

	1.Treaty partners	2. Compliance with the standard	3. Signature of a complying instrument	4. Minimum standard provision used
1	Belgium	Yes MLI		PPT
2	Cabo Verde	Yes other		PPT
3	Canada	Yes MLI		PPT

[124] Règlement n°08/2008/CM des pays de l'Union économique et monétaire Ouest Africaine (UEMOA) du 26 septembre 2008 portant adoption des règles visant à éviter la double imposition au sein de l'UEMOA et des règles d'assistance en matière fiscale.

[125] For its agreements listed under the MLI, Senegal is implementing the preamble statement (Article 6 of the MLI) and the PPT (Article 7 of the MLI). Senegal has also adopted for the simplified LOB under Article 7(6) of the MLI and expressed a statement, in accordance with Article 7(17)(a) of the MLI, that while it accepts the application of the PPT under the MLI, it intends where possible to adopt an LOB provision through bilateral negotiation. Senegal has made a reservation pursuant to Article 6(4) of the MLI not to apply Article 6(1) of the MLI with respect to agreements, which already contain the relevant preamble language (covering one agreement). Senegal has also made a reservation pursuant to Article 7(15)(b) of the MLI not to apply Article 7(1) of the MLI with respect to agreements which already contain a PPT (covering one agreement).

[126] Revisions to the UEMOA require an agreement from its eight treaty partners.

4	France	Yes MLI		PPT
5	Italy	No	Yes MLI	PPT
6	Lebanon*	No	No	PPT
7	Luxembourg	Yes other		PPT
8	Malaysia	Yes MLI		PPT
9	Mauritania	No	No	PPT
10	Morocco	No	Yes MLI	PPT
11	Norway	No	No	PPT
12	ECOWAS Supplementary Act treaty partners (Benin, Burkina Faso, Cabo Verde, Côte d'Ivoire, The Gambia*, Ghana*, Guinea-Bissau*, Guinea Conakry*, Liberia, Mali*, Niger*, Nigeria, Sierra Leone, Togo)	Yes other		PPT
13	Portugal	Yes MLI		PPT
14	Qatar	Yes MLI		PPT
15	Spain	Yes MLI		PPT
16	Tunisia	No	Yes MLI	PPT
17	United Arab Emirates	Yes MLI		PPT
18	United Kingdom	Yes MLI		PPT

Other agreements

	1.Treaty partners	1.Treaty partners
1	Chinese Taipei*	No
2	UEMOA treaty partners (Benin, Burkina Faso, Côte d'Ivoire, Guinea-Bissau*, Mali*, Niger*, Togo)	Yes (Benin, Burkina Faso, Côte d'Ivoire, Togo) No (Guinea-Bissau*, Mali*, Niger*)

Serbia

A. Progress in the implementation of the minimum standard

Serbia has 64 tax agreements in force, as reported in its response to the Peer Review questionnaire. Forty-three of those agreements comply with the minimum standard.

Serbia signed the MLI in 2017 and deposited its instrument of ratification on 5 June 2018, listing its non-compliant agreements. The MLI entered into force for Serbia on 1 October 2018. The agreements modified by the MLI come into compliance with the minimum standard once the provisions of the MLI take effect.

Serbia is implementing the minimum standard through the inclusion of the preamble statement and the PPT.[127]

B. Conclusion

No jurisdiction has raised any concerns about their agreements with Serbia.

Summary of the jurisdiction response - Serbia

	1.Treaty partners	2. Compliance with the standard	3. Signature of a complying instrument	4. Minimum standard provision used
1	Albania	Yes MLI		PPT
2	Armenia	No	Yes MLI	PPT
3	Austria	Yes MLI		PPT
4	Azerbaijan	No	No	PPT
5	Belarus	No	No	PPT
6	Belgium	Yes MLI		PPT
7	Bosnia-Herzegovina	Yes MLI		PPT
8	Bulgaria	Yes MLI		PPT
9	Canada	Yes MLI		PPT
10	China (People's Republic of)	Yes MLI		PPT
11	Croatia	Yes MLI		PPT
12	Cyprus*	Yes MLI		PPT
13	Czechia	Yes MLI		PPT
14	Democratic People's Republic of Korea*	No	No	PPT
15	Denmark	Yes MLI		PPT
16	Egypt	Yes MLI		PPT
17	Estonia	No	Yes MLI	PPT
18	Finland	Yes MLI		PPT
19	France	Yes MLI		PPT
20	Georgia	Yes MLI		PPT
21	Germany	No	No	PPT
22	Greece	Yes MLI		PPT
23	Hong Kong (China)	Yes other		PPT

127 For its agreements listed under the MLI, Serbia is implementing the preamble statement (Article 6 of the MLI) and the PPT (Article 7 of the MLI).

24	Hungary	Yes MLI		PPT
25	India	Yes MLI		PPT
26	Indonesia	Yes MLI		PPT
27	Iran*	No	No	PPT
28	Ireland	Yes MLI		PPT
29	Israel	Yes other		PPT
30	Italy	No	Yes MLI	PPT
31	Japan	Yes other		PPT
32	Kazakhstan	Yes MLI		PPT
33	Korea	Yes MLI		PPT
34	Kuwait	No	Yes MLI	PPT
35	Latvia	Yes MLI		PPT
36	Libya*	No	No	PPT
37	Lithuania	Yes MLI		PPT
38	Luxembourg	Yes MLI		PPT
39	Malta	Yes MLI		PPT
40	Moldova*	No	No	PPT
41	Montenegro	No	No	PPT
42	Morocco	No	Yes MLI	PPT
43	Netherlands	Yes MLI		PPT
44	North Macedonia	No	Yes MLI	PPT
45	Norway	Yes MLI		PPT
46	Pakistan	Yes MLI		PPT
47	Poland	Yes MLI		PPT
48	Qatar	Yes MLI		PPT
49	Romania	No	Yes MLI	PPT
50	Russian Federation	Yes MLI		PPT
51	San Marino	Yes other		PPT
52	Singapore	Yes other		PPT
53	Slovak Republic	Yes MLI		PPT
54	Slovenia	Yes MLI		PPT
55	Spain	Yes MLI		PPT
56	Sri Lanka	No	No	PPT
57	Sweden	No	No	PPT
58	Switzerland	No	No	PPT
59	Tunisia	No	Yes MLI	PPT
60	Türkiye	No	Yes MLI	PPT
61	Ukraine	Yes MLI		PPT
62	United Arab Emirates	Yes MLI		PPT
63	United Kingdom	Yes MLI		PPT
64	Viet Nam	No	Yes MLI	PPT

Seychelles

A. Progress in the implementation of the minimum standard

The Seychelles has 29 tax agreements in force, as reported in its response to the Peer Review questionnaire. Twenty of those agreements comply with the minimum standard.

The Seychelles signed the MLI in 2017 and deposited its instrument of ratification on 14 December 2021, listing its non-compliant agreements. The MLI entered into force for the Seychelles on 1 April 2022. The agreements modified by the MLI come into compliance with the minimum standard once the provisions of the MLI take effect.

The Seychelles is implementing the minimum standard through the inclusion of the preamble statement and the PPT.[128]

B. Conclusion

No jurisdiction has raised any concerns about their agreements with the Seychelles.

Summary of the jurisdiction response - Seychelles

	1.Treaty partners	2. Compliance with the standard	3. Signature of a complying instrument	4. Minimum standard provision used
1	Bahrain	Yes MLI		PPT
2	Barbados	Yes MLI		PPT
3	Belgium	Yes MLI		PPT
4	Bermuda	No	No	
5	Botswana	No	No	
6	China (People's Republic of)	Yes MLI		PPT
7	Cyprus*	Yes MLI		PPT
8	Eswatini	No	No	
9	Ethiopia*	No	No	
10	Guernsey	Yes MLI		PPT
11	Indonesia	Yes MLI		PPT
12	Isle of Man	Yes MLI		PPT
13	Jersey	Yes MLI		PPT
14	Kenya	No	Yes MLI	PPT
15	Kuwait	No	Yes MLI	PPT
16	Luxembourg	Yes MLI		PPT
17	Malaysia	Yes MLI		PPT
18	Mauritius	Yes MLI		PPT
19	Monaco	Yes MLI		PPT
20	Oman	Yes MLI		PPT
21	Qatar	Yes MLI		PPT
22	San Marino	Yes MLI		PPT

128 For its agreements listed under the MLI, the Seychelles is implementing the preamble statement (Article 6 of the MLI) and the PPT (Article 7 of the MLI). The Seychelles expressed a statement that while it accepts the application of the PPT under the MLI, it intends where possible to adopt an LOB provision through bilateral negotiation.

23	Singapore	Yes MLI		PPT
24	South Africa	Yes MLI		PPT
25	Sri Lanka	No	No	
26	Thailand	Yes MLI		PPT
27	United Arab Emirates	Yes MLI		PPT
28	Viet Nam	No	Yes MLI	PPT
29	Zambia	No	No	

Sierra Leone

A. Progress in the implementation of the minimum standard

Sierra Leone has four tax agreements in force, as reported in its response to the Peer Review questionnaire, including the multilateral Supplementary Act A/SA, 5/12/18 adopting community rules for the elimination of double taxation with respect to taxes on income, capital and inheritance and the prevention of tax evasion and avoidance within the ECOWAS Member States (the ECOWAS Supplementary Act) concluded with fourteen treaty partners. One of those agreements, the ECOWAS Supplementary Act, complies with the minimum standard.

Sierra Leone has not signed the MLI.

Sierra Leone is implementing the minimum standard through the inclusion of the preamble statement and the PPT.

B. Conclusion

Recommendation

It is recommended that Sierra Leone formulates a plan for the implementation of the minimum standard in the agreements for which no steps have yet been taken and that were concluded with members of the BEPS Inclusive Framework (Norway, South Africa, and the United Kingdom)

Summary of the jurisdiction response – Sierra Leone

	1.Treaty partners	2. Compliance with the standard	3. Signature of a complying instrument	4. Minimum standard provision used
1	ECOWAS Supplementary Act treaty partners (Benin, Burkina Faso, Cabo Verde, Côte d'Ivoire, The Gambia*, Ghana*, Guinea-Bissau*, Guinea Conakry*, Liberia, Mali*, Niger*, Nigeria, Senegal, Togo)	Yes other		PPT

Other agreements

	1.Treaty partners	2. Inclusive Framework member
1	Norway	Yes
2	South Africa	Yes
3	United Kingdom	Yes

Singapore

A. Progress in the implementation of the minimum standard

Singapore has 93 tax agreements in force, as reported in its response to the Peer Review questionnaire. Sixty-two of those agreements comply with the minimum standard.

Singapore signed the MLI in 2017 and deposited its instrument of ratification on 21 December 2018, listing its non-compliant agreements concluded with other members of the Inclusive Framework. The MLI entered into force for Singapore on 1 April 2019. The agreements modified by the MLI come into compliance with the minimum standard once the provisions of the MLI take effect.

Singapore is implementing the minimum standard in its tax agreements through the inclusion of the preamble statement and the PPT.[129]

B. Conclusion

No jurisdiction has raised any concerns about their agreements with Singapore.

Summary of the jurisdiction response - Singapore

	1.Treaty partners	2. Compliance with the standard	3. Signature of a complying instrument	4. Minimum standard provision used
1	Albania	Yes MLI		PPT
2	Armenia	Yes other		PPT
3	Australia	Yes MLI		PPT
4	Austria	Yes MLI		PPT
5	Bahrain	Yes MLI		PPT
6	Bangladesh*	No	No	PPT
7	Barbados	Yes MLI		PPT
8	Belarus	No	No	PPT
9	Belgium	Yes MLI		PPT
10	Brazil	Yes other		PPT+LOB
11	Brunei Darussalam	No	No	PPT
12	Bulgaria	Yes MLI		PPT
13	Cambodia*	No	No	PPT
14	Canada	Yes MLI		PPT
15	China (People's Republic of)	Yes MLI		PPT
16	Chinese Taipei*	No	No	PPT
17	Cyprus*	Yes MLI		PPT
18	Czechia	Yes MLI		PPT
19	Denmark	Yes MLI		PPT
20	Ecuador*	No	No	PPT
21	Egypt	Yes MLI		PPT
22	Estonia	No	Yes MLI	PPT
23	Ethiopia*	No	No	PPT

[129] For its agreements listed under the MLI, Singapore is implementing the preamble statement (Article 6 of the MLI) and the PPT (Article 7 of the MLI).

24	Fiji*	No	Yes MLI	PPT
25	Finland	Yes MLI		PPT
26	France	Yes MLI		PPT
27	Georgia	Yes MLI		PPT
28	Germany	Yes other		PPT
29	Ghana*	No	No	PPT
30	Greece	Yes other		PPT
31	Guernsey	Yes MLI		PPT
32	Hungary	Yes MLI		PPT
33	India	Yes MLI		PPT
34	Indonesia	Yes other		PPT
35	Ireland	Yes MLI		PPT
36	Isle of Man	Yes MLI		PPT
37	Israel	Yes MLI		PPT
38	Italy	No	Yes MLI	PPT
39	Japan	Yes MLI		PPT
40	Jersey	Yes MLI		PPT
41	Jordan	Yes other		PPT
42	Kazakhstan	Yes MLI		PPT
43	Korea	Yes other		PPT
44	Kuwait	No	Yes MLI	PPT
45	Lao People's Democratic Republic*	No	No	PPT
46	Latvia	Yes MLI		PPT
47	Libya*	No	No	PPT
48	Liechtenstein	Yes MLI		PPT
49	Lithuania	Yes MLI		PPT
50	Luxembourg	Yes MLI		PPT
51	Malaysia	Yes MLI		PPT
52	Malta	Yes MLI		PPT
53	Mauritius	Yes MLI		PPT
54	Mexico	No	Yes MLI	PPT
55	Mongolia	No	Yes MLI	PPT
56	Morocco	No	Yes MLI	PPT
57	Myanmar*	No	No	PPT
58	Netherlands	Yes MLI		PPT
59	New Zealand	Yes MLI		PPT
60	Nigeria	No	Yes MLI	PPT
61	Norway	No	No	PPT
62	Oman	Yes MLI		PPT
63	Pakistan	Yes MLI		PPT
64	Panama	Yes MLI		PPT
65	Papua New Guinea	No	Yes MLI	PPT
66	Philippines	No	No	PPT
67	Poland	Yes MLI		PPT
68	Portugal	Yes MLI		PPT
69	Qatar	Yes MLI		PPT
70	Romania	No	Yes MLI	PPT
71	Russian Federation	Yes MLI		PPT
72	Rwanda*	No	No	PPT
73	San Marino	Yes MLI		PPT
74	Saudi Arabia	Yes MLI		PPT
75	Serbia	Yes other		PPT
76	Seychelles	Yes MLI		PPT

77	Slovak Republic	Yes MLI		PPT
78	Slovenia	Yes MLI		PPT
79	South Africa	Yes MLI		PPT
80	Spain	Yes MLI		PPT
81	Sri Lanka	No	No	PPT
82	Sweden	No	No	PPT
83	Switzerland	No	No	PPT
84	Thailand	Yes MLI		PPT
85	Tunisia	No	Yes MLI	PPT
86	Türkiye	No	Yes MLI	PPT
87	Turkmenistan*	Yes other		PPT
88	Ukraine	Yes MLI		PPT
89	United Arab Emirates	Yes MLI		PPT
90	United Kingdom	Yes MLI		PPT
91	Uruguay	Yes MLI		PPT
92	Uzbekistan	No	No	PPT
93	Viet Nam	No	Yes MLI	PPT

Slovak Republic

A. Progress in the implementation of the minimum standard

The Slovak Republic has 70 tax agreements in force as reported in its response to the Peer Review questionnaire. Forty-one of those agreements comply with the minimum standard.

The Slovak Republic signed the MLI in 2017 and deposited its instrument of ratification on 20 September 2018. The MLI entered into force for the Slovak Republic on 1 January 2019. The agreements modified by the MLI come into compliance with the minimum standard once the provisions of the MLI take effect.

The Slovak Republic has not listed its agreements with Armenia, Oman and the United Arab Emirates but indicated in its response to the Peer Review questionnaire that steps have been taken (other than under the MLI) to implement the minimum standard in those agreements, as well as the agreements with Brazil, Ethiopia* and Iran*. Armenia, Oman and the United Arab Emirates have listed their agreements with the Slovak Republic under the MLI.

The Slovak Republic is implementing the minimum standard through the inclusion of the preamble statement and the PPT combined with the LOB.[130]

B. Conclusion

No jurisdiction has raised any concerns about their agreements with the Slovak Republic.

Armenia, Oman and the United Arab Emirates have listed their agreements with the Slovak Republic under the MLI, which amount to requests to implement the minimum standard.

Summary of the jurisdiction response – Slovak Republic

	1.Treaty partners	2. Compliance with the standard	3. Signature of a complying instrument	4. Minimum standard provision used
1	Armenia	No	No	PPT+LOB
2	Australia	Yes MLI		PPT
3	Austria	Yes MLI		PPT
4	Belarus	No	No	
5	Belgium	Yes MLI		PPT
6	Bosnia-Herzegovina	Yes MLI		PPT
7	Brazil	No	No	PPT+LOB
8	Bulgaria	Yes MLI		PPT
9	Canada	Yes MLI		PPT
10	China (People's Republic of)	Yes MLI		PPT
11	Croatia	Yes MLI		PPT
12	Cyprus*	Yes MLI		PPT
13	Czechia	Yes MLI		PPT
14	Denmark	Yes MLI		PPT+LOB

130 For its agreements listed under the MLI, the Slovak Republic is implementing the preamble statement (Article 6 of the MLI) and the PPT (Article 7 of the MLI). The Slovak Republic has also adopted for the simplified LOB under Article 7(6) of the MLI.

15	Estonia	Yes MLI		PPT
16	Ethiopia*	No	No	PPT+LOB
17	Finland	Yes MLI		PPT
18	France	Yes MLI		PPT
19	Georgia	Yes MLI		PPT
20	Germany	No	Yes MLI	PPT
21	Greece	Yes MLI		PPT+LOB
22	Hungary	Yes MLI		PPT
23	Iceland	Yes MLI		PPT+LOB
24	India	Yes MLI		PPT+LOB
25	Indonesia	Yes MLI		PPT
26	Iran*	No	No	PPT
27	Ireland	Yes MLI		PPT
28	Israel	Yes MLI		PPT
29	Italy	No	Yes MLI	PPT
30	Japan	Yes MLI		PPT
31	Kazakhstan	Yes MLI		PPT+LOB
32	Korea	Yes MLI		PPT
33	Kuwait	No	Yes MLI	PPT
34	Latvia	Yes MLI		PPT
35	Libya*	No	No	
36	Lithuania	Yes MLI		PPT
37	Luxembourg	Yes MLI		PPT
38	Malaysia	Yes MLI		PPT
39	Malta	Yes MLI		PPT
40	Mexico	No	Yes MLI	PPT+LOB
41	Moldova*	No	No	
42	Montenegro	No	No	
43	Netherlands	Yes MLI		PPT
44	Nigeria	No	Yes MLI	PPT
45	North Macedonia	No	Yes MLI	PPT
46	Norway	No	No	
47	Oman	No	No	
48	Poland	Yes MLI		PPT
49	Portugal	Yes MLI		PPT
50	Romania	No	Yes MLI	PPT
51	Russian Federation	Yes MLI		PPT+LOB
52	Serbia	Yes MLI		PPT
53	Singapore	Yes MLI		PPT
54	Slovenia	Yes MLI		PPT
55	South Africa	Yes MLI		PPT
56	Spain	Yes MLI		PPT
57	Sri Lanka	No	No	
58	Sweden	No	Yes MLI	PPT
59	Switzerland	No	No	
60	Syrian Arab Republic*	No	No	
61	Tunisia	No	Yes MLI	PPT
62	Türkiye	No	Yes MLI	PPT
63	Turkmenistan*	No	No	
64	Ukraine	Yes MLI		PPT
65	United Arab Emirates	No	No	
66	United Kingdom	Yes MLI		PPT
67	United States	No	No	

68	Uzbekistan	No	No	
69	Viet Nam	No	Yes MLI	PPT

Other agreements

	1.Treaty partners	2. Inclusive Framework member
1	Chinese Taipei*	No

Slovenia

A. Progress in the implementation of the minimum standard

Slovenia has 60 tax agreements in force as reported in its response to the Peer Review questionnaire. Forty-two of those agreements comply with the minimum standard.

Slovenia signed the MLI in 2017 and deposited its instrument of ratification of the MLI on 22 March 2018. The MLI entered into force for Slovenia on 1 July 2018. The agreements modified by the MLI come into compliance with the minimum standard once the provisions of the MLI take effect.

Slovenia has not listed its agreements with Germany and Montenegro under the MLI but indicated in its response to the Peer Review questionnaire that steps have been taken (other than under the MLI) to implement the minimum standard in those agreements.

Slovenia has signed a bilateral complying instrument with respect to its agreement with Switzerland.

Slovenia is implementing the minimum standard through the inclusion of the preamble statement and the PPT.[131]

B. Conclusion

No jurisdiction has raised any concerns about their agreements with Slovenia.

Summary of the jurisdiction response - Slovenia

	1.Treaty partners	2. Compliance with the standard	3. Signature of a complying instrument	4. Minimum standard provision used
1	Albania	Yes MLI		PPT
2	Armenia	No	Yes MLI	PPT
3	Austria	Yes MLI		PPT
4	Azerbaijan	No	No	PPT
5	Belarus	No	No	PPT
6	Belgium	Yes MLI		PPT
7	Bosnia-Herzegovina	Yes MLI		PPT
8	Bulgaria	Yes MLI		PPT
9	Canada	Yes MLI		PPT
10	China (People's Republic of)	Yes MLI		PPT
11	Croatia	Yes MLI		PPT
12	Cyprus*	Yes MLI		PPT
13	Czechia	Yes MLI		PPT
14	Denmark	Yes MLI		PPT
15	Estonia	No	Yes MLI	PPT
16	Finland	Yes MLI		PPT
17	France	Yes MLI		PPT
18	Georgia	Yes MLI		PPT
19	Germany	No	No	PPT

131 For its agreements listed under the MLI, Slovenia is implementing the preamble statement (Article 6 of the MLI) and the PPT (Article 7 of the MLI).

20	Greece	Yes MLI		PPT
21	Hungary	Yes MLI		PPT
22	Iceland	Yes MLI		PPT
23	India	Yes MLI		PPT
24	Iran*	No	No	PPT
25	Ireland	Yes MLI		PPT
26	Israel	Yes MLI		PPT
27	Italy	No	Yes MLI	PPT
28	Japan	Yes other		PPT
29	Kazakhstan	Yes MLI		PPT
30	Korea	Yes MLI		PPT
31	Kosovo*	No	No	PPT
32	Kuwait	No	Yes MLI	PPT
33	Latvia	Yes MLI		PPT
34	Lithuania	Yes MLI		PPT
35	Luxembourg	Yes MLI		PPT
36	Malta	Yes MLI		PPT
37	Moldova*	No	No	PPT
38	Montenegro	No	No	PPT
39	Morocco	No	Yes MLI	PPT
40	Netherlands	Yes MLI		PPT
41	North Macedonia	No	Yes MLI	PPT
42	Norway	Yes MLI		PPT
43	Poland	Yes MLI		PPT
44	Portugal	Yes MLI		PPT
45	Qatar	Yes MLI		PPT
46	Romania	No	Yes MLI	PPT
47	Russian Federation	Yes MLI		PPT
48	Serbia	Yes MLI		PPT
49	Singapore	Yes MLI		PPT
50	Slovak Republic	Yes MLI		PPT
51	Spain	Yes MLI		PPT
52	Sweden	Yes other		PPT
53	Switzerland	No	Yes other	PPT
54	Thailand	Yes MLI		PPT
55	Türkiye	No	Yes MLI	PPT
56	Ukraine	Yes MLI		PPT
57	United Arab Emirates	Yes MLI		PPT
58	United Kingdom	Yes MLI		PPT
59	United States	No	No	
60	Uzbekistan	No	No	PPT

South Africa

A. Progress in the implementation of the minimum standard

South Africa has 79 tax agreements in force as reported in its response to the Peer Review questionnaire. Forty-four of those agreements comply with the minimum standard.

South Africa signed the MLI in 2017 and deposited its instrument of ratification on 30 September 2022. The MLI enters into force for South Africa on 1 January 2023. The agreements modified by the MLI come into compliance with the minimum standard once the provisions of the MLI take effect.

South Africa has not listed its agreements with Germany, Grenada, Sierra Leone and Zambia under the MLI. These agreements will therefore not, at this stage, be modified by the MLI.

South Africa indicated in its response to the Peer Review questionnaire that steps have been taken (other than under the MLI) to implement the minimum standard in its agreements with Germany, Malawi* and Zambia.

South Africa is implementing the minimum standard through the inclusion of the preamble statement and the PPT.[132]

B. Conclusion

South Africa has developed a plan for the implementation of the minimum standard in its agreements with Grenada and Sierra Leone. South Africa indicated in its response to the Peer Review questionnaire that bilateral negotiations would be pursued with respect to those agreements.

Summary of the jurisdiction response – South Africa

	1.Treaty partners	2. Compliance with the standard	3. Signature of a complying instrument	4. Minimum standard provision used
1	Algeria*	No	No	PPT
2	Australia	Yes MLI		PPT
3	Austria	Yes MLI		PPT
4	Belarus	No	No	PPT
5	Belgium	Yes MLI		PPT
6	Botswana	No	No	PPT
7	Brazil	No	No	PPT
8	Bulgaria	Yes MLI		PPT
9	Cameroon	Yes MLI		PPT
10	Canada	Yes MLI		PPT
11	Chile	Yes MLI		PPT
12	China (People's Republic of)	Yes MLI		PPT
13	Chinese Taipei*	No	No	PPT
14	Croatia	Yes MLI		PPT
15	Cyprus*	Yes MLI		PPT

[132] For its agreements listed under the MLI, South Africa is implementing the preamble statement (Article 6 of the MLI) and the PPT (Article 7 of the MLI).

16	Czechia	Yes MLI		PPT
17	Democratic Republic of the Congo	No	No	PPT
18	Denmark	Yes MLI		PPT
19	Egypt	Yes MLI		PPT
20	Eswatini	No	No	PPT
21	Ethiopia*	No	No	PPT
22	Finland	Yes MLI		PPT
23	France	Yes MLI		PPT
24	Germany	No	No	PPT
25	Ghana*	No	No	PPT
26	Greece	Yes MLI		PPT
27	Hong Kong (China)	Yes MLI		PPT
28	Hungary	Yes MLI		PPT
29	India	Yes MLI		PPT
30	Indonesia	No	Yes MLI	PPT
31	Iran*	No	No	PPT
32	Ireland	Yes MLI		PPT
33	Israel	Yes MLI		PPT
34	Italy	No	Yes MLI	PPT
35	Japan	Yes MLI		PPT
36	Kenya	No	Yes MLI	PPT
37	Korea	Yes MLI		PPT
38	Kuwait	No	Yes MLI	PPT
39	Lesotho*	Yes MLI		PPT
40	Luxembourg	Yes MLI		PPT
41	Malawi*	No	No	PPT
42	Malaysia	Yes MLI		PPT
43	Malta	Yes MLI		PPT
44	Mauritius	Yes MLI		PPT
45	Mexico	No	Yes MLI	PPT
46	Mozambique*	No	No	PPT
47	Namibia	No	No	PPT
48	Netherlands	Yes MLI		PPT
49	New Zealand	Yes MLI		PPT
50	Nigeria	No	Yes MLI	PPT
51	Norway	Yes MLI		PPT
52	Oman	Yes MLI		PPT
53	Pakistan	Yes MLI		PPT
54	Poland	Yes MLI		PPT
55	Portugal	Yes MLI		PPT
56	Qatar	Yes MLI		PPT
57	Romania	No	Yes MLI	PPT
58	Russian Federation	No	Yes MLI	PPT
59	Rwanda*	No	No	PPT
60	Saudi Arabia	Yes MLI		PPT
61	Seychelles	Yes MLI		PPT
62	Singapore	Yes MLI		PPT
63	Slovak Republic	Yes MLI		PPT
64	Spain	No	Yes MLI	PPT
65	Sweden	No	Yes MLI	PPT
66	Switzerland	No	Yes MLI	PPT
67	Tanzania*	No	No	PPT
68	Thailand	Yes MLI		PPT

69	Tunisia	No	Yes MLI	PPT
70	Türkiye	No	Yes MLI	PPT
71	Uganda*	No	No	PPT
72	Ukraine	Yes MLI		PPT
73	United Arab Emirates	Yes MLI		PPT
74	United Kingdom	Yes MLI		PPT
75	United States	No	No	LOB included in DTA
76	Zambia	No	No	PPT
77	Zimbabwe*	No	No	PPT

Other agreements

	1.Treaty partners	2. Inclusive Framework member
1	Grenada	Yes
2	Sierra Leone	Yes

Spain

A. Progress in the implementation of the minimum standard

Spain has 93 tax agreements in force as reported in its response to the Peer Review questionnaire. Fifty-four of those agreements comply with the minimum standard.

Spain signed the MLI in 2017 and deposited its instrument of ratification on 28 September 2021. The MLI entered into force for Spain on 1 January 2022. The agreements modified by the MLI come into compliance with the minimum standard once the provisions of the MLI take effect.

Spain reserved the right to delay the entry into effect of the provisions of the MLI until Spain has completed its internal procedures for this purpose with respect to each of its listed agreements.[133] Spain notified that it completed its internal procedures for the entry into effect of the MLI with respect to its agreements with Albania, Andorra, Australia, Austria, Barbados, Belgium, Bosnia-Herzegovina, Canada, Chile, Costa Rica, Croatia, Cyprus*, Czechia, Egypt, Estonia, Finland, France, Georgia, Germany, Greece, Hungary, Iceland, India, Indonesia, Ireland, Israel, Kazakhstan, Korea, Latvia, Lithuania, Luxembourg, Malaysia, Malta, New Zealand, Oman, Pakistan, Panama, Poland, Portugal, Qatar, Romania, Russian Federation, Saudi Arabia, Serbia, Singapore, the Slovak Republic, Slovenia, the United Arab Emirates, the United Kingdom and Uruguay on 1 June 2022, with respect to its agreements with Hong Kong (China), Senegal and Thailand on 30 November 2022, with respect to its agreements with Bulgaria and South Africa on 1 June 2023 and with respect to its agreements with Mexico, Tunisia and Viet Nam on 10 November 2023.

Spain has signed a bilateral complying instrument with respect to its agreement with Ukraine.

Spain has not listed its agreements with Netherlands, Norway, and Sweden under the MLI, but indicated in its response to the Peer Review questionnaire that steps have been taken (other than under the MLI) to implement the minimum standard in those agreements.

Spain is implementing the minimum standard through the inclusion of the preamble statement and the PPT, combined with the LOB for its agreements with Japan and Mexico.[134]

B. Conclusion

No jurisdiction has raised any concerns about their agreements with Spain.

Summary of the jurisdiction response – Spain

	1.Treaty partners	2. Compliance with the standard	3. Signature of a complying instrument	4. Minimum standard provision used
1	Albania	Yes MLI		PPT
2	Algeria*	No	No	

[133] The reservation was made under Article 35(7)(a) of the MLI.

[134] For its agreements listed under the MLI, Spain is implementing the preamble statement (Article 6 of the MLI) and the PPT (Article 7 of the MLI). Spain has made a reservation pursuant to Article 6(4) not to apply Article 6(1) of the MLI with respect to agreements that already contain the relevant preamble language (covering three agreements). Spain has also made a reservation pursuant to Article 7(15)(b) of the MLI not to apply Article 7(1) of the MLI with respect to agreements that already contain a PPT (covering three agreements).

3	Andorra	Yes MLI		PPT
4	Argentina	No	Yes MLI	PPT
5	Armenia	No	Yes MLI	PPT
6	Australia	Yes MLI		PPT
7	Austria	Yes MLI		PPT
8	Azerbaijan	No	No	
9	Barbados	Yes MLI		PPT
10	Belarus	No	No	
11	Belgium	Yes MLI		PPT
12	Bolivia*	No	No	
13	Bosnia-Herzegovina	Yes MLI		PPT
14	Brazil	No	No	
15	Bulgaria	No	Yes MLI	PPT
16	Cabo Verde	No	No	
17	Canada	Yes MLI		PPT
18	Chile	Yes MLI		PPT
19	China (People's Republic of)	Yes other		PPT
20	Colombia	No	Yes MLI	PPT
21	Costa Rica	Yes MLI		PPT
22	Croatia	Yes MLI		PPT
23	Cuba*	No	No	
24	Cyprus*	Yes MLI		PPT
25	Czechia	Yes MLI		PPT
26	Dominican Republic	No	No	
27	Ecuador*	No	No	
28	Egypt	Yes MLI		PPT
29	El Salvador*	No	No	
30	Estonia	Yes MLI		PPT
31	Finland	Yes MLI		PPT
32	France	Yes MLI		PPT
33	Georgia	Yes MLI		PPT
34	Germany	No	Yes MLI	PPT
35	Greece	Yes MLI		PPT
36	Hong Kong (China)	Yes MLI		PPT
37	Hungary	Yes MLI		PPT
38	Iceland	Yes MLI		PPT
39	India	Yes MLI		PPT
40	Indonesia	Yes MLI		PPT
41	Iran*	No	No	
42	Ireland	Yes MLI		PPT
43	Israel	Yes MLI		PPT
44	Italy	No	Yes MLI	PPT
45	Jamaica	No	Yes MLI	PPT
46	Japan	Yes other		PPT+LOB
47	Kazakhstan	Yes MLI		PPT
48	Korea	Yes MLI		PPT
49	Kuwait	No	Yes MLI	PPT
50	Latvia	Yes MLI		PPT
51	Lithuania	Yes MLI		PPT
52	Luxembourg	Yes MLI		PPT
53	Malaysia	Yes MLI		PPT
54	Malta	Yes MLI		PPT
55	Mexico	Yes other		PPT+LOB

56	Moldova*	No	No	
57	Morocco	No	Yes MLI	PPT
58	Netherlands	No	No	
59	New Zealand	Yes MLI		PPT
60	Nigeria	No	Yes MLI	PPT
61	North Macedonia	No	Yes MLI	PPT
62	Norway	No	No	
63	Oman	Yes MLI		PPT
64	Pakistan	Yes MLI		PPT
65	Panama	Yes MLI		PPT
66	Philippines	No	No	
67	Poland	Yes MLI		PPT
68	Portugal	Yes MLI		PPT
69	Qatar	Yes MLI		PPT
70	Romania	Yes other		PPT
71	Russian Federation	No	Yes MLI	PPT
72	Saudi Arabia	Yes MLI		PPT
73	Senegal	Yes MLI		PPT
74	Serbia	Yes MLI		PPT
75	Singapore	Yes MLI		PPT
76	Slovak Republic	Yes MLI		PPT
77	Slovenia	Yes MLI		PPT
78	South Africa	No	Yes MLI	PPT
79	Sweden	No	No	
80	Switzerland	No	No	
81	Tajikistan*	No	No	
82	Thailand	Yes MLI		PPT
83	Trinidad and Tobago	No	No	
84	Tunisia	No	Yes MLI	PPT
85	Türkiye	No	Yes MLI	PPT
86	Ukraine	No	Yes other	PPT
87	United Arab Emirates	Yes MLI		PPT
88	United Kingdom	Yes MLI		PPT
89	United States	No	No	
90	Uruguay	Yes MLI		PPT
91	Uzbekistan	No	No	
92	Venezuela*	No	No	
93	Viet Nam	No	Yes MLI	

Sri Lanka

A. Progress in the implementation of the minimum standard

Sri Lanka has 43 tax agreements in force as reported in its response to the Peer Review questionnaire. None of those agreements, comply with the minimum standard.

Sri Lanka has not signed the MLI.

Sri Lanka has signed a bilateral complying instrument with respect to its agreement with Czechia.

Sri Lanka indicated in its response to the Peer Review questionnaire that steps have been taken (other than under the MLI) to implement the minimum standard in its agreements with Belgium, Denmark, India, Luxembourg, Netherlands, Pakistan, Romania and Switzerland.

Sri Lanka is implementing the minimum standard through the inclusion of the preamble statement and the PPT, combined with the LOB for its agreement with India.

In their responses to the Peer Review questionnaire, Japan and Indonesia indicated that their agreements with Sri Lanka did not give rise to material treaty shopping concerns for their respective jurisdictions.

B. Conclusion

Sri Lanka has developed a plan for the implementation of the minimum standard in its agreements with Australia, Bahrain, Belarus, Canada, China (People's Republic of), Finland, France, Germany, Indonesia, Italy, Japan, Korea, Malaysia, Mauritius, Norway, Oman, Poland, Qatar, Russian Federation, Seychelles, Singapore, the Slovak Republic, Sweden, Thailand, the United Arab Emirates, the United Kingdom and Viet Nam. Sri Lanka indicated in its response to the Peer Review questionnaire that bilateral negotiations would be pursued with respect to those agreements.

Summary of the jurisdiction response – Sri Lanka

	1.Treaty partners	2. Compliance with the standard	3. Signature of a complying instrument	4. Minimum standard provision used
1	Belgium	No	No	PPT
2	Czechia	No	Yes other	PPT
3	Denmark	No	No	PPT
4	India	No	No	PPT+LOB
5	Luxembourg	No	No	PPT
6	Netherlands	No	No	PPT
7	Pakistan	No	No	PPT
8	Romania	No	No	PPT
9	Switzerland	No	No	PPT
10	United States	No	No	D-LOB

Other agreements

	1.Treaty partners	2. Inclusive Framework member
1	Australia	Yes

2	Bahrain	Yes
3	Bangladesh*	No
4	Belarus	Yes
5	Canada	Yes
6	China (People's Republic of)	Yes
7	Finland	Yes
8	France	Yes
9	Germany	Yes
10	Indonesia	Yes
11	Iran*	No
12	Italy	Yes
13	Japan	Yes
14	Korea	Yes
15	Kuwait	Yes
16	Malaysia	Yes
17	Mauritius	Yes
18	Nepal*	No
19	Norway	Yes
20	Oman	Yes
21	Palestine*	No
22	Philippines	Yes
23	Poland	Yes
24	Qatar	Yes
25	Russian Federation	Yes
26	Seychelles	Yes
27	Singapore	Yes
28	Slovak Republic	Yes
29	Sweden	Yes
30	Thailand	Yes
31	United Arab Emirates	Yes
32	United Kingdom	Yes
33	Viet Nam	Yes

Sweden

A. Progress in the implementation of the minimum standard

Sweden has 83 tax agreements in force as reported in its response to the Peer Review questionnaire, including the multilateral Nordic Convention concluded with Denmark, the Faroe Islands, Finland, Iceland and Norway (the "Nordic Convention").[135] Nine of those agreements, including the Nordic Convention, comply with the minimum standard.

Sweden signed the MLI in 2017 and deposited its instrument of ratification on 22 June 2018. The MLI entered into force for Sweden on 1 October 2018. The agreements modified by the MLI come into compliance with the minimum standard once the provisions of the MLI take effect.

Sweden reserved the right to delay the entry into effect of the provisions of the MLI until Sweden has completed its internal procedures for this purpose with respect to each of its listed agreements.[136] Sweden has not yet notified that it completed its internal procedures for the entry into effect of the MLI with respect to any of its agreements.

Sweden has not listed its agreements with Australia, Austria, Bosnia-Herzegovina, Croatia, Montenegro, Serbia, Singapore and Spain under the MLI but indicated in its response to the Peer Review questionnaire that steps have been taken (other than under the MLI) to implement the minimum standard in its agreements with Australia, Austria, Bosnia-Herzegovina, Croatia, Serbia, Singapore and Spain. Australia, Bosnia-Herzegovina, Croatia, Serbia and Singapore have listed their agreements with Sweden under the MLI.

Sweden has signed a bilateral complying instrument with respect to its agreement with Brazil, France and Germany.

Sweden indicated in its response to the Peer Review questionnaire that the agreements with Kosovo* and Montenegro do not give rise to material treaty-shopping concerns for Sweden.

Sweden is implementing the minimum standard through the inclusion of the preamble statement and the PPT.[137]

B. Conclusion

Australia, Bosnia-Herzegovina, Croatia, Serbia and Singapore have listed their agreements with Sweden under the MLI, which amount to requests to implement the minimum standard.

Sweden is working towards finalising its internal procedures for the entry into effect of the MLI (which involves the appropriate enactment of a separate, dedicated law reflecting the effects of the MLI with respect to each agreement that is a covered tax agreement under the MLI). To ensure that the minimum standard is implemented as swiftly as possible, Sweden is concurrently pursuing bilateral negotiations.

---

[135] See the Multilateral convention concluded by Denmark, Finland, the Faroe Islands, Iceland, Norway and Sweden: for the avoidance of double taxation with respect to taxes on income and on capital (1996, 1997, 2008 and 2018).

[136] The reservation was made under Article 35(7)(a) of the MLI.

[137] For its agreements listed under the MLI, Sweden is implementing the preamble statement (Article 6 of the MLI) and the PPT (Article 7 of the MLI).

Recommendation

It is recommended that Sweden completes the steps to have the MLI take effect with respect to its agreements listed under the MLI as those agreements will only be modified by the MLI (and come into compliance with the minimum standard) once the provisions of the MLI take effect.

Summary of the jurisdiction response - Sweden

	1.Treaty partners	2. Compliance with the standard	3. Signature of a complying instrument	4. Minimum standard provision used
1	Albania	No	Yes MLI	PPT
2	Argentina	No	Yes MLI	PPT
3	Armenia	No	Yes MLI	PPT
4	Australia	No	No	
5	Austria	No	No	
6	Azerbaijan	No	No	
7	Bangladesh*	No	No	
8	Barbados	No	Yes MLI	
9	Belarus	No	No	
10	Belgium	No	Yes MLI	PPT
11	Bolivia*	No	No	
12	Bosnia-Herzegovina	No	No	
13	Botswana	No	No	
14	Brazil	No	Yes other	PPT+LOB
15	Bulgaria	No	Yes MLI	PPT
16	Canada	No	Yes MLI	PPT
17	Chile	No	Yes MLI	PPT
18	China (People's Republic of)	No	Yes MLI	PPT
19	Croatia	No	No	
20	Cyprus*	No	Yes MLI	PPT
21	Czechia	No	Yes MLI	PPT
22	Denmark	Yes other		PPT
23	Egypt	No	Yes MLI	PPT
24	Estonia	No	Yes MLI	PPT
25	Faroe Islands	Yes other		PPT
26	Finland	Yes other		PPT
27	France	No	Yes other	
28	Gambia*	No	No	
29	Georgia	No	Yes MLI	PPT
30	Germany	No	Yes other	
31	Hungary	No	Yes MLI	PPT
32	Iceland	Yes other		PPT
33	India	No	Yes MLI	PPT
34	Indonesia	No	Yes MLI	PPT
35	Ireland	No	Yes MLI	PPT
36	Israel	No	Yes MLI	PPT
37	Italy	No	Yes MLI	PPT
38	Jamaica	No	Yes MLI	PPT

39	Japan	No	Yes MLI	PPT+LOB
40	Kazakhstan	No	Yes MLI	PPT
41	Kenya	No	Yes MLI	PPT
42	Korea	No	Yes MLI	PPT
43	Latvia	No	Yes MLI	PPT
44	Lithuania	No	Yes MLI	PPT
45	Luxembourg	No	Yes MLI	PPT
46	Malaysia	No	Yes MLI	PPT
47	Malta	No	Yes MLI	PPT
48	Mauritius	No	Yes MLI	PPT
49	Mexico	No	Yes MLI	PPT
50	Namibia	No	Yes MLI	PPT
51	Netherlands	No	Yes MLI	PPT
52	New Zealand	No	Yes MLI	PPT
53	Nigeria	No	Yes MLI	PPT
54	North Macedonia	No	Yes MLI	PPT
55	Norway	Yes other		PPT
56	Pakistan	No	Yes MLI	PPT
57	Philippines	No	No	
58	Poland	No	Yes MLI	PPT
59	Romania	No	Yes MLI	PPT
60	Russian Federation	Yes other		PPT
61	Saudi Arabia	No	Yes MLI	PPT
62	Serbia	No	No	
63	Singapore	No	No	
64	Slovak Republic	No	Yes MLI	PPT
65	Slovenia	Yes other		PPT
66	South Africa	No	Yes MLI	PPT
67	Spain	No	No	
68	Sri Lanka	No	No	
69	Switzerland	Yes other		PPT
70	Tanzania*	No	No	
71	Thailand	No	Yes MLI	PPT
72	Trinidad and Tobago	No	No	
73	Tunisia	No	Yes MLI	PPT
74	Türkiye	No	Yes MLI	PPT
75	Ukraine	No	Yes MLI	PPT
76	United Kingdom	Yes other		PPT
77	United States	No	No	
78	Venezuela*	No	No	
79	Viet Nam	No	Yes MLI	PPT
80	Zambia	No	No	
81	Zimbabwe*	No	No	

Other agreements

	1.Treaty partners	2. Inclusive Framework member
1	Kosovo*	No
2	Montenegro	Yes

Switzerland

A. Progress in the implementation of the minimum standard

Switzerland has 108 tax agreements in force as reported in its response to the Peer Review questionnaire. Twenty-four of those agreements comply with the minimum standard.

Switzerland signed the MLI in 2017 and deposited its instrument of ratification on 29 August 2019, listing twelve of its agreements. The MLI entered into force for Switzerland on 1 December 2019. The agreements modified by the MLI come into compliance with the minimum standard once the provisions of the MLI take effect.

Switzerland reserved the right to delay the entry into effect of the provisions of the MLI until Switzerland has completed its internal procedures for this purpose with respect to each of its listed agreements.[138] Switzerland notified that it completed its internal procedures for the entry into effect of the MLI with respect to its agreements with Luxembourg on 27 May 2020, with respect to its agreements with Czechia and Lithuania on 18 December 2020, and with respect to its agreement with Iceland on 16 December 2022.

Switzerland has not listed its agreements with Albania, Antigua and Barbuda, Australia, Barbados, Belarus, Belgium, Belize, British Virgin Islands, Bulgaria, Canada, China (People's Republic of), Colombia, Côte d'Ivoire, Croatia, Denmark, Dominica, Egypt, Estonia, Finland, France, Georgia, Germany, Greece, Grenada, Hong Kong (China), Hungary, India, Indonesia, Israel, Jamaica, Kazakhstan, Korea, Liechtenstein, Malaysia, Malta, Mongolia, Montenegro, Montserrat, Morocco, Oman, Pakistan, Peru, Poland, Qatar, Romania, Russia, Saint Kitts and Nevis, Saint Lucia, Saint Vincent and the Grenadines, Serbia, Singapore, Slovak Republic, Spain, Sri Lanka, Thailand, Tunisia, Uruguay and Viet Nam. These agreements will therefore not, at this stage, be modified under the MLI. Albania, Australia, Barbados, Belize, China (People's Republic of), Colombia, Croatia, Egypt, Finland, France, Greece, Hong Kong (China), Hungary, India, Indonesia, Jamaica, Kazakhstan, Malaysia, Mongolia, Morocco, Oman, Pakistan, Peru, Poland, Romania, Serbia, Singapore, Slovak Republic, Spain, Tunisia, Uruguay and Viet Nam have listed their agreement with Switzerland under the MLI.

Switzerland has signed a bilateral complying instrument with respect to its agreements with Kuwait, North Macedonia, Slovenia, Tajikistan* and the United Arab Emirates.

Switzerland indicated in its response to the Peer Review questionnaire that steps have been taken (other than under the MLI) to implement the minimum standard in its agreements with Albania, Algeria*, Australia, Austria, Bangladesh*, Belarus, Belgium, Bulgaria, Canada, China (People's Republic of), Colombia, Côte d'Ivoire, Croatia, Denmark, Egypt, Estonia, Finland, France, Georgia, Germany, Greece, Hong Kong (China), Hungary, India, Indonesia, Israel, Jamaica, Kazakhstan, Kyrgyzstan*, Malaysia, Mongolia, Montenegro, Morocco, Oman, Pakistan, Peru, Philippines, Poland, Qatar, Romania, Russia, Serbia, Singapore, the Slovak Republic, Spain, Sri Lanka, Thailand, Trinidad and Tobago, Tunisia, the United States, Uruguay and Viet Nam.

Switzerland indicated in its response to the Peer Review questionnaire that the agreements with Antigua and Barbuda, Azerbaijan, Barbados, Belize, British Virgin Islands, Chinese Taipei*, Dominica, Ecuador*, Gambia*, Ghana*, Grenada, Malawi*, Moldova*, Montserrat, Saint Kitts and Nevis, Saint Lucia, Saint Vincent and the Grenadines, Turkmenistan*, Uzbekistan and Venezuela* do not give rise to material treaty-shopping concerns for Switzerland.

[138] The reservation was made under Article 35(7)(a) of the MLI.

Switzerland is implementing the minimum standard through the inclusion of the preamble statement and the PPT.[139]

In their responses to the Peer Review Questionnaire, Saint Kitts and Nevis, Saint Lucia and Saint Vincent and the Grenadines indicated that their agreements with Switzerland did not give rise to material treaty shopping concerns for their respective jurisdictions.

B. Conclusion

Albania, Australia, Barbados, Belize, China (People's Republic of), Colombia, Croatia, Egypt, Finland, France, Greece, Hong Kong (China), Hungary, India, Indonesia, Kazakhstan, Malaysia, Mongolia, Morocco, Oman, Pakistan, Peru, Poland, Romania, Serbia, Singapore, Slovak Republic, Spain, Tunisia, Uruguay and Viet Nam have listed their agreements with Switzerland under the MLI, which amount to requests to implement the minimum standard.

Switzerland is encouraged to complete (and notify that it has completed) its internal procedures for the entry into effect of the MLI with respect to its agreements that are covered tax agreements under the MLI and for which no such notification has yet been made.

Summary of the jurisdiction response - Switzerland

	1.Treaty partners	2. Compliance with the standard	3. Signature of a complying instrument	4. Minimum standard provision used
1	Albania	No	No	PPT
2	Algeria*	No	No	PPT
3	Argentina	No	Yes MLI	PPT
4	Armenia	Yes other		PPT
5	Australia	No	No	PPT
6	Austria	No	Yes MLI	PPT
7	Bahrain	Yes other		PPT
8	Bangladesh*	No	No	PPT
9	Belarus	No	No	PPT
10	Belgium	No	No	PPT
11	Brazil	Yes other		PPT
12	Bulgaria	No	No	PPT
13	Canada	No	No	PPT
14	Chile	No	Yes MLI	PPT
15	China (People's Republic of)	No	No	PPT
16	Colombia	No	No	PPT
17	Côte d'Ivoire	No	No	PPT
18	Croatia	No	No	PPT
19	Cyprus*	Yes other		PPT
20	Czechia	Yes MLI		PPT
21	Denmark	No	No	PPT
22	Egypt	No	No	PPT
23	Estonia	No	No	PPT
24	Finland	No	No	PPT
25	France	No	No	PPT

[139] For its agreements listed under the MLI, Switzerland is implementing the preamble statement (Article 6 of the MLI) and the PPT (Article 7 of the MLI).

26	Georgia	No	No	PPT
27	Germany	No	No	PPT
28	Greece	No	No	PPT
29	Hong Kong (China)	No	No	PPT
30	Hungary	No	No	PPT
31	Iceland	Yes MLI		PPT
32	India	No	No	PPT
33	Indonesia	No	No	PPT
34	Iran*	Yes other		PPT
35	Ireland	Yes other		PPT
36	Israel	No	No	PPT
37	Italy	No	Yes MLI	PPT
38	Jamaica	No	No	PPT
39	Japan	Yes other		PPT+LOB
40	Kazakhstan	No	No	PPT
41	Korea	Yes other		PPT
42	Kosovo*	Yes other		PPT
43	Kuwait	No	Yes other	PPT
44	Kyrgyzstan*	No	No	PPT
45	Latvia	Yes other		PPT
46	Liechtenstein	Yes other		PPT
47	Lithuania	Yes MLI		PPT
48	Luxembourg	Yes MLI		PPT
49	Malaysia	No	No	PPT
50	Malta	Yes other		PPT
51	Mexico	No	Yes MLI	PPT
52	Mongolia	No	No	PPT
53	Montenegro	No	No	PPT
54	Morocco	No	No	PPT
55	Netherlands	Yes other		PPT
56	New Zealand	Yes other		PPT
57	North Macedonia	No	Yes other	PPT
58	Norway	Yes other		PPT
59	Oman	No	No	PPT
60	Pakistan	No	No	PPT
61	Peru	No	No	PPT
62	Philippines	No	No	PPT
63	Poland	No	No	PPT
64	Portugal	No	Yes MLI	PPT
65	Qatar	No	No	PPT
66	Romania	No	No	PPT
67	Russian Federation	No	No	PPT
68	Saudi Arabia	Yes other		PPT
69	Serbia	No	No	PPT
70	Singapore	No	No	PPT
71	Slovak Republic	No	No	PPT
72	Slovenia	No	Yes, other	PPT
73	South Africa	No	Yes MLI	PPT
74	Spain	No	No	PPT
75	Sri Lanka	No	No	PPT
76	Sweden	Yes other		PPT
77	Tajikistan*	No	Yes other	PPT
78	Thailand	No	No	PPT

79	Trinidad and Tobago	No	No	PPT
80	Tunisia	No	No	PPT
81	Türkiye	No	Yes MLI	PPT
82	Ukraine	Yes other		PPT
83	United Arab Emirates	No	Yes other	PPT
84	United Kingdom	Yes other		PPT
85	United States	No	No	D-LOB
86	Uruguay	No	No	PPT
87	Viet Nam	No	No	PPT
88	Zambia	Yes other		PPT

Other agreements

	1.Treaty partners	2. Inclusive Framework member
1	Antigua and Barbuda	Yes
2	Azerbaijan	Yes
3	Barbados	Yes
4	Belize	Yes
5	British Virgin Islands	Yes
6	Chinese Taipei*	No
7	Dominica	Yes
8	Ecuador*	No
9	Gambia*	No
10	Ghana*	No
11	Grenada	Yes
12	Malawi*	No
13	Moldova*	No
14	Montserrat	Yes
15	Saint Kitts and Nevis	Yes
16	Saint Lucia	Yes
17	Saint Vincent and the Grenadines	Yes
18	Turkmenistan*	No
19	Uzbekistan	Yes
20	Venezuela*	No

Thailand

A. Progress in the implementation of the minimum standard

Thailand has 61 tax agreements in force as reported in its response to the Peer Review questionnaire. Thirty-four of those agreements comply with the minimum standard.

Thailand signed the MLI in 2022 and deposited its instrument of ratification on 31 March 2022, listing its non-compliant agreements concluded with other members of the Inclusive Framework. The MLI entered into force for Thailand on 1 July 2022. The agreements modified by the MLI come into compliance with the minimum standard once the provisions of the MLI take effect.

Thailand indicated in its response to the Peer Review questionnaire that steps have been taken (other than under the MLI) to implement the minimum standard in its agreements with the Netherlands and Norway.

Thailand is implementing the minimum standard through the inclusion of the preamble statement and the PPT.[140]

B. Conclusion

No jurisdiction has raised any concerns about their agreements with Thailand.

Summary of the jurisdiction response - Thailand

	1.Treaty partners	2. Compliance with the standard	3. Signature of a complying instrument	4. Minimum standard provision used
1	Armenia	No	Yes MLI	PPT
2	Australia	Yes MLI		PPT
3	Austria	No	No	PPT
4	Bahrain	Yes MLI		PPT
5	Bangladesh*	No	No	PPT
6	Belarus	No	No	PPT
7	Belgium	Yes MLI		PPT
8	Bulgaria	Yes MLI		PPT
9	Cambodia*	No	No	PPT
10	Canada	Yes MLI		PPT
11	Chile	Yes MLI		PPT
12	China (People's Republic of)	Yes MLI		PPT
13	Cyprus*	Yes MLI		PPT
14	Czechia	No	No	PPT
15	Denmark	Yes MLI		PPT
16	Estonia	No	Yes MLI	PPT
17	Finland	Yes MLI		PPT
18	France	Yes MLI		PPT
19	Germany	No	No	PPT
20	Hong Kong (China)	Yes MLI		PPT

140 For its agreements listed under the MLI, Thailand is implementing the preamble statement (Article 6 of the MLI) and the PPT (Article 7 of the MLI).

21	Hungary	Yes MLI		PPT
22	India	Yes MLI		PPT
23	Indonesia	Yes MLI		PPT
24	Ireland	Yes MLI		PPT
25	Israel	Yes MLI		PPT
26	Italy	No	Yes MLI	PPT
27	Japan	Yes MLI		PPT
28	Korea	Yes MLI		PPT
29	Kuwait	No	Yes MLI	PPT
30	Lao People's Democratic Republic*	No	No	PPT
31	Luxembourg	Yes MLI		PPT
32	Malaysia	Yes MLI		PPT
33	Mauritius	Yes MLI		PPT
34	Myanmar*	No	No	PPT
35	Nepal*	No	No	PPT
36	Netherlands	No	No	
37	New Zealand	Yes MLI		PPT
38	Norway	No	No	
39	Oman	Yes MLI		PPT
40	Pakistan	Yes MLI		PPT
41	Philippines	No	No	PPT
42	Poland	Yes MLI		PPT
43	Romania	No	Yes MLI	PPT
44	Russian Federation	No	Yes MLI	PPT
45	Seychelles	Yes MLI		PPT
46	Singapore	Yes MLI		PPT
47	Slovenia	Yes MLI		PPT
48	South Africa	Yes MLI		PPT
49	Spain	Yes MLI		PPT
50	Sri Lanka	No	No	PPT
51	Sweden	No	Yes MLI	PPT
52	Switzerland	No	No	PPT
53	Tajikistan*	No	No	PPT
54	Türkiye	No	Yes MLI	PPT
55	Ukraine	Yes MLI		PPT
56	United Arab Emirates	Yes MLI		PPT
57	United Kingdom	Yes MLI		PPT
58	United States	No	No	D-LOB
59	Uzbekistan	No	No	PPT
60	Viet Nam	No	Yes MLI	PPT

Other agreements

	1.Treaty partners	2. Inclusive Framework member
1	Chinese Taipei*	No

Togo

A. Progress in the implementation of the minimum standard

Togo has three tax agreements in force as reported in its response to the Peer Review questionnaire, including the multilateral Regulation 08/2008/COM adopting the rules for the avoidance of double taxation within the West African Economic and Monetary Union and the rule for assistance in tax matters (the UEMOA) concluded with seven treaty partners,[141] and the multilateral Supplementary Act A/SA, 5/12/18 adopting community rules for the elimination of double taxation with respect to taxes on income, capital and inheritance and the prevention of tax evasion and avoidance within the ECOWAS Member States (the ECOWAS Supplementary Act) concluded with fourteen treaty partners. One of those agreements, the ECOWAS Supplementary Act, complies with the minimum standard.

Togo has not signed the MLI.

Togo is implementing the minimum standard through the inclusion of the preamble statement and the PPT.

B. Conclusion

Togo is currently developing a plan, in consultation with the Secretariat, for the implementation of the minimum standard in the agreement with France.

The UEMOA does not at this stage comply with the minimum standard and discussions to bring this agreement up to date should be contemplated.[142]

Summary of the jurisdiction response - Togo

	1.Treaty partners	2. Compliance with the standard	3. Signature of a complying instrument	4. Minimum standard provision used
1	ECOWAS Supplementary Act treaty partners (Benin, Burkina Faso, Cabo Verde, Côte d'Ivoire, The Gambia*, Ghana*, Guinea-Bissau*, Guinea Conakry*, Liberia, Mali*, Niger*, Nigeria, Senegal, Sierra Leone)	Yes other		PPT

Other agreements

	1.Treaty partners	2. Inclusive Framework member

[141] Règlement n°08/2008/CM des pays de l'Union économique et monétaire Ouest Africaine (UEMOA) du 26 septembre 2008 portant adoption des règles visant à éviter la double imposition au sein de l'UEMOA et des règles d'assistance en matière fiscale.

[142] Revisions to the UEMOA require an agreement from its eight treaty partners.

1	France	Yes
2	UEMOA treaty partners (Benin, Burkina Faso, Côte d'Ivoire, Guinea-Bissau*, Mali*, Niger*, Senegal)	Yes (Benin, Burkina Faso, Côte d'Ivoire, Senegal) No (Guinea-Bissau*, Mali*, Niger*)

Trinidad and Tobago

A. Progress in the implementation of the minimum standard

Trinidad and Tobago has 16 tax agreements in force, as reported in its response to the Peer Review questionnaire, including the multilateral agreement among the members of the CARICOM concluded with ten treaty partners (the CARICOM Agreement). [143]

None of those agreements comply with the minimum standard.

Trinidad and Tobago has not signed the MLI.

Trinidad and Tobago indicated in its response to the Peer Review questionnaire that steps have been taken (other than under the MLI) to implement the minimum standard in the CARICOM Agreement.

Trinidad and Tobago indicated in its response to the Peer Review questionnaire that it intends to implement the minimum standard through the inclusion of the preamble statement and the PPT combined with the simplified LOB.

In its response to the Peer Review questionnaire, Italy indicated that its agreement with Trinidad and Tobago did not give rise to material treaty shopping concerns for Italy.

B. Conclusion

Trinidad and Tobago has developed a plan, in consultation with the Secretariat, for the implementation of the minimum standard in its agreements with Brazil, Canada, China (People's Republic of), France, Germany, India, Italy, Luxembourg, Norway, Spain, Sweden, Switzerland, and the United Kingdom. Trinidad indicated in its response to the Peer Review questionnaire that bilateral negotiations would be pursued with respect to those agreements.

Summary of the jurisdiction response – Trinidad and Tobago

	1.Treaty partners	2. Compliance with the standard	3. Signature of a complying instrument	4. Minimum standard provision used
1	United States	No	No	
2	CARICOM Agreement treaty partners (Antigua and Barbuda, Barbados, Belize, Dominica, Grenada, Guyana*, Jamaica, Saint Kitts and Nevis, Saint Lucia, Saint Vincent and the Grenadines)	No	No	

[143] Agreement Among the Governments of the Member States of the Caribbean Community for the Avoidance of Double Taxation and the Prevention of Fiscal Evasion with Respect to Taxes on Income, Profits or Gains and Capital Gains and for the Encouragement of Regional Trade and Investment, St. Michael Barbados, 6 July 1994; between: Antigua and Barbuda (18 February 1998), Barbados (7 July 1995), Belize (30 November 1994), Dominica (19 June 1996), Grenada (1 March 1996), Guyana* (26 November 1997), Jamaica (16 February 1995), St. Kitts/Nevis (8 May 1997), St. Lucia (22 May 1995) St. Vincent (12 February 1998) and Trinidad & Tobago (29 November 1994).

Other agreements

	1.Treaty partners	2. Inclusive Framework member
1	Brazil	Yes
2	Canada	Yes
3	China (People's Republic of)	Yes
4	France	Yes
5	Germany	Yes
6	India	Yes
7	Italy	Yes
8	Luxembourg	Yes
9	Norway	Yes
10	Spain	Yes
11	Sweden	Yes
12	Switzerland	Yes
13	United Kingdom	Yes
14	Venezuela*	Yes

Tunisia

A. Progress in the implementation of the minimum standard

Tunisia has 56 tax agreements in force as reported in its response to the Peer Review questionnaire, including the Arab Maghreb Union Income Agreement concluded with four treaty partners (the UMA Agreement). None of those agreements comply with the minimum standard.

Tunisia signed the MLI in 2018 and deposited its instrument of ratification on 24 July 2023, listing its non-compliant agreements. The MLI enters into force for Tunisia on 1 November 2023. The agreements modified by the MLI come into compliance with the minimum standard once the provisions of the MLI take effect.

Tunisia indicated in its response to the Peer Review questionnaire that steps have been taken (other than under the MLI) to implement the minimum standard in its agreements with Austria, Norway, Sudan* and Switzerland.

Tunisia is implementing the minimum standard through the inclusion of the preamble statement and the PPT.[144]

B. Conclusion

No jurisdiction has raised any concerns about their agreements with Tunisia.

Summary of the jurisdiction response - Tunisia

	1.Treaty partners	2. Compliance with the standard	3. Signature of a complying instrument	4. Minimum standard provision used
1	Algeria	No	No	
2	Austria	No	No	PPT
3	Belgium	No	Yes MLI	PPT
4	Burkina Faso	No	Yes MLI	PPT
5	Cameroon	No	Yes MLI	PPT
6	Canada	No	Yes MLI	PPT
7	China	No	Yes MLI	PPT
8	Côte d'Ivoire	No	Yes MLI	PPT
9	Czechia	No	No	
10	Denmark	No	Yes MLI	PPT
11	Egypt	No	Yes MLI	PPT
12	Ethiopia	No	No	
13	France	No	Yes MLI	PPT
14	Germany	No	No	
15	Greece	No	Yes MLI	PPT
16	Hungary	No	Yes MLI	PPT
17	Indonesia	No	No	
18	Iran	No	No	

[144] For its agreements listed under the MLI, Tunisia is implementing the preamble statement (Article 6 of the MLI) and the PPT (Article 7 of the MLI).

19	Italy	No	Yes MLI	PPT
20	Jordan	No	Yes MLI	PPT
21	Korea	No	Yes MLI	PPT
22	Kuwait	No	Yes MLI	PPT
23	Lebanon	No	No	
24	Libya	No	No	
25	Luxembourg	No	Yes MLI	PPT
26	Mali	No	No	
27	Malta	No	Yes MLI	PPT
28	Mauritania	No	No	
29	Mauritius	No	Yes MLI	PPT
30	Morocco	No	No	PPT
31	Netherlands	No	Yes MLI	PPT
32	Norway	No	No	PPT
33	Oman	No	Yes MLI	PPT
34	Pakistan	No	Yes MLI	PPT
35	Poland	No	Yes MLI	PPT
36	Portugal	No	Yes MLI	PPT
37	Qatar	No	Yes MLI	PPT
38	Romania	No	Yes MLI	PPT
39	Saudi Arabia	No	Yes MLI	PPT
40	Senegal	No	Yes MLI	PPT
41	Serbia	No	Yes MLI	PPT
42	Singapore	No	Yes MLI	PPT
43	Slovak Republic	No	Yes MLI	PPT
44	South Africa	No	Yes MLI	PPT
45	Spain	No	Yes MLI	PPT
46	Sudan	No	No	PPT
47	Sweden	No	Yes MLI	PPT
48	Switzerland	No	No	PPT
49	Syria	No	No	
50	Türkiye	No	Yes MLI	PPT
51	UMA Agreement (Algeria*, Mauritania, Morocco and Libya*)			
52	United Arab Emirates	No	Yes MLI	PPT
53	United Kingdom	No	Yes MLI	PPT
54	United States	No	No	
55	Viet Nam	No	Yes MLI	PPT
56	Yemen	No	No	

Türkiye

A. Progress in the implementation of the minimum standard

Türkiye has 89 tax agreements in force as reported in its response to the Peer Review questionnaire. Three of those agreements comply with the minimum standard.

Türkiye signed the MLI in 2017 and listed its non-compliant agreements. The agreements modified by the MLI come into compliance with the minimum standard once the provisions of the MLI take effect.

Türkiye has signed a bilateral complying instrument with respect to its agreement with Korea.

Türkiye indicated in its response to the Peer Review questionnaire that steps have been taken (other than under the MLI) to implement the minimum standard in its agreement with Azerbaijan.

Türkiye is implementing the minimum standard through the inclusion of the preamble statement and the PPT.[145]

B. Conclusion

Recommendation

It is recommended that Türkiye completes the steps to have the MLI take effect with respect to its agreements listed under the MLI as those agreements will only be modified by the MLI (and come into compliance with the minimum standard) once the provisions of the MLI take effect.

Summary of the jurisdiction response – Türkiye

	1.Treaty partners	2. Compliance with the standard	3. Signature of a complying instrument	4. Minimum standard provision used
1	Albania	No	Yes MLI	PPT
2	Algeria*	No	No	PPT
3	Australia	No	Yes MLI	PPT
4	Austria	No	Yes MLI	PPT
5	Azerbaijan	No	No	PPT
6	Bahrain	No	Yes MLI	PPT
7	Bangladesh*	No	No	PPT
8	Belarus	No	No	PPT
9	Belgium	No	Yes MLI	PPT
10	Bosnia-Herzegovina	No	Yes MLI	PPT
11	Brazil	No	No	PPT
12	Bulgaria	No	Yes MLI	PPT
13	Canada	No	Yes MLI	PPT
14	Chad*	No	No	PPT

[145] For its agreements listed under the MLI, Türkiye is implementing the preamble statement (Article 6 of the MLI) and the PPT (Article 7 of the MLI).

15	China (People's Republic of)	No	Yes MLI	PPT
16	Croatia	No	Yes MLI	PPT
17	Czechia	No	Yes MLI	PPT
18	Denmark	No	Yes MLI	PPT
19	Egypt	No	Yes MLI	PPT
20	Estonia	No	Yes MLI	PPT
21	Ethiopia*	No	No	PPT
22	Finland	No	Yes MLI	PPT
23	France	No	Yes MLI	PPT
24	Gambia*	No	No	PPT
25	Georgia	No	Yes MLI	PPT
26	Germany	No	Yes MLI	PPT
27	Greece	No	Yes MLI	PPT
28	Hungary	No	Yes MLI	PPT
29	India	No	Yes MLI	PPT
30	Indonesia	No	Yes MLI	PPT
31	Iran*	No	No	PPT
32	Ireland	No	Yes MLI	PPT
33	Israel	No	Yes MLI	PPT
34	Italy	No	Yes MLI	PPT
35	Japan	No	Yes MLI	PPT
36	Jordan	No	Yes MLI	PPT
37	Kazakhstan	No	Yes MLI	PPT
38	Korea	No	Yes other	PPT
39	Kosovo*	No	No	PPT
40	Kuwait	Yes other		PPT
41	Kyrgyzstan*	No	No	PPT
42	Latvia	No	Yes MLI	PPT
43	Lebanon*	No	No	PPT
44	Lithuania	No	Yes MLI	PPT
45	Luxembourg	No	Yes MLI	PPT
46	Malaysia	No	Yes MLI	PPT
47	Malta	No	Yes MLI	PPT
48	Mexico	No	Yes MLI	PPT
49	Moldova*	No	No	PPT
50	Mongolia	No	Yes MLI	PPT
51	Montenegro	No	No	PPT
52	Morocco	No	Yes MLI	PPT
53	Netherlands	No	Yes MLI	PPT
54	New Zealand	No	Yes MLI	PPT
55	North Macedonia	No	Yes MLI	PPT
56	Norway	No	Yes MLI	PPT
57	Oman	No	Yes MLI	PPT
58	Pakistan	No	Yes MLI	PPT
59	Philippines	No	No	PPT
60	Poland	No	Yes MLI	PPT
61	Portugal	No	Yes MLI	PPT
62	Qatar	No	Yes MLI	PPT
63	Romania	No	Yes MLI	PPT
64	Russian Federation	No	Yes MLI	PPT
65	Rwanda*	Yes other		PPT
66	Saudi Arabia	No	Yes MLI	PPT
67	Serbia	No	Yes MLI	PPT

68	Singapore	No	Yes MLI	PPT
69	Slovak Republic	No	Yes MLI	PPT
70	Slovenia	No	Yes MLI	PPT
71	South Africa	No	Yes MLI	PPT
72	Spain	No	Yes MLI	PPT
73	Sudan*	No	No	PPT
74	Sweden	No	Yes MLI	PPT
75	Switzerland	No	Yes MLI	PPT
76	Syrian Arab Republic*	No	No	PPT
77	Tajikistan*	No	No	PPT
78	Thailand	No	Yes MLI	PPT
79	Tunisia	No	Yes MLI	PPT
80	Turkish Republic of Northern Cyprus*	No	No	PPT
81	Turkmenistan*	No	No	PPT
82	Ukraine	No	Yes MLI	PPT
83	United Arab Emirates	No	Yes MLI	PPT
84	United Kingdom	No	Yes MLI	PPT
85	United States	No	No	
86	Uzbekistan	No	No	PPT
87	Venezuela*	Yes other		PPT
88	Viet Nam	No	Yes MLI	PPT
89	Yemen*	No	No	PPT

Turks and Caicos Islands

A. Progress in the implementation of the minimum standard

The Turks and Caicos Islands has no tax agreements in force, as reported in its response to the Peer Review questionnaire.

B. Conclusion

No jurisdiction has raised any concerns about the Turks and Caicos Islands.

Ukraine

A. Progress in the implementation of the minimum standard

Ukraine has 73 tax agreements in force as reported in its response to the Peer Review questionnaire. Forty-one of those agreements comply with the minimum standard.

Ukraine signed the MLI in 2018 and deposited its instrument of ratification on 8 August 2019. The MLI entered into force for Ukraine on 1 December 2019. The agreements modified by the MLI come into compliance with the minimum standard once the provisions of the MLI take effect.

Ukraine has signed a bilateral complying instrument with respect to its agreements with Qatar and Spain.

Ukraine indicated in its response to the Peer Review questionnaire that steps have been taken (other than under the MLI) to implement the minimum standard in its agreements with Germany and Montenegro.

Ukraine is implementing the minimum standard through the inclusion of the preamble statement and the PPT.[146]

B. Conclusion

No jurisdiction has raised any concerns about their agreements with Ukraine.

Summary of the jurisdiction response - Ukraine

	1.Treaty partners	2. Compliance with the standard	3. Signature of a complying instrument	4. Minimum standard provision used
1	Algeria*	No	No	PPT
2	Armenia	No	Yes MLI	PPT
3	Austria	Yes other		PPT
4	Azerbaijan	No	No	PPT
5	Belgium	Yes MLI		PPT
6	Brazil	No	No	PPT
7	Bulgaria	Yes MLI		PPT
8	Canada	Yes MLI		PPT
9	China (People's Republic of)	Yes MLI		PPT
10	Croatia	Yes MLI		PPT
11	Cyprus*	Yes MLI		PPT
12	Czechia	No	No	PPT
13	Denmark	Yes MLI		PPT
14	Egypt	Yes MLI		PPT
15	Estonia	Yes MLI		PPT
16	Finland	Yes MLI		PPT
17	France	Yes MLI		PPT
18	Georgia	No	No	PPT
19	Germany	No	No	PPT
20	Greece	Yes MLI		PPT

[146] For its agreements listed under the MLI, Ukraine is implementing the preamble statement (Article 6 of the MLI) and the PPT (Article 7 of the MLI).

21	Hungary	Yes MLI		PPT
22	Iceland	Yes MLI		PPT
23	India	Yes MLI		PPT
24	Indonesia	No	No	PPT
25	Iran*	No	No	PPT
26	Ireland	Yes MLI		PPT
27	Israel	Yes MLI		PPT
28	Italy	No	Yes MLI	PPT
29	Japan	Yes MLI		PPT
30	Jordan	Yes MLI		PPT
31	Kazakhstan	Yes MLI		PPT
32	Korea	Yes MLI		PPT
33	Kuwait	No	No	PPT
34	Kyrgyzstan*	No	No	PPT
35	Latvia	Yes MLI		PPT
36	Lebanon*	No	No	PPT
37	Libya*	No	No	PPT
38	Lithuania	Yes MLI		PPT
39	Luxembourg	Yes MLI		PPT
40	Malaysia	Yes MLI		PPT
41	Malta	Yes MLI		PPT
42	Mexico	No	Yes MLI	PPT
43	Moldova*	No	No	PPT
44	Mongolia	No	Yes MLI	PPT
45	Montenegro	No	No	PPT
46	Morocco	No	Yes MLI	PPT
47	Netherlands	Yes other		PPT
48	North Macedonia	No	Yes MLI	PPT
49	Norway	No	No	PPT
50	Pakistan	Yes MLI		PPT
51	Poland	Yes MLI		PPT
52	Portugal	Yes MLI		PPT
53	Qatar	No	Yes other	PPT
54	Romania	No	Yes MLI	PPT
55	Saudi Arabia	Yes MLI		PPT
56	Serbia	Yes MLI		PPT
57	Singapore	Yes MLI		PPT
58	Slovak Republic	Yes MLI		PPT
59	Slovenia	Yes MLI		PPT
60	South Africa	Yes MLI		PPT
61	Spain	No	Yes other	PPT
62	Sweden	No	Yes MLI	PPT
63	Switzerland	Yes other		PPT
64	Syrian Arab Republic*	No	No	PPT
65	Tajikistan*	No	No	PPT
66	Thailand	Yes MLI		PPT
67	Türkiye	No	Yes MLI	PPT
68	Turkmenistan*	No	No	PPT
69	United Arab Emirates	Yes MLI		PPT
70	United Kingdom	Yes other		PPT
71	United States	No	No	
72	Uzbekistan	No	No	PPT
73	Viet Nam	No	Yes MLI	PPT

United Arab Emirates

A. Progress in the implementation of the minimum standard

The United Arab Emirates has 110 tax agreements in force as reported in its response to the Peer Review questionnaire. Fifty-four of those agreements comply with the minimum standard.

The United Arab Emirates signed the MLI in 2018 and deposited its instrument of ratification on 29 May 2019. The MLI entered in force for the United Arab Emirates on 1 September 2019. The agreements modified by the MLI come into compliance with the minimum standard once the provisions of the MLI take effect.

The United Arab Emirates has not listed its agreements with San Marino and Gabon. These agreements will therefore not, at this stage, be modified by the MLI. San Marino has listed its agreement with the United Arab Emirates under the MLI.

The United Arab Emirates has signed a bilateral complying instrument with respect to its agreements with Czechia and Switzerland.

The United Arab Emirates indicated in its response to the Peer Review questionnaire that steps have been taken (other than under the MLI) to implement the minimum standard in its agreement with Saint Vincent and the Grenadines.

The United Arab Emirates is implementing the minimum standard through the inclusion of the preamble statement and the PPT.[147]

B. Conclusion

San Marino has listed its agreement with the United Arab Emirates under the MLI, which amounts to a request to implement the minimum standard.

The United Arab Emirates has developed a plan for the implementation of the minimum standard in its agreement with San Marino. The United Arab Emirates indicated in its response to the Peer Review questionnaire that it intends to expand its list of agreements to be covered under the MLI to include that agreement. Separately, the United Arab Emirates is currently developing a plan, in consultation with the Secretariat, for the implementation of the minimum standard in its agreement with Gabon.

Summary of the jurisdiction response – United Arab Emirates

	1.Treaty partners	2. Compliance with the standard	3. Signature of a complying instrument	4. Minimum standard provision used
1	Albania	Yes MLI		PPT
2	Algeria*	No	No	PPT
3	Andorra	Yes MLI		PPT
4	Angola	Yes other		PPT
5	Antigua and Barbuda	No	No	PPT
6	Argentina	No	Yes MLI	PPT

[147] For its agreements listed under the MLI, the United Arab Emirates is implementing the preamble statement (Article 6 of the MLI) and the PPT (Article 7 of the MLI).

7	Armenia	No	Yes MLI	PPT
8	Austria	Yes other		PPT
9	Azerbaijan	No	No	PPT
10	Bangladesh*	No	No	PPT
11	Barbados	Yes MLI		PPT
12	Belarus	No	No	PPT
13	Belgium	Yes MLI		PPT
14	Belize	No	Yes MLI	PPT
15	Bermuda	No	No	PPT
16	Bosnia-Herzegovina	Yes MLI		PPT
17	Botswana	Yes other		PPT
18	Brazil	Yes other		PPT
19	Brunei Darussalam	No	No	PPT
20	Bulgaria	No	Yes MLI	PPT
21	Burundi*	No	No	PPT
22	Cameroon	No	Yes MLI	PPT
23	Canada	Yes MLI		PPT
24	Chile	Yes other		PPT
25	China (People's Republic of)	No	Yes MLI	PPT
26	Colombia	No	No	PPT
27	Comoros*	No	No	PPT
28	Costa Rica	No	Yes MLI	PPT
29	Croatia	Yes MLI		PPT
30	Cyprus*	Yes MLI		PPT
31	Czechia	No	Yes other	PPT
32	Egypt	Yes other		PPT
33	Estonia	No	Yes MLI	PPT
34	Ethiopia*	No	No	PPT
35	Fiji*	No	No	PPT
36	Finland	Yes MLI		PPT
37	France	Yes MLI		PPT
38	Georgia	No	No	PPT
39	Greece	Yes MLI		PPT
40	Guinea*	No	No	PPT
41	Hong Kong (China)	Yes MLI		PPT
42	Hungary	Yes MLI		PPT
43	India	Yes MLI		PPT
44	Indonesia	Yes other		PPT
45	Ireland	Yes MLI		PPT
46	Israel	Yes other		PPT
47	Italy	No	Yes MLI	PPT
48	Japan	Yes MLI		PPT
49	Jersey	Yes MLI		PPT
50	Jordan	Yes MLI		PPT
51	Kazakhstan	Yes MLI		PPT
52	Kenya	No	Yes MLI	PPT
53	Korea	Yes MLI		PPT
54	Kosovo*	No	No	PPT
55	Kyrgyzstan*	No	No	PPT
56	Latvia	Yes MLI		PPT
57	Lebanon*	No	No	PPT
58	Liechtenstein	Yes MLI		PPT
59	Lithuania	Yes MLI		PPT

60	Luxembourg	Yes MLI		PPT
61	Malaysia	Yes MLI		PPT
62	Maldives	No	No	PPT
63	Malta	Yes MLI		PPT
64	Mauritania	No	No	PPT
65	Mauritius	Yes MLI		PPT
66	Mexico	No	Yes MLI	PPT
67	Moldova*	No	No	PPT
68	Montenegro	No	No	PPT
69	Morocco	No	Yes MLI	PPT
70	Mozambique*	No	No	PPT
71	Netherlands	Yes MLI		PPT
72	New Zealand	Yes MLI		PPT
73	North Macedonia	No	Yes MLI	PPT
74	Pakistan	Yes MLI		PPT
75	Panama	Yes MLI		PPT
76	Paraguay	No	No	PPT
77	Philippines	No	No	PPT
78	Poland	Yes MLI		PPT
79	Portugal	Yes MLI		PPT
80	Romania	No	Yes MLI	PPT
81	Russian Federation	Yes MLI		PPT
82	Saint Vincent and the Grenadines	No	No	PPT
83	Saudi Arabia	Yes other		PPT
84	Senegal	Yes MLI		PPT
85	Serbia	Yes MLI		PPT
86	Seychelles	No	Yes MLI	PPT
87	Singapore	Yes MLI		PPT
88	Slovak Republic	No	No	PPT
89	Slovenia	Yes MLI		PPT
90	South Africa	Yes MLI		PPT
91	Spain	Yes MLI		PPT
92	Sri Lanka	No	No	PPT
93	Sudan*	No	No	PPT
94	Switzerland	No	Yes other	PPT
95	Syrian Arab Republic*	No	No	PPT
96	Tajikistan*	No	No	PPT
97	Thailand	Yes MLI		PPT
98	Tunisia	No	Yes MLI	PPT
99	Türkiye	No	Yes MLI	PPT
100	Turkmenistan*	No	No	PPT
101	Ukraine	Yes MLI		PPT
102	United Kingdom	Yes MLI		PPT
103	Uruguay	Yes MLI		PPT
104	Uzbekistan	No	No	PPT
105	Venezuela*	No	No	PPT
106	Viet Nam	No	Yes MLI	PPT
107	Yemen*	No	No	PPT
108	Zambia	Yes other		PPT

Other agreements

	1.Treaty partners	2. Inclusive Framework member
1	San Marino	Yes
2	Gabon	Yes

United Kingdom

A. Progress in the implementation of the minimum standard

The United Kingdom has 132 tax agreements in force as reported in its response to the Peer Review questionnaire. Seventy-three of those agreement comply with the minimum standard.

The United Kingdom signed the MLI in 2017 and deposited its instrument of ratification on 29 June 2018. The MLI entered into force for the United Kingdom on 1 October 2018. The agreements modified by the MLI come into compliance with the minimum standard once the provisions of the MLI take effect.

The United Kingdom indicated in its response to the Peer Review questionnaire that steps have been taken (other than under the MLI) to implement the minimum standard in its agreement with Montserrat.

The United Kingdom is implementing the minimum standard through the inclusion of the preamble statement and the PPT.[148]

B. Conclusion

No jurisdiction has raised any concerns about their agreements with the United Kingdom.

Summary of the jurisdiction response – United Kingdom

	1.Treaty partners	2. Compliance with the standard	3. Signature of a complying instrument	4. Minimum standard provision used
1	Albania	Yes MLI		PPT
2	Algeria*	No	No	PPT
3	Antigua and Barbuda	No	No	PPT
4	Argentina	No	Yes MLI	PPT
5	Armenia	No	Yes MLI	PPT
6	Australia	Yes MLI		PPT
7	Austria	Yes other		PPT
8	Azerbaijan	No	No	PPT
9	Bahrain	Yes MLI		PPT
10	Bangladesh*	No	No	PPT
11	Barbados	Yes MLI		PPT
12	Belarus	Yes other		PPT
13	Belgium	Yes MLI		PPT
14	Belize	Yes MLI		PPT
15	Bolivia*	No	No	PPT
16	Bosnia-Herzegovina	Yes MLI		PPT
17	Botswana	No	No	PPT
18	Brunei Darussalam	No	No	PPT
19	Bulgaria	Yes MLI		PPT

148 For its agreements listed under the MLI, the United Kingdom is implementing the preamble statement (Article 6 of the MLI) and the PPT (Article 7 of the MLI). The United Kingdom has made a reservation pursuant to Article 6(4) of the MLI not to apply Article 6(1) of the MLI with respect to agreements that already contain the relevant preamble language (covering three agreements).

20	Canada	Yes MLI		PPT
21	Chile	Yes MLI		PPT
22	China (People's Republic of)	Yes MLI		PPT
23	Chinese Taipei*	Yes other		PPT
24	Colombia	Yes other		PPT
25	Côte d'Ivoire	No	Yes MLI	PPT
26	Croatia	Yes MLI		PPT
27	Cyprus*	Yes other		PPT
28	Czechia	Yes MLI		PPT
29	Denmark	Yes MLI		PPT
30	Egypt	Yes MLI		PPT
31	Estonia	No	Yes MLI	PPT
32	Eswatini	No	No	PPT
33	Ethiopia*	No	No	PPT
34	Faroe Islands	No	No	PPT
35	Fiji*	No	Yes MLI	PPT
36	Finland	Yes MLI		PPT
37	France	Yes MLI		PPT
38	Gambia*	No	No	PPT
39	Georgia	Yes MLI		PPT
40	Germany	Yes other		PPT
41	Ghana*	No	No	PPT
42	Gibraltar	Yes other		PPT
43	Greece	Yes MLI		PPT
44	Grenada	No	No	PPT
45	Guernsey	Yes other		PPT
46	Guyana*	No	No	PPT
47	Hong Kong (China)	Yes MLI		PPT
48	Hungary	Yes MLI		PPT
49	Iceland	Yes MLI		PPT
50	India	Yes MLI		PPT
51	Indonesia	Yes MLI		PPT
52	Ireland	Yes MLI		PPT
53	Isle of Man	Yes other		PPT
54	Israel	Yes other		PPT
55	Italy	No	Yes MLI	PPT
56	Jamaica	No	Yes MLI	PPT
57	Japan	Yes MLI		PPT+LOB
58	Jersey	Yes other		PPT
59	Jordan	Yes MLI		PPT
60	Kazakhstan	Yes MLI		PPT
61	Kenya	No	Yes MLI	PPT
62	Kiribati*	No	No	PPT
63	Korea	Yes MLI		PPT
64	Kosovo*	No	No	PPT
65	Kuwait	No	Yes MLI	PPT
66	Kyrgyzstan*	No	No	PPT
67	Latvia	Yes MLI		PPT
68	Lesotho*	Yes MLI		PPT
69	Libya*	No	No	PPT
70	Liechtenstein	Yes MLI		PPT
71	Lithuania	Yes MLI		PPT
72	Luxembourg	Yes MLI		PPT

73	Malawi*	No	No	PPT
74	Malaysia	Yes MLI		PPT
75	Malta	Yes MLI		PPT
76	Mauritius	Yes MLI		PPT
77	Mexico	No	Yes MLI	PPT
78	Moldova*	No	No	PPT
79	Mongolia	No	Yes MLI	PPT
80	Montenegro	No	No	PPT
81	Montserrat	No	No	PPT
82	Morocco	No	Yes MLI	PPT
83	Myanmar*	No	No	PPT
84	Namibia	No	Yes MLI	PPT
85	Netherlands	Yes MLI		PPT
86	New Zealand	Yes MLI		PPT
87	Nigeria	No	Yes MLI	PPT
88	North Macedonia	No	Yes MLI	PPT
89	Norway	Yes MLI		PPT
90	Oman	Yes MLI		PPT
91	Pakistan	Yes MLI		PPT
92	Panama	Yes MLI		PPT
93	Papua New Guinea	No	Yes MLI	PPT
94	Philippines	No	No	PPT
95	Poland	Yes MLI		PPT
96	Portugal	Yes MLI		PPT
97	Qatar	Yes MLI		PPT
98	Romania	No	Yes MLI	PPT
99	Russian Federation	Yes MLI		PPT
100	Saint Kitts and Nevis	No	No	PPT
101	Saudi Arabia	Yes MLI		PPT
102	Senegal	Yes MLI		PPT
103	Serbia	Yes MLI		PPT
104	Sierra Leone	No	No	PPT
105	Singapore	Yes MLI		PPT
106	Slovak Republic	Yes MLI		PPT
107	Slovenia	Yes MLI		PPT
108	Solomon Islands*	No	No	PPT
109	South Africa	Yes MLI		PPT
110	Spain	Yes MLI		PPT
111	Sri Lanka	No	No	PPT
112	Sudan*	No	No	PPT
113	Sweden	Yes other		PPT
114	Switzerland	Yes other		PPT
115	Tajikistan*	No	No	PPT
116	Thailand	Yes MLI		PPT
117	Trinidad and Tobago	No	No	PPT
118	Tunisia	No	Yes MLI	PPT
119	Türkiye	No	Yes MLI	PPT
120	Turkmenistan*	No	No	PPT
121	Tuvalu*	No	No	PPT
122	Uganda*	No	No	PPT
123	Ukraine	Yes MLI		PPT
124	United Arab Emirates	Yes MLI		PPT
125	United States	No	No	

126	Uruguay	Yes MLI		PPT
127	Uzbekistan	Yes other		PPT
128	Venezuela*	No	No	PPT
129	Viet Nam	No	Yes MLI	PPT
130	Zambia	No	No	PPT
131	Zimbabwe*	No	No	PPT

Other agreements

	1.Treaty partners	2. Inclusive Framework member
1	Falkland Islands*	No

United States

A. Progress in the implementation of the minimum standard

The United States has 65 tax agreements in force as reported in its response to the Peer Review questionnaire. None of those agreements comply with the minimum standard.

The United States made a general statement in its response to the Peer Review questionnaire that it intends to implement a detailed LOB rule as part of its commitment to implement the minimum standard in all of its bilateral agreements. The detailed LOB is not available through the MLI and requires substantive bilateral discussions and modifications with respect to each treaty.

The United States has implemented LOB clauses in most of its agreements. It started to include anti-treaty-shopping measures in 1962,[149] and since the seventies, LOB clauses (which initially targeted investment or holding companies) have appeared in agreements concluded by the United States. All of the United States' agreements are supplemented by its domestic anti-conduit regulations.[150]

The 2016 US Model Convention contains an express statement that the tax treaty should not create opportunities for non-taxation or reduced taxation through tax evasion or avoidance (including through treaty-shopping arrangements aimed at obtaining reliefs provided in this Convention for the indirect benefit of residents of third states).

The United States' agreements with the following 45 jurisdictions contain an LOB rule and are supplemented by domestic anti-conduit rules: Australia, Austria, Bangladesh*, Barbados, Belgium, Bulgaria, Canada, China (People's Republic of), Cyprus*, Czechia, Denmark, Estonia, Finland, France, Germany, Iceland, India, Indonesia, Ireland, Israel, Italy, Jamaica, Japan, Kazakhstan, Latvia, Lithuania, Luxembourg, Malta, Mexico, Netherlands, New Zealand, Portugal, Russian Federation, the Slovak Republic, Slovenia, South Africa, Spain, Sri Lanka, Sweden, Switzerland, Thailand, Tunisia, Türkiye, Ukraine, Venezuela*. A signed convention with Poland contains an LOB rule and is supplemented by domestic anti-conduit rules. The agreements with Egypt, Korea, Morocco, Norway, and Trinidad and Tobago have a limited anti-treaty shopping rule and are supplemented by domestic anti-conduit rules. The agreement with the United Kingdom contains an LOB and anti-conduit rules and is supplemented by domestic anti-conduit rules.

B. Conclusion

No jurisdiction has raised any concerns about their agreements with the United States.

---

[149] With respect to the United States' agreement with Luxembourg.

[150] See I.R.C. §7701(l), added to the Internal Revenue Code by section 13238 of the Omnibus Budget Reconciliation Act of 1993, P.L. 103-66 (allowing the Internal Revenue Service to re-characterise any multiple-party financing transaction as being a transaction directly among any two or more of its parties whenever appropriate to prevent the avoidance of the United States' tax); Treas. Reg. § 1.881-3 (as amended in 2020) (providing additional guidance relating to conduit financing arrangements). In addition, the United States has judicial doctrines such as substance-over-form and economic substance that may achieve a similar result in addressing conduit arrangements.

Summary of the jurisdiction response – United States

	1.Treaty partners	2. Compliance with the standard	3. Signature of a complying instrument	4. Minimum standard provision used
1	Armenia	No	No	
2	Australia	No	No	
3	Austria	No	No	
4	Azerbaijan	No	No	
5	Bangladesh*	No	No	
6	Barbados	No	No	
7	Belarus	No	No	
8	Belgium	No	No	
9	Bulgaria	No	No	
10	Canada	No	No	
11	China (People's Republic of)	No	No	
12	Cyprus*	No	No	
13	Czechia	No	No	
14	Denmark	No	No	
15	Egypt	No	No	
16	Estonia	No	No	
17	Finland	No	No	
18	France	No	No	
19	Georgia	No	No	
20	Germany	No	No	
21	Greece	No	No	
22	Iceland	No	No	
23	India	No	No	
24	Indonesia	No	No	
25	Ireland	No	No	
26	Israel	No	No	
27	Italy	No	No	
28	Jamaica	No	No	
29	Japan	No	No	
30	Kazakhstan	No	No	
31	Korea	No	No	
32	Kyrgyzstan*	No	No	
33	Latvia	No	No	
34	Lithuania	No	No	
35	Luxembourg	No	No	
36	Malta	No	No	
37	Mexico	No	No	
38	Moldova*	No	No	
39	Morocco	No	No	
40	Netherlands	No	No	
41	New Zealand	No	No	
42	Norway	No	No	
43	Pakistan	No	No	
44	Philippines	No	No	
45	Poland	No	No	
46	Portugal	No	No	
47	Romania	No	No	
48	Russian Federation	No	No	
49	Slovak Republic	No	No	

50	Slovenia	No	No	
51	South Africa	No	No	
52	Spain	No	No	
53	Sri Lanka	No	No	
54	Sweden	No	No	
55	Switzerland	No	No	
56	Tajikistan*	No	No	
57	Thailand	No	No	
58	Trinidad and Tobago	No	No	
59	Tunisia	No	No	
60	Türkiye	No	No	
61	Turkmenistan*	No	No	
62	Ukraine	No	No	
63	United Kingdom	No	No	
64	Uzbekistan	No	No	
65	Venezuela*	No	No	

Uruguay

A. Progress in the implementation of the minimum standard

Uruguay has 23 tax agreements in force as reported in its response to the Peer Review questionnaire. Seventeen of those agreements comply with the minimum standard.

Uruguay signed the MLI in 2017 and deposited its instrument of ratification on 6 February 2020, listing its non-compliant agreements. The MLI entered into force for Uruguay on 1 June 2020. The agreements modified by the MLI come into compliance with the minimum standard once the provisions of the MLI take effect.

Uruguay is implementing the minimum standard through the inclusion of the preamble statement and the PPT combined with the LOB.[151]

B. Conclusion

No jurisdiction has raised any concerns about their agreements with Uruguay.

Summary of the jurisdiction response – Uruguay

	1.Treaty partners	2. Compliance with the standard	3. Signature of a complying instrument	4. Minimum standard provision used
1	Belgium	Yes MLI		PPT
2	Chile	Yes other		PPT+LOB
3	Ecuador*	No	No	PPT+LOB
4	Finland	Yes MLI		PPT
5	Germany	No	No	
6	Hungary	Yes MLI		PPT
7	India	Yes MLI		PPT+LOB
8	Italy	Yes other		PPT
9	Japan	Yes other		PPT
10	Korea	Yes MLI		PPT
11	Liechtenstein	Yes MLI		PPT
12	Luxembourg	Yes MLI		PPT
13	Malta	Yes MLI		PPT
14	Mexico	No	Yes MLI	PPT+LOB
15	Paraguay	Yes other		PPT+LOB
16	Portugal	Yes MLI		PPT
17	Romania	No	Yes MLI	PPT
18	Singapore	Yes MLI		PPT
19	Spain	Yes MLI		PPT
20	Switzerland	No	No	
21	United Arab Emirates	Yes MLI		PPT
22	United Kingdom	Yes MLI		PPT
23	Viet Nam	No	Yes MLI	PPT

[151] For its agreements listed under the MLI, Uruguay is implementing the preamble statement (Article 6 of the MLI) and the PPT (Article 7 of the MLI). Uruguay has also adopted for the simplified LOB under Article 7(6) of the MLI.

Uzbekistan

A. Progress in the implementation of the minimum standard

Uzbekistan has 55 tax agreements in force as reported in its response to the Peer Review questionnaire. Five of those agreements comply with the minimum standard.

Uzbekistan has not signed the MLI.

Uzbekistan indicated in its response to the Peer Review questionnaire that steps have been taken (other than under the MLI) to implement the minimum standard in its agreements with Austria, Bulgaria and Italy.

Uzbekistan is implementing the minimum standard through the inclusion of the preamble statement and the PPT, combined with the LOB for the agreement with Japan.

In its response to the Peer Review questionnaire, Switzerland indicated that its agreement with Switzerland did not give rise to material treaty shopping concerns, for their respective jurisdictions.

B. Conclusion

Uzbekistan is currently developing a plan, in consultation with the Secretariat, for the implementation of the minimum standard in its agreements with Azerbaijan, Bahrain, Belarus, Belgium, Canada, China (People's Republic of), Czechia, Egypt, Estonia, Finland, France, Georgia, Germany, Greece, Hungary, India, Indonesia, Ireland, Israel, Jordan, Kazakhstan, Latvia, Lithuania, Malaysia, Oman, Pakistan, Poland, Romania, Russian Federation, Saudi Arabia, Singapore, Slovak Republic, Slovenia, Spain, Switzerland, Thailand, Türkiye, Ukraine, United Arab Emirates and Viet Nam.

Summary of the jurisdiction response – Uzbekistan

	1.Treaty partners	2. Compliance with the standard	3. Signature of a complying instrument	4. Minimum standard provision used
1	Austria	No	No	
2	Bulgaria	No	No	
3	Italy	No	No	
4	Japan	Yes other		PPT+LOB
5	Korea	Yes other		PPT
6	Luxembourg	Yes other		PPT
7	Netherlands	Yes other		PPT
8	United Kingdom	Yes other		PPT

Other agreements

	1.Treaty partners	2. Inclusive Framework member
1	Azerbaijan	Yes
2	Bahrain	Yes
3	Belarus	Yes
4	Belgium	Yes
5	Canada	Yes
6	China	Yes
7	Cyprus*	No
8	Czechia	Yes

9	Egypt	Yes
10	Estonia	Yes
11	Finland	Yes
12	France	Yes
13	Georgia	Yes
14	Germany	Yes
15	Greece	Yes
16	Hungary	Yes
17	India	Yes
18	Indonesia	Yes
19	Iran*	No
20	Ireland	Yes
21	Israel	Yes
22	Jordan	Yes
23	Kazakhstan	Yes
24	Kuwait	Yes
25	Kyrgyzstan*	No
26	Latvia	Yes
27	Lithuania	Yes
28	Malaysia	Yes
29	Moldova*	No
30	Oman	Yes
31	Pakistan	Yes
32	Poland	Yes
33	Romania	Yes
34	Russian Federation	Yes
35	Saudi Arabia	Yes
36	Singapore	Yes
37	Slovak Republic	Yes
38	Slovenia	Yes
39	Spain	Yes
40	Switzerland	Yes
41	Tajikistan*	No
42	Thailand	Yes
43	Türkiye	Yes
44	Turkmenistan*	No
45	Ukraine	Yes
46	United Arab Emirates	Yes
47	Viet Nam	Yes

Viet Nam

A. Progress in the implementation of the minimum standard

Viet Nam has 76 tax agreements in force as reported in its response to the Peer Review questionnaire. None of those agreements comply with the minimum standard.

Viet Nam signed the MLI in 2022 and deposited its instrument of ratification on 23 May 2023, listing its non-compliant agreements concluded with other members of the Inclusive Framework. The MLI entered into force for Viet Nam on 1 September 2023. The agreements modified by the MLI come into compliance with the minimum standard once the provisions of the MLI take effect.

Viet Nam is implementing the minimum standard through the inclusion of the preamble statement and the PPT.[152]

B. Conclusion

No jurisdiction has raised any concerns about their agreements with Viet Nam.

Summary of the jurisdiction response – Viet Nam

	1.Treaty partners	2. Compliance with the standard	3. Signature of a complying instrument	4. Minimum standard provision used
1	Australia	No	Yes MLI	PPT
2	Austria	No	No	PPT
3	Azerbaijan	No	No	PPT
4	Bangladesh*	No	No	PPT
5	Belarus	No	No	PPT
6	Belgium	No	Yes MLI	PPT
7	Brunei Darussalam	No	No	PPT
8	Bulgaria	No	Yes MLI	PPT
9	Cambodia*	No	No	PPT
10	Canada	No	Yes MLI	PPT
11	China (People's Republic of)	No	Yes MLI	PPT
12	Croatia	No	Yes MLI	PPT
13	Cuba*	No	No	PPT
14	Czechia	No	No	PPT
15	Democratic People's Republic of Korea*	No	No	PPT
16	Denmark	No	Yes MLI	PPT
17	Estonia	No	Yes MLI	PPT
18	Finland	No	Yes MLI	PPT
19	France	No	Yes MLI	PPT
20	Germany	No	No	PPT
21	Hong Kong (China)	No	Yes MLI	PPT
22	Hungary	No	Yes MLI	PPT

152 For its agreements listed under the MLI, Viet Nam is implementing the preamble statement (Article 6 of the MLI) and the PPT (Article 7 of the MLI).

23	Iceland	No	Yes MLI	PPT
24	India	No	Yes MLI	PPT
25	Indonesia	No	Yes MLI	PPT
26	Iran*	No	No	PPT
27	Ireland	No	Yes MLI	PPT
28	Israel	No	Yes MLI	PPT
29	Italy	No	Yes MLI	PPT
30	Japan	No	No	PPT
31	Kazakhstan	No	Yes MLI	PPT
32	Korea	No	Yes MLI	PPT
33	Kuwait	No	Yes MLI	PPT
34	Lao People's Democratic Republic*	No	No	PPT
35	Latvia	No	Yes MLI	PPT
36	Luxembourg	No	Yes MLI	PPT
37	Macau (China)	No	No	PPT
38	Malaysia	No	Yes MLI	PPT
39	Malta	No	Yes MLI	PPT
40	Mongolia	No	Yes MLI	PPT
41	Morocco	No	Yes MLI	PPT
42	Mozambique*	No	No	PPT
43	Myanmar*	No	No	PPT
44	Netherlands	No	Yes MLI	PPT
45	New Zealand	No	Yes MLI	PPT
46	Norway	No	No	PPT
47	Oman	No	Yes MLI	PPT
48	Pakistan	No	Yes MLI	PPT
49	Palestine*	No	No	PPT
50	Panama	No	Yes MLI	PPT
51	Philippines	No	No	PPT
52	Poland	No	Yes MLI	PPT
53	Portugal	No	Yes MLI	PPT
54	Qatar	No	Yes MLI	PPT
55	Romania	No	Yes MLI	PPT
56	Russian Federation	No	Yes MLI	PPT
57	San Marino	No	Yes MLI	PPT
58	Saudi Arabia	No	Yes MLI	PPT
59	Serbia	No	Yes MLI	PPT
60	Seychelles	No	Yes MLI	PPT
61	Singapore	No	Yes MLI	PPT
62	Slovak Republic	No	Yes MLI	PPT
63	Spain	No	Yes MLI	PPT
64	Sri Lanka	No	No	PPT
65	Sweden	No	Yes MLI	PPT
66	Switzerland	No	No	PPT
67	Thailand	No	Yes MLI	PPT
68	Tunisia	No	No	PPT
69	Türkiye	No	Yes MLI	PPT
70	Ukraine	No	Yes MLI	PPT
71	United Arab Emirates	No	Yes MLI	PPT
72	United Kingdom	No	Yes MLI	PPT
73	Uruguay	No	Yes MLI	PPT
74	Uzbekistan	No	No	PPT
75	Venezuela*	No	No	PPT

Other agreements

	1.Treaty partners	2. Inclusive Framework member
1	Chinese Taipei*	No

Zambia

A. Progress in the implementation of the minimum standard

Zambia has 23 tax agreements in force as reported in its response to the Peer Review questionnaire. One of those agreements, the agreement with Switzerland, complies with the minimum standard.

Zambia has not signed the MLI.

Zambia indicated in its response to the Peer Review questionnaire that steps have been taken (other than under the MLI) to implement the minimum standard in its agreements with India and South Africa.

Zambia is implementing the minimum standard through the inclusion of the preamble statement and the PPT.

In their responses to the Peer Review questionnaire, Germany and Japan indicated that their agreements with Zambia did not give rise to material treaty shopping concerns, for their respective jurisdictions.

B. Conclusion

Zambia is currently developing a plan, in consultation with the Secretariat, for the implementation of the minimum standard in its agreements with Botswana, Canada, China (People's Republic of), Denmark, Finland, France, Germany, Ireland, Italy, Japan, Kenya, Morocco, Netherlands, Norway, Romania, the Seychelles, Sweden and the United Kingdom.

Summary of the jurisdiction response - Zambia

	1.Treaty partners	2. Compliance with the standard	3. Signature of a complying instrument	4. Minimum standard provision used
1	India	No	No	
2	South Africa	No	No	PPT
3	Switzerland	Yes other		PPT

Other agreements

	1.Treaty partners	2. Inclusive Framework member
1	Botswana	Yes
2	Canada	Yes
3	China (People's Republic of)	Yes
4	Denmark	Yes
5	Finland	Yes
6	France	Yes
7	Germany	Yes
8	Ireland	Yes
9	Italy	Yes
10	Japan	Yes
11	Kenya	Yes
12	Morocco	Yes
13	Netherlands	Yes

14	Norway	Yes
15	Romania	Yes
16	Seychelles	Yes
17	Sweden	Yes
18	Tanzania*	No
19	Uganda*	No
20	United Kingdom	Yes

www.ingramcontent.com/pod-product-compliance
Ingram Content Group UK Ltd.
Pitfield, Milton Keynes, MK11 3LW, UK
UKHW051457290926
15471UKWH00008B/1254

9 789264 341326